IS THERE STILL ROOM IN YOUR LIFE FOR ME? *a novel*

WILL MANWILL

First Edition: April 2021

Library of Congress Control Number: 2021902254

ISBN 978-1-7366198-2-7 (hardcover) – ISBN 978-1-7366198-0-3 (paperback) – ISBN: 978-1-7366198-1-0 (e-book)

Editor: Hollie Westring

Cover Design and Formatting by: Dane Low, Adrian Low, John Low, Team EbookLaunch – http://www.EbookLaunch.com/

www.willmanwill.com

www.twitter.com/wmanwill • www.instagram.com/will_manwill

To my family –

the one I was born into and the one I found

PART I

JAKE RUIZ

CHAPTER 1

Jake Ruiz had been in a lot of ride shares, but this one took the cake. The driver—Claire, had somehow managed to successfully steer the front axle of her car into every dip, divot, and puddle on Pine Street as if she was intentionally trying to not miss a single one. And now here he was…teetering on the edge of vomiting in the backseat of her Hyundai that smelled like a cherry-flavored vape pen and bubblegum. He'd say there was no way he was going to give her five stars, but who was he kidding? Jake Ruiz always played by the rules, and that included giving drivers five stars out of fear they would give him a bad review in return and ruin his impeccable record as a customer.

Claire slammed on her brakes, and her car fishtailed slightly on the wet Seattle streets before it came to a grinding halt in front of Chiapas, the restaurant he was supposed to be at for dinner with his best friend, Gigi, a half hour ago.

"Here we are! Have a great evening!" Claire called out as Jake already had one foot on the curb. He couldn't get out of Claire's death vehicle fast enough.

"Uh…thanks," Jake said before shutting the door. He stood on the sidewalk, looking down at his phone. His finger hovered over a 1-star rating for just a moment before he gave Claire five stars and then closed the app. Through the window, he could see Gigi in the booth that they frequented whenever they went to Chiapas, and she was clearly pissed off.

"Hey, I'm so sorry! The sitter was late and then Charlie threw a tantrum as I was heading out the door." One of the best things Jake had learned five years ago when he became a parent was that having a child was like having a built-in excuse for practically anything. He didn't pull the card often, but he knew when to use it after reading a room. And

Gigi's face required a good excuse for why he was late. Fortunately for him, just the mention of his son's name wiped the irritation right off her face. Charlie was the most adorable kid, and the awful thing was that he knew it. Charlie was a master of working that five-year-old charm and getting almost anything from Jake's friends. Jake had become acutely aware of the little con artist, so Charlie's tricks didn't work on him. But the excuse that there was an issue with Charlie wasn't too far from the truth. Jake did have a problem leaving tonight, but there was nothing wrong with Charlie. It was Jake. Jake was nervous to set foot out of the house without Charlie.

"It's fine," Gigi said, her voice softening. "I was about to give up your seat to that guy in the purple hoodie. He offered to buy me a drink."

"Oh yeah?" Jake said, looking over at the bar where Gigi was pointing to a college-age blond guy drinking with some friends. He figured Gigi wasn't being serious. The guy was cute in all the obvious ways. He and his friends looked like their social media profiles were probably littered with a bunch of thirst trap photos and their biggest dilemma of the week was learning the choreography for their latest TikTok video. Even from the other side of the restaurant, Jake could tell the guy was easily over a decade younger than their thirty-six-year-old selves.

"Why do you ask like that? I'm being serious!" Gigi said defensively.

"Can I get you something to drink?" asked the waiter, who had just approached their table.

"I'll have the jalapeño margarita with halo del santo on the rim," Jake said.

"Of course. I'll get that going for you." The waiter's eyebrows furrowed and he stared at Jake a bit longer than a non-awkward exchange would allow, and then walked away.

"What was that about?" Jake asked Gigi.

"I don't know. Maybe he thinks you're eighteen trying to buy liquor. Anyway, can we get back to my story?" she said with the full force of irritation restored in her voice. It was as though the entire Charlie excuse had never happened.

"Okay, I'm sorry. Now tell me about Purple Hoodie Guy."

"He came up here and asked me if he could buy me a margarita," she began.

"And?"

"And then he asked if I was his roommate Connor's mom," Gigi said, slumping back into the booth.

Jake pursed his lips, trying to suppress laughter, but instead let out what could only be described as an inverted snort.

"I hate you," Gigi said through gritted teeth. "First, you're late, then you use your stinking adorable son as an excuse so I won't be mad at you, and then you laugh at my misery."

"Sorry, sorry, sorry! I promise I…" Jake stopped mid-sentence as Gigi lifted a lime margarita and took a sip. "Gigi, is that a salt rim?"

"Ugh, dammit," Gigi said, nearly slamming the glass back onto the table.

"Trying something new?" Jake asked. In all the time he knew Gigi, she despised a salt rim on margaritas. She was also a creature of habit and never strayed away from her usual drinks. So, the fact that she was drinking a lime margarita on the rocks and not her usual blended strawberry margarita gave away the fact that Gigi was drinking something bought for her.

"Okay, I may have played along… What? I'll never turn down a free drink."

"What did he say?"

"He said that Connor isn't going to be at their dorm room for the rest of the night and…" Gigi paused momentarily as she pretended to gag before acting like someone just threw some ice cubes down the back of her shirt, squirming in her chair. "And then he said he has a thing for moms."

"Oh Gigi…" Jake said. It was like listening to someone describe a car crash—you didn't want to hear the story, but at the same time, you had to know the ending. "What did you do?"

"After he bought me the drink, I told him that Connor is on my speed dial and if he didn't leave, I'd call him and tell him his roommate is trying to be his new stepdaddy," Gigi said, taking another sip of her margarita, but this time she did it proudly. "When did we get so old?"

"I ask myself that all the time," Jake said as he grabbed a chip and dug it into the guacamole. "Mmmm… Why is their table guac like crack?"

"I don't know, but I'm glad we only do these meetups rarely now. Otherwise, I'd be eating my weight in guac," Gigi said. Jake couldn't tell if she was making a subtle dig at him or if it was a completely innocent comment. It was true that they hadn't done a dinner like this with just the two of them in a while. In fact, Jake could count the exact number of nights out with Gigi over the last year on two fingers. But even if he wanted to feel guilty from this comment, he didn't. Fifteen months ago, Jake's entire world was turned upside down with a single phone call where he was informed that his husband had just died. And since then, Jake struggled with going anywhere without Charlie. He constantly worried that something might happen to him, too, and leave Charlie without any parent.

It was as if Gigi had processed what she had said and exactly why just the two of them had not been able to meet up. "Oh God, I'm sorry. Can I just blame that comment on this really awful free margarita?"

"Of course, but you only get one of those comments tonight. And sadly, you just spent it on that one. So, for the rest of the night you can't complain about how your social life has taken a toll because of me becoming a widower."

"Oh damn, metaphorical gut punch to the ovaries, Ruiz."

"Ew, Gigi."

"One jalapeño margarita," the waiter said after arriving with Jake's drink. He stood there and looked at Jake, who looked at Gigi for validation that this odd interaction was actually happening. Jake wasn't sure why the waiter was still standing there. Gigi had already ordered their usual food, which was basically the entire list of appetizers and margaritas. Nothing else. Maybe he wanted Jake to try the drink, so to see if that would appease the waiter and have him disappear, Jake took a sip. The waiter just stood there, smiling.

"I'm sorry. Was there something else?" Jake asked, not trying hard to mask his annoyance.

"Sorry, are you Jake Ruiz?" the waiter asked.

"I am," Jake said hesitantly.

"I knew it!" the waiter said excitedly. "I've dined at every single one of your restaurants! You are like...the best chef in Seattle! Viva la Vida is my favorite restaurant in the city."

"Well, thank you. That's very kind," Jake said. His cheeks had become ten shades darker from the sudden recognition. He was known throughout the city and in many social circles, but getting recognized while out in public didn't happen as often as one would think. Sure, he was a popular chef and restaurateur, but he wasn't some kind of celebrity A-lister, so he often was able to keep a somewhat lower profile.

"You're actually one of the reasons I'm going to culinary school right now," the waiter said proudly. "I'm sorry, this is probably crossing the line, but can I take a picture with you?"

Gigi let out an exasperated cough before shifting in her seat loudly. Jake shot a look at her before nodding to the waiter, who already had unlocked his phone and was navigating to the camera.

"Gouda!" the waiter said, holding up his phone to take a selfie. The flash caused Jake and Gigi to go blind momentarily in the dim restaurant.

"Let me see that," Gigi said, grabbing the waiter's phone out of his hand. "Alex, is it? I think we are on a new level now, so you'll understand that I need to approve before this before it goes on the 'Gram… Ugh. That flash washed my skin out. Throw a filter on that before you post, okay?"

"Sure thing. Thank you so much, Mr. Ruiz! I can't wait to tell my boyfriend I met you!" The waiter quickly left the table, probably realizing he had ten other tables he had neglected.

"Bet you didn't know you were out on the town with a celebrity, did you?" Jake looked at Gigi with a big smile on his face. She just pretended like she was about to projectile vomit.

"Anyways, what is the matter with Charlie?" Gigi asked.

"Nothing really. It was…me. I couldn't leave," Jake said quietly as he had way too many thoughts going through his mind right now for what was supposed to be a casual, fun evening.

"Oh honey…" Gigi said, reaching across the table and holding his hand. It wasn't lost on her what her best friend was going through. She tried to be there as much as she could but realized maybe the best thing she could do for Jake was give him some space. "Well, you're here now. And I'm so happy to see you."

"Thanks. Sorry—you know how my brain works. I think about what might happen if Charlie lost his other dad and then it's a snowball effect. Before I know it, my brain justifies sitting in sweats at night and watching Netflix."

"Jeez, that's about the saddest thing you've ever said. And I've heard you say a lot of sad things," Gigi said.

"I'm serious, Gigi. How am I ever going to be able to go on a date again?" Jake thought back to his last, and only, date since his husband had died. It had been seven months since the funeral and Jake had been set up by the bar manager of one of his restaurants. Just thinking about the date gave Jake a slight feeling of PTSD. He met up with Luke, a software engineer who worked for a startup in South Lake Union, and before the appetizers had even been delivered, Jake had broken down in tears and rushed out of the restaurant.

"Well, I think the chances of you finding a man will be higher if you crawl out of your hermit shell and put something other than sweats on. Hey, if it makes you feel any better, I'm pretty sure our waiter was about to proposition you for a three-way with his boyfriend if he stood at our table any longer." The two began to laugh before clinking their margaritas together.

"Sweetie…" Gigi said as she held up her margarita. "I hope you know you're going to have to help me finish this drink. I need to find your waiter boyfriend and get me something else to drink that won't burn my esophagus on the way down."

"I've got my own to work on, thank you very much," Jake said, holding up his drink.

"Not even a free sip, courtesy of Connor's roommate, Mr. Purple Hoodie?" Gigi said, beginning to swirl her margarita glass in only what Jake could assume was Gigi trying to be seductive.

"Stop, you're creeping me out," Jake said before he felt his phone begin to vibrate. He worried it was the sitter. He pulled his phone out and looked at the caller ID.

MOM

Jake set the phone back down on the table and Gigi leaned over to look at it.

"Yeesh, what is Dragon doing calling you?" Gigi asked. She had coined the awful nickname for Jake's mom when they were sophomores in high school after his mom found out they had been drinking in the woods with other kids from school. Jake's mom forbid him from hanging out with Gigi for two weeks and forced him to "confess" his sins in front of a packed Bible study group, which was supremely embarrassing. After that, Gigi started calling her the *Dragon*.

"I have no idea," Jake said before sending it to voicemail.

"Has she called you recently?" Gigi asked. The relationship Jake had with his parents was a complicated one mostly because of the fact he fell in love with and married a man.

"Mmmm… She called me a few months ago to see if I wanted an old jukebox that was in their garage."

"Don't fall for it. It's a trap. You'll get there and then they'll probably kidnap you and send you to one of those 'pray-the-gay-away' camps in Utah," Gigi said, half joking. At least, Jake thought she was half joking, but if there was one woman Gigi despised, it was his mother. She had liked his parents up until that night during their sophomore year, and then it was a sharp decline on that relationship that never recovered.

BZZZZZZZ. BZZZZZZZ

MOM

"Do you want me to answer it and pretend to be your new female lover and get her really excited? And then we can crush her dreams?"

"Oh my God… You've put some thought into that, haven't you?"

"No – I don't know what you're talking about!" Gigi said, her eyes darted in a hundred different directions before she grabbed her drink and took a long sip from it.

"Hold on one second," Jake said to Gigi right before he accepted the call. "Hello?"

"Jacob. It's your mamá, Consuela."

"Yeah, I know, Mom. Caller ID…"

"Oh, right. Jacob, you need to come home."

Jake had rarely spoken with his mother the last several years, so for her to call out of the blue with such a demand was just absolutely insane. Actually, it was about on par for exactly the kind of person Jake's mother was.

"Mom, I don't know why you're saying this now, but I'm not—"

"It's your father, Jacob. He's in the hospital. They…" Jake's mom paused, and he could hear sobbing through the phone. "They don't know if he will make it through the night."

"Dad…" It was the only word that escaped Jake's mouth before he sat there, paralyzed from the words his mother had spoken. Unlike his mother, Jake's relationship with his father was slightly better. It was still a strained relationship with his father, but compared to what he had with Consuela Ruiz, it was a big improvement. "I'll get on a flight to Spokane tonight."

CHAPTER 2

Traveling back to his hometown felt more like a race around the world for Jake. First, there was the trip back to his home to pick up Charlie, who was already fast asleep. Then there was a second ride share that took Jake and Charlie to the airport to catch the last flight out of Seattle to Spokane. Jake found it slightly funny that he spent more time getting to the airport and through security than he did actually in the air to Spokane, which only lasted a little more than an hour. The bouncing from one mode of transportation to the next, while trying to keep Charlie asleep, provided a needed distraction for Jake. It wasn't until the ninety-minute drive to his hometown of Newport, Washington, that Jake began thinking about his father.

Carlos Ruiz was a friendly man and for some God unknown reason, decided to plant his family's roots in the remote town of Newport that sat on the border of Idaho and Washington, about ninety minutes from the Canadian border. The town, which was home to a little more than 2,000 people, had virtually no restaurants until Carlos opened his.

Jake's family had purchased the building when he was five years old and converted the old pharmacy into Los Ruiz Restaurant and Karaoke Lounge. The second part of the name wasn't added until about a year after opening, when Jake's father realized that karaoke was a way to get people to stay and spend more money. Forget the fact that it was an unconventional combination and an even more bizarre restaurant name. Growing up, his parents expected their only child to help in the restaurant. Eventually, Jake's friends got jobs there, including Gigi, and the place became more of a teen hangout. At one point, it almost felt like Los Ruiz Restaurant and Karaoke Lounge was the hotspot of Newport.

Jake slowed down as he made his way into town and drove past Los Ruiz on the way to the hospital. The entire building's facade was now dilapidated. The vibrant colors that had made the building stand out were now faded, even evident in the darkness. Weeds had now grown through the cracks of the asphalt. The landscaping that his mother had once spent hours every week making sure looked impeccable was now overgrown with weeds and littered with trash. Patches of terracotta roofing tiles were missing and many of the pieces looked like they had cracked and broken over the years. If Jake hadn't known better, it looked as though the restaurant was out of business. In truth, the family restaurant seemed to be a perfect symbol of his actual family. They had deteriorated as a family unit when Jake decided to tell them he was gay. His parents wouldn't talk with him in the years that followed his coming out—something that had taken a severe emotional toll on both sides. As he looked at the weeds and dilapidated building, he couldn't help but feel angry for so many reasons, none of which he felt like addressing at this particular moment in time.

"Dad? Where are we?" Charlie mumbled, half asleep. Jake unfastened Charlie from the car seat and picked him up.

"It's okay, buddy. We had to take a trip to see someone. Try to go back to sleep, okay?" Jake said, patting his son on the back as he made his way into the hospital entrance. He didn't want to tell Charlie who they were seeing. Charlie had only met Jake's parents once when they went to a cousin's wedding, and he doubted Charlie would remember them.

"Hi there, I'm here to see my father," Jake said, approaching the nurse's station.

"Name?" the nurse asked without looking up. Something about her seemed oddly familiar and given the size of the town, Jake knew her from somewhere. He just wasn't sure where.

"Carlos Ruiz. He was brought in earlier tonight."

"Jake, is that you?" The nurse looked up, surprised. "Well, I'll be damned! You had quite the glow up!"

"I'm sorry, but…" Jake was embarrassed he still had no idea who she was.

"It's me. Stacy Morrell. Well, Stacy Morrell-Jones-Clovis now. Class of 2003?" she said, appearing to be a little embarrassed he hadn't recognized her.

"Of course! Stacy! How are you? I'm so sorry I didn't recog—"

"Oh, don't apologize. Three kids, two husbands, and eighty pounds later, I'm not quite the Newport Junior Miss I was back when we were in high school. But you... You haven't changed a bit. You look like a supermodel!"

"Thanks," Jake said, feeling his cheeks grow red.

"And who's that little guy?" Stacy asked, craning her neck, trying to get a better look at Charlie.

"This is my son."

"Your son? I didn't even know. You know, I heard a rumor that you married a... Oh well, never mind that. I guess it was just a silly rumor! Is your wife out in the car?" Stacy had just crossed about a hundred different lines and reminded Jake why he avoided his hometown like the plague.

"Stacy, can I just find out where my father is?"

"Of course. He's in 107. Just down the hall."

"Thanks! Oh, and Stacy?"

"Yes, Jake?"

"That rumor you heard? That was true. I was fortunate enough to find an amazing man to marry and raise *our* child with, until he passed away. Have a good night!" Jake watched all the color drain from the face of Stacy Morrell-*whatever-the-hell-her-other-names* were. She didn't say another word and just sat back down in her chair. Jake knew this wouldn't be the last interaction of this kind while he was here and was already emotionally exhausted. At least, he thought he was until he opened the door of Room 107. Consuela, Jake's mother, had her head resting on the bed his father was laying in while a doctor looked at a machine.

"Visiting hours are... Jake?" the doctor said, looking up from the machine.

How many times is this going to happen? Jake thought. He looked at the man dressed in a white doctor's jacket and recognized him. Colt Humphrey. Colt had been in Jake's class and they had grown up together. In fact, they had been best friends up until fourth or fifth grade, when Colt became more interested in sports and Jake hadn't. Colt was lean and muscular with dirty blond hair, and a patch of freckles that Jake knew only appeared during the summer months when Colt would spend most of his time on his family's jet ski on Sacheen Lake. He was one of the first, if not *the* first, guys who made Jake realize how very much he was *not* into girls. After they graduated and left Newport, Jake would sometimes think about Colt. He wondered if his looks faded and he had become overweight and unattractive. But here stood Colt in front of Jake now, as handsome as ever, with zero body fat and a full head of dirty blond hair still intact. And by the looks of it, Colt had followed in his father's footsteps, becoming a physician. By all accounts, Colt Humphrey appeared to still have it all, and Jake couldn't help but feel the slightest tinge of guilt as he looked at Colt, who flashed a smile that reminded Jake of everything he had once felt about him. To say it was a crush would have made those feelings Jake once had seem so trivial.

"Colt?"

"It's *Dr.* Colton Humphrey now," Colt said with a tone of supreme arrogance, but then quietly laughed. He walked up to Jake and placed his hand on Jake's shoulder. The innocent gesture sent a wave of warmth down Jake's shoulder, and he felt a small flutter in his stomach. "Is this your little guy?"

"It is. This is Charlie," Jake said, pivoting so Colt could see his son.

"Ah, he's adorable, Ruiz," Colt said with a wide smile. Jake grew frustrated that even Colt's teeth were flawless. He wondered if there was anything that couldn't go right for this guy. "Listen, I know we haven't talked in a while, but I heard what happened to your husband. I'm really sorry."

"Thanks," Jake said, taken aback by the gesture.

"I'm sure he was a great husband and father," Colt said with a smile.

"He really was. Thank you. That means a lot," Jake said, looking at Colt. For a fleeting moment, Jake felt like he had traveled back in time and was the scared and confused teenager he had once been with feelings for someone he could never have. And just as quickly as he had felt those feelings, they faded. "How's my father?"

"Stable now," Colt said, turning his head back toward the hospital bed. "We have him in a medically induced coma right now. Your mom hasn't left his side."

"What happened?" Jake asked. In all the chaos of picking up Charlie and flying across the state, his mother hadn't shared this information with Jake.

"He had a stroke at the restaurant. One of the workers drove him here right after, which is lucky. If he had arrived any later, it could have been much worse."

"So, he'll be fine then?"

"He'll recover. It may take some time, but to be honest, Jake, I don't know if he'll be able to get back to working for quite some time." This would likely be one of the last concerns for other people, but Jake knew that Colt understood how important the family restaurant was to his parents. It was their entire lives now. In fact, it was now their child.

"Well, thank you for taking care of him, Colt. I mean Dr. Colton," Jake said, smiling at the doctor.

"I'm just messin' with you, dude. For you, I'll always be Colt." Those words had an effect on Jake that he knew Colt had not intended. He locked on Colt's hazel eyes, staring for longer than was customary before looking downward and noticing Colt's hand. There was no wedding band. Just the mere thought made Jake feel guilty for so many reasons. He was there to see his father, and more importantly, he was still in what Gigi referred to as "widow mode." That disastrous first date with Luke was proof of that. So, for Jake to now be focusing on Dr. Colt Humphrey's faultless facial features while his father was lying in a hospital bed just a few feet away made Jake feel like a really deplorable human being. "How long are you in town for?"

"I don't really know," Jake said, looking at his mother and realizing he had not yet planned how long he would be in town. Given the volatile history with his mother, it wouldn't be long. Jake figured the first indication that his mother was about to have one of her episodes, he would be on the first flight back to Seattle.

"Hey, I don't know if it's weird, but you're welcome to stay in my guest house. It has a kitchen and its own bathroom and bedroom. And best of all, it doesn't have bedbugs like the Moose Knuckle," Colt said with a laugh, reminding Jake that there only one motel in Newport—the Moose Nugget Motel that they all had nicknamed the Moose Knuckle. Jake never had a reason to stay there in the past and from the looks of the exterior, he had no desire to ever find out what the inside of the Moose Knuckle looked like.

"Thanks, but I called Gigi's mom, and I'm going to stay with her," Jake said. Had he known an offer would have been on the table to stay at Colt's house, he probably would not have been so quick to call Helen Clayton for room and board. But before he realized what he was doing, Jake opened his mouth to create a way to keep that invitation open. "Well, if it gets too crowded there, I may take you up on that offer."

"The invitation will still be there. You're welcome anytime. Tell Helen I said hello," Colt said.

"So, you have an entire guest house?" Jake asked, processing what Colt had offered. Jake had felt a major sense of accomplishment when he was able to add an additional half bathroom to the first floor of his Phinney Ridge home and here was Colt, talking about an entire extra house.

"You remember my parents' old place?"

"Who doesn't? Do you remember the bonfire?" Jake said, laughing at the memory of a bonfire party they had in high school at Colt's house that could only be described as a compound. It was the closest thing to a mansion in Newport. And unfortunately, that mansion nearly burned to the ground when Colt had decided to build the bonfire a little too close to his parents' house.

"Oh my God. My parents were pissed. I almost gave my dad a heart attack when he saw the melted siding," Colt said, running his hand through his hair.

"We were all really stupid back then," Jake said reassuringly.

"You weren't. I guess I should have listened to you when you warned me about putting it that close to the house," Colt said, looking off in the distance, obviously replaying the memory in his head. "Anyway, that's my house now."

"Your house? Did your parents make you buy it after you nearly torched it?"

"Nah. Mom and Dad decided to move down to Phoenix. They said the winters were getting to be a little too much, so they bought a place down there. They're usually back around this time by now, but they decided to travel around Europe for the next couple months."

"Rough life. So your parents stay with you the entire summer? I bet your wife likes that," Jake said. He would be kidding himself if he tried saying he hadn't said that to get more details about Colt's personal life.

"I'm not married. I'm dating someone but haven't quite settled down yet," Colt said. Jake hated that he was elated to hear Colt wasn't married, and was not quite sure why. "Anyway, I'm sure you want to catch up with your mom. And Jake?"

"Yeah?" Jake spun around a little too eagerly as Colt made his way to the door.

"That red button on that cord? You can press that if your mom becomes—well..."

"Herself? Thanks. I'll definitely keep that in mind," Jake said, looking over at the call button.

Jake couldn't help but appreciate his view as he watched Colt walk out of the hospital room. Colt Humphrey was still as gorgeous as ever and somehow, after all this time, seemed to still make Jake's stomach flutter. He knew this brief encounter with Colt would lead to an hours' long call with Gigi where they would dissect the entire conversation as though they were forensic experts. But Jake still had Charlie in his arms, which were going dead from holding him the entire time and his father was in a coma from suffering a stroke. Gigi would have to wait, but Jake knew she would be livid with him if he waited too long to tell her. Jake stared blankly at the door that led back to the hall. How many men could say their childhood crush turned out to be just as handsome, just as successful, just as charming, and seemingly flawless all these years later? Colt never peaked. This just gave Jake affirmation that he has always had good taste in men. Nothing could interrupt the thoughts that Jake was now pondering. Thoughts about another person that Jake realized he hadn't had since his husband's death.

"*Cochino*. Must you flirt with every man?" Jake spun around, nearly waking up Charlie. His mother's head was still on his father's bed and her eyes were still closed, but it was clear that Consuela Ruiz witnessed or heard more than Jake would have ever hoped she would hear.

Jake took a deep breath as he readied himself for what would undoubtedly be the exact opposite of the perfectly pleasant interaction he had just had with Colt. A conversation with *Dragon*.

CHAPTER 3 – OCTOBER 27, 2006

"Jacob, come help your *mamita*." The mouthwatering scent of Consuela Ruiz' chilaquiles filled the Ruiz home as Jake walked into the kitchen. He didn't realize how incredibly hungry he was until he smelled breakfast. "*Mijo*, can you set the table?"

"Sure thing," Jake said, giving his mother a kiss on the cheek before sliding past her to grab the plates. "Oh, is it cool if Gigi comes over? She just got in town for the week."

"*Ay, mijo!* I wish you told me sooner. I would have cooked more chilaquiles."

"Sorry, Mom. I kind of forgot."

"It's okay. I'll cook up a little more and it should be enough for everyone."

"Where's Pa?"

"Your *papa* should be here in a minute. He's got to get to the restaurant early today. They're finally delivering the new booths!"

"Oh nice!" Jake sat on the table and watched his mom cook in the kitchen. It seemed like his entire life revolved around the kitchen and family dinners. Jake was in his final year at college, studying business, and couldn't help but worry he had made a mistake. Sure, he was incredibly smart and already had an internship lined up for when he graduated, but he couldn't help but feel as though his heart was in cooking and food. His parents wanted so much more for him than they had growing up and pushed him to study business. This was the least he could do for his parents, because Jake already knew there were so many other parts about his life that would inevitably cause complete disappointment for them.

"Jacob, what are you doing today? You going to come help me with this furniture delivery today down at the restaurant?" Without any greeting, Carlos, Jacob's father, walked right into the kitchen and spoke with his son as though he had been in the room the entire time.

"Hey, Pops. You need me to? Gigi and I were planning on meeting up with a couple friends in Spokane for Halloween, but that's not for a while."

"Gigi this…Gigi that. Honestly, *mijo*, I'm not the biggest fan of that girl. She's always going off and getting you into trouble, but when are you two just going to make it official?" Consuela asked as she started pan-frying bacon.

"Bacon con chilaquiles?" Carlos asked with a raised eyebrow.

Consuela held up a spatula, silencing any potential complaint that Jake's father was about to make about the breakfast menu.

"Make what official, Mom?"

"Boyfriend and girlfriend, *mijo*! It's obvious you like her!"

Jake clenched his jaw and felt his stomach begin to race. He had already come out to Gigi long ago, followed by several of his friends at college last year, but he still had not found the courage to tell his parents that if they were expecting him to settle down with a girl, they would be waiting their entire lives. He told himself not too long ago that he would tell his parents when the opportunity arose. And there had been countless times such as this one, where the window of opportunity presented itself, but Jake quickly shut it.

"Gigi's just a friend, Mom," Jake said.

"They are all 'just friends.' Jacob, you are getting old and letting all the good girls slip right through your fingers!"

"MOM!" Jake said in a drawn-out plea to stop. "I'm only twenty-one."

"Exactly! Your father and I had already been married for three years by the time we were twenty-one. *Mijo*, all I'm saying…"

"Things are different now, Mom. For one, there's electricity and modes of transportation aren't pulled by horses. Besides, I'm focusing on school. The rest can come later," Jake said. He heard his dad quietly suppress laughter at the comment, knowing full well that Consuela would not find humor in Jake's retort.

"*Ay.* Carlos, do you see how your son treats me? That temper... It comes from your side!" If the comment wasn't an indication that Consuela was now irritated, the furious scraping of the spatula against her cast-iron skillet was. This was how Jake's mom was. She would be fine one moment and then the next, she would erupt. It seemed to Jake that Consuela Ruiz loved to pick a fight, whether it be with him or his father.

"Jacob, that's enough. Show your mom respect," Carlos said passively as he flipped on the TV, trying to find the preshow coverage for the Seahawks game against Kansas City.

"Seriously, Dad? I didn't say anything!" He couldn't believe his parents sometimes.

Jake had played out at least a thousand times how he would tell his mom and dad that he was gay. *Treat it like a bandage and just rip it off,* he told himself. He already had an idea how they would react. Consuela would likely begin quoting biblical scriptures and storm off, cursing in Spanish, while his father would likely say nothing and walk away. And somehow, Jacob knew the non-response from his father would hurt so much more than all the screaming in the world from his mother. But if he timed coming out to a Seahawks game, perhaps the news would go right over his dad's head.

The front door to the house opened and Jake heard Gigi call out, "Hello, it's your favorite adopted daughter!"

The sudden arrival of Gigi had Carlos pop out of his recliner to go greet her.

"Is that you, Virginia?" Carlos walked up to Gigi and squeezed her so tightly that he lifted her up from the ground.

"Hi, Mr. Ruiz," Gigi said through strangled air as he set her back down.

"How long has it been, *mija?* Two years at least! Too long!" Carlos said, wiggling his index finger at her as if she were in trouble.

"At least! And I see you are keeping that figure trim!" Gigi said, patting Carlos's round belly. Carlos chuckled and put his hands on his hips as he turned from side to side as if he were a supermodel in a photoshoot.

"Virginia..." Jake's mom said as she walked into the living room, acknowledging Gigi's presence and giving her a hug that was about as affectionate as a doctor hugging someone dying of the Bubonic plague.

"Hi, Mrs. Ruiz," Gigi said.

"Come. Breakfast is ready," Consuela said.

It had been almost two years since Jake's parents had seen Gigi, but the moment she entered his house, it was as if time had not passed. Jake had hoped the two of them would end up choosing the same college, but when he was accepted to Gonzaga University in Spokane, Gigi told him it was still far too close to Newport and she needed to go farther away. She ended up going to Western Washington University in Bellingham, which was about as far away as you could get from Newport and still go to college in state. The conversations between Jake's parents, Jake, and Gigi seemed to revert to sharing memories of the two growing up and the antics they had caused. And it was a mostly pleasant conversation until Jake's father brought up the unthinkable.

"Ah, you two got into quite the trouble. Like that time you and your class had the party in the woods," Carlos said, chuckling with a raised eyebrow.

Consuela cleared her throat so loudly that it sounded like she was about to cough up a lung and half the chilaquiles she had already eaten.

"It's a good thing you had your Bible study group pray that all away before that 'sin' really set in. Right, Mrs. Ruiz?" Gigi said with the subtlest tone of sarcasm that Jake's parents would most likely be oblivious to.

"It is, Virginia. You know what the Bible says in Galatians…Acts of the flesh like drunkenness, orgies, and idolatry will not allow you to enter the kingdom of Heaven."

"Orgies? Well, I can assure that party wasn't nearly as fun as you make it out to be. But I can certainly see how Jake consuming half of a warm beer could certainly tarnish his soul. Ow!" Gigi said after Jake had kicked her under the table a bit too hard. There was no reason to poke the bear that was Jake's mother.

"Well, this was delicious. Thank you for breakfast," Gigi said, wiping her mouth. "Jake, should we get going?"

"Sure. Do you think we could stop at the restaurant first? Dad has some new furniture being delivered that I was going to help him with."

"Yeah, of course! I'm happy to help, too, if you'd like, Mr. Ruiz."

"Ah Virginia, I'll never turn down free help!"

19

"Free? I figured you'd pay me in some tamales," Gigi said jokingly.

"I think I can arrange that, *mija*."

Had Gigi known she would be helping unload about twenty booths from a packed semitruck after breakfast, she would have likely negotiated for more than a couple tamales. It took nearly an hour to unload all the booths from the truck, and true to his word, Mr. Ruiz fed the two of them before they headed into Spokane. He also gave Gigi an additional tray of warm tamales that were bound to sit in her car the entire day and end up having to be thrown away.

"Okay, I didn't realize that your dad was going to make us unload everything. Don't they have drivers that do that?"

"You know Dad. He probably ordered them from some sketchy place where the truck unloading was an extra cost. Sorry I got you roped into that. So, what's the plan for tonight?"

"Well, you remember Stacy Morrell? She's living with Bradley Jones and Jenny Watson, and I told them we'd drop by and say hi before we go out tonight with your Bulldog friends."

"Oh, so I'll be playing Straight Jake this afternoon then," Jake said disappointedly. His college friends and Gigi had known about Jake's sexuality, but it was something that was not widely known by his high school friends, mostly out of fear that the news would make its way through the gossip chain and right into Los Ruiz Restaurant and Karaoke Lounge.

"Only until you put on your Halloween costume..." Gigi said suspiciously.

"Oh, what did you do, Gigi?" Jake hadn't been concerned for what Gigi had picked out this year until now. It had been a custom since they were freshman in high school that they would alternate each year on who picked out their "couples" costume for Halloween. It had started innocently with Pebbles and Bamm-Bamm, but as the years progressed, the costumes seemed to get shorter and more scandalous.

"It's a blast from the past," Gigi said, beginning to hum the theme song to *The Flintstones*.

"I thought you were adamantly against costume repeating."

"Oh, I was, but when I was going through my old costume trunk at Helen's, I found our first costume and thought it would be fun to do it again. Don't worry, I've made some...alterations."

"Oh jeez, how short is it?" Jake asked. Knowing how liberal Gigi was in cutting fabric, he was worried that his dick would fall out of his costume before the end of the night.

"Don't worry, I cut it short enough to make any guy want to immediately take you home, but not short enough to give away any spoilers. I'm so excited for tonight! This is our first time to go to a gay bar together!"

"Oh yeah! So, what happens if we run into anyone from Newport there?" The thought had crossed Jake's mind. It wasn't as if this was his first time to one of the gay bars in downtown Spokane, but usually it was with a group of his college friends and Max, Jake's only gay friend at Gonzaga. He had always figured if he ran into someone from Newport, he would just say he was there with his friends, but Max had decided to go down to San Diego to see his boyfriend for Halloween this weekend, so Jake wasn't sure what he would say.

"Relax. If we run into anyone, you can just say that I dragged you there," Gigi said reassuringly.

"Have I told you what an amazing friend you are?"

"Not nearly enough! Now remember—I get all the straight guys and you get all the gay boys," Gigi said. This reminded Jake of when they were growing up and the two would share a pack of Runts. Both would fight over who got the pink ones, but Gigi would always separate the oranges to keep for herself and give Jake the green ones. Neither liked the banana-flavored ones, which would end up getting thrown away. And now she applied that same distribution model to boys, divvying them amongst the two of them.

That afternoon, Gigi took Jake on a tour de "Newport alumni" that was neither enjoyable nor entertaining. In the three years since graduating high school, Jake had felt like he had changed and grown in so many ways. And yet, whenever he found himself around his former classmates, it was like revisiting some weird human time capsule. His old friends seemed to gravitate to the "good old times" like elderly people thinking back to a fonder time decades ago. But instead, they were reminiscing of a time that was four years ago. Jake didn't have memories like this and couldn't help but wonder if it was because near the very end of high school he was always walking on eggshells, afraid to let his true self be known.

"You guys want a beer?" Bradley Jones asked Jake and Gigi.

"Um, it's, like, not even one p.m.," Jake said.

"Come on, Ruiz. It's Halloween weekend. If you start early, you'll last longer through the night."

"I'm not sure that's how that works, Brad. I'm good," Jake said.

"That's science, Jake," Gigi said in an authoritative voice as if it were an indisputable fact. "I'm the world's foremost expert on day drinking. I'll take one!"

"So where are you guys going tonight?" Stacy Morrell asked the two of them. Stacy had been one of the most popular girls in Jake's class. She and Jake had the same circle of friends, but he hadn't kept in touch with Stacy as much as Gigi had. This was mostly because Jake saw Stacy as the equivalent of a human train wreck. Sure, she was pretty and pleasant enough, but the slightest drop of alcohol in Stacy was like throwing a lit match into a tank of gasoline.

"Oh, we are just going to go barhopping with some of Jake's friends from college. But I really want to go to Dempsey's!"

"The gay bar?" Bradley asked, handing Gigi a PBR. She grabbed the can with hesitation, not realizing that when she said yes to Bradley's offer, it meant she was starting her night off with PBR.

"Thank you," Gigi said, not even trying to hide the hesitation in her voice. "Yeah, I really want to go. I hear it's a lot of fun. You want to come, Bradley?"

"That's a no for me," Bradley said. "Not really my scene."

"Dancing, hilarious drag queens with big giant boobs, and fun with friends aren't really your scene? Jenny, you've really got yourself one dud of a boyfriend," Gigi said, looking at Jenny Watson, who laughed at the dig.

"I'm just saying I don't want to go there and have someone think I'm gay," Bradley said, trying to justify his reasoning with an even worse excuse.

"Bradley, we've all seen how you dress. Trust me, no one in their right mind is going to think someone in a camo shirt, mesh athletic shorts, wearing tube socks with sandals is gay. If anything, they will think you're blind and got lost in your dresser. Besides, there are plenty of straight guys and girls who go there, so no one would think that. But relax, it was just an invitation," Gigi said. "I didn't realize you weren't comfortable with your masculinity like Jake is. He's coming."

"Ruiz? You're going?" Bradley asked as though this had changed the game.

"Yeah. Why not?" Jake said nonchalantly as if he weren't the one who had proposed going to the gay bar tonight in the first place.

"Eh, I don't know. Besides, Jenny, Stacy, and I were going to go to a house party up on South Hill tonight."

"Oh, I do love the gay bar," Stacy said a little too excitedly. Jake began to panic, worrying that Stacy would change her plans and invite herself to join Jake and Gigi. Jake knew if that happened, his night would quickly change from having fun to having to babysit Stacy.

"Do you…want to come with us?" Jake said with the most obvious hesitation in his voice.

"Not tonight. But maybe we can go together another time?" Stacy looked at Jake in a way that Jake almost felt like she was saying, "I understand. I know." Maybe Stacy wasn't as oblivious as Jake had always thought she was. And that made Jake nervous.

"Fine. Your loss. What's the best taxi service?" Gigi asked the group, clearly ready to get on with the evening without their high school friends.

"Use AAA Taxi. It's the cheapest." Bradley said.

"Yeah, and if you throw up in the backseat, they only charge you an extra fifty dollars!" Stacy chimed in, as though that were some sort of selling point. Jake already knew Stacy could only know this fact from personal experience.

"You know, I was a little on the fence, but that sold me, Stacy," Gigi said, dialing the number for their taxi to take them downtown. After she got off the phone, she grabbed an extremely large duffel bag and pushed Jake into Stacy's room so they could change. They had known each other for far too long to change in front of each other and have it be some sort of awkward thing. Bradley, Jenny, and Stacy didn't think anything of it either. They had their suspicions that Jake and Gigi were secretly dating, so this just seemed to validate their thoughts.

"Can you believe Bradley?" Jake whispered as he started undressing to put on his costume.

"Can I believe that a guy who grew up in the middle of nowhere is homophobic *and* a bad dresser? No… I mean, look where we are Jake… It's not like we are in San Francisco or NYC."

"It's just... I don't know. I guess I figured moving away from Newport would have helped him grow into his own person. Besides, I always thought Bradley was more accepting and liberal."

"Oh? How so?" Gigi let go of her hair that she had been putting bobby pins in before she put on her red wig to see where Jake was going with this.

"I don't know. I mean, his parents are very earth-friendly and they hosted Jozef."

"You seriously think someone would not be homophobic because their parents recycle their milk jugs and host high school students from Slovakia?" Gigi asked incredulously.

"Well, when you say it like that, it sounds crazy."

"Any way you say that, it sounds crazy. It makes no sense. Do you also not remember how religious his parents are? Do you not remember him coming to class when we were in second grade after Bush lost the election saying that his parents said the end of the world was coming because Clinton was going to be president?"

Jake had forgotten about Bradley's meltdown where he started crying and shoved his desk over after the election and told all his classmates they needed to ask for forgiveness so they could get into heaven. Once word had traveled of his antics, Consuela Ruiz urged Jake to try and become better friends with Bradley and had even arranged several play dates between their two families. It was a memory that was buried so deeply in Jake's mind that he had forgotten about it until Gigi had brought it up. The two started laughing at the resurfaced memory.

"Oh my God. How do you remember stuff like that?" Jake asked.

Gigi pointed to her head and then said, "This thing is a steel trap."

"Um...GIGI! What did you do?" Jake broke their whispered conversation as he yelled out her name. He was looking down at the bottom half of his costume, or what was left of it. The last time he had worn this costume, Bamm-Bamm had jagged brown shorts that went just above his knee and a padded foam chest to cover his actual body. Now all that was left was a vest to go over his actual exposed chest and a pair of shorts that traveled maybe six inches down from the waistband and had at best a two-inch inseam. "Gigi, I can't wear this. My balls are going to fall out of this."

"Relax…here." She walked over and readjusted the length of the shorts by pulling them down a bit.

"Oh great. Now my ass will fall out from the back," Jake said, adjusting the shorts carefully to avoid anything falling out from the front or back.

"Seriously, Jake. This isn't an issue. It's Halloween! People expect to see everyone in skimpy costumes."

"Well, they are definitely going to see a lot of me then," Jake said as he reassessed the costume. There was no way he was going to feel comfortable tonight. "Let's just get downtown so we can start drinking and maybe the alcohol buzz will make me feel less awkward."

"Now that's the spirit!" Gigi said, handing Jake his club – the only part of the costume that avoided Gigi's free-spirited, scissor-wielding hands.

When their taxi finally dropped Jake and Gigi off downtown, they realized how very wrong Gigi was that people would be in costume this early in the day. As far as they could see, they were the only two in costume, and there was hardly anyone downtown yet.

"Gigi, I am going to kill you," Jake said between gritted teeth as the two walked down the street. It may as well have been any other day in the year, because there was no indication it was Halloween weekend.

"Hey, it's cool. We're the first people downtown. Nothing wrong with that. Come on… Let's go to Blue Spark and I'll buy the first round of drinks. Sound good?"

"It better be decent liquor and something strong," Jake said as he walked alongside Gigi, consciously checking to make sure a rogue testicle didn't fall out with every step he took along the street. Once they got to Blue Spark, Jake felt at least a bit better after noticing another table of people their age already in costume as well. Jake looked at the table and recognized one of the guys. There was no way he could ever forget that face. The face of his childhood crush.

"Oh my God, look who it is," Gigi said, pointing to the table. She had recognized him too. "Come on, let's go say hi."

"Do you think that's a good idea?"

"Why not?" Gigi asked.

"Because…" Jake said, crossing his arms wildly as though he were some sort of air traffic controller ushering in a plane to the narrow airstrip that was his shorts. "I'm practically naked, Gigi."

"We really need to get you a drink, Consuela," Gigi said, comparing Jake's high-strung behavior to his mother's.

"Well, well, well. Look who it is," a voice that had just approached them from behind now sent a minor chill down Jake's back. Jake and Gigi spun around to see the most gorgeous man in black rimmed glasses and a dark wig hiding his dirty blond hair.

Chapter 4 – Present Day

"Hi, Mamá," Jake said quietly, laying Charlie down on the empty patient bed next to his father.

"*Cállate, mijo!* You want to kill your father?" Consuela said in a harsh whisper. Jake took a deep breath. As tired as he already was, he knew Consuela Ruiz was about to exhaust him to new levels.

"Sorr—"

"TTT...TTT...TTT!" Consuela whispered, holding up her forefinger, effectively bringing Jake into submission and silence.

"Can we talk out in the hall?" Jake asked ever so quietly before his mother could silence him again. She opened one eye and slowly stood up. Jake realized in that moment how very appropriate Gigi's nickname for his mother was. He had just awoken a sleeping dragon.

"Jacob, it's the middle of the night," Consuela said, almost sounding as if she were irritated, but Jake knew there was no way she could be upset that her only son packed up in a matter of minutes and hopped on the last flight out of Seattle to Spokane with his son and then drove an additional ninety minutes to get to the hospital. No, there was no way Consuela could be irritated. Except that she was. Jake knew his mother all too well and how very selfish and self-centered Consuela Ruiz could be.

"Really, Mom? I can't just teleport myself here instantly from Seattle. I got here as fast as I could," Jake said.

"Well, you are just lucky that your father has enough strength to hold on long enough to say goodbye to you!"

"Mom, enough with the guilt trip. Colt said he is stable now and that it wasn't even as bad as you made it sound."

"Oh, he did, did he? Well, I'm telling you he isn't. Your father is weak, *mijo.*"

"Of course he is, Mom. He just had a stroke!"

"Don't you take that tone with me. I'm not the one who abandoned their family," Consuela said. She didn't dance around the issue. Instead, she took an express train to a topic that was guaranteed to create a heated argument for both sides.

"Maybe y'all should take this outside," Stacy Morrell-*blah-blah-extra-names* said from the nurse's station.

"Shut up, Stacy," Jake and his mother said in unison. The shock on Stacy's face had her fall back into her chair so quickly it was as if someone had come up behind her and kicked in the back of her locked knees.

"Jesus, Mom. I can't continue to have the same fight with you," Jake said.

Consuela slapped her son on the shoulder. "Don't you DARE take the Lord's name in vain, Jacob Carlos Ruiz."

"I'm sorry, but you can't tell me that I was the one who abandoned my family when you and Dad decided to not speak to me for years. You're really going to say I'm the one who abandoned my family, when I was the first to extend an olive branch and send you an invitation to my wedding?"

"You were just rubbing your sinful lifestyle in our faces!"

"No, I was trying to reach out to you and Dad. I can't help it if that was the message you chose to see from that gesture. And what do you think now? You think I'm rubbing in my sinful lifestyle by bringing him here?" Jake asked, pointing through the window at Charlie, who was fast asleep, oblivious to the ensuing argument between Jake and his mother.

"You know that is not what I think. You've only let me see my grandson once…" Consuela began, trying to play the guilt card.

"And that's because you've invalidated half of his family. You've discredited the family that we had built, and you have never acknowledged someone Charlie knew as his father and someone he misses every day! As far as I'm concerned, Charlie only has one grandmother, and that isn't you," Jake hissed back.

"It's not too late, *mijo*. Now that you're single, you can repent. Take a life of celibacy and raise your son."

Jake stood there, floored at what his mother had said. He looked up and saw Stacy at the nurse's station who looked equally stunned and speechless, which was saying a lot since Stacy never seemed to be able to shut her mouth.

"Text me when you're not at the hospital so I can see Dad," Jake said.

"Oh, you're not seeing your father," Consuela said firmly.

"Excuse me?" Jake looked at his mother incredulously. Surely the woman who called him a mere few hours ago and demanded that he return to his hometown was not telling him now that he could not see his father. But this was Consuela Ruiz. She was stubborn, selfish, hateful, and always made sure she had control of a situation. Even if it came at the expense of others. "Are you seriously telling me I can't see my father after I flew here from Seattle?"

"That is EXACTLY what I'm saying. You're no son to him," Consuela screamed. The vein on her forehead was bulging and she looked like a rabid dog, ready to foam from the mouth at any moment. Jake envied his friends who all had great relationships with their parents, because at this very moment, he wanted to throw his mother down a flight of stairs.

"Stacy, can she do this? I can see my father, right?" Jake said, turning to face Stacy, who looked like a deer in headlights that was about to be plowed over by an eighteen wheeler.

"Um…well." Stacy paused after speaking as if she were in slow motion. All the color had drained from her face and she looked like she was going to faint at any moment. She took a deep breath and looked around, likely hoping Colt or someone else way above her pay grade would be able to jump in and handle the situation. "I believe your mother is your father's power of attorney. I would need to check with my supervisor, but if she thinks you being here may not be in the best interest of your dad's recovery…"

"It is NOT in Carlos's best interest," Consuela said, cutting Stacy off. Stacy bit her upper lip and slipped through an employee door and out of sight. She clearly did not want to be a witness or casualty to Consuela Ruiz's wrath.

"This isn't over, Mother. I'm calling my lawyer first thing tomorrow," Jake said. He walked past his her and back into his father's room to get Charlie. When he emerged again, Consuela was standing there motionless. Her eyes were closed and she was taking deep breaths that sounded like grunts. Jake recognized what she was doing. She was either trying to calm herself down or was trying to contain herself from going on a blackout rage. He had seen both outcomes from the deep breaths, and if that was any indication, he needed to get his son and himself away from Consuela as quickly as possible.

Jake didn't care what time it was in Seattle. He had to call Gigi. Too much had transpired in such a short period of time that Jake knew he had to talk with someone.

"Hello?" Gigi said in an extremely quiet whisper.

"Gigi? I'm so sorry for calling so late," Jake said quietly as well, hoping not to wake up Charlie.

"It's fine, it's fine. But hold on one second," Gigi said quietly. He could hear her fumble around for a few minutes without a word coming from her.

"How's your father?" Gigi asked. This time, she was talking in a loud voice that echoed.

"Where are you? You sound like you're in a tunnel." Jake said.

"Sorry. It must be my cell service. I'm just on the balcony," Gigi said, giving an unconvincing response. Had the events of the evening not unfolded, Jake would have pressed a bit harder on Gigi to find out what was going on, but he didn't have the time.

Jake told the story of how Consuela Ruiz apparently awoke with a vendetta to settle, and not even his father having a stroke could abate her temper.

"Seriously, what is wrong with her? Your mother is a straight-up bitch, Jacob, and if I were there, I'd be in jail right now for assault," Gigi said. "I'm so sorry, Jake. I wish I could give you a giant hug. You know you don't deserve to hear that...and she doesn't deserve you!"

"Thanks. I guess I just kind of didn't expect that would happen." Jake paused, feeling guilty at the thought that was about to come out of his mouth. "I guess I thought my dad's stroke might possibly bring us together. And now that I'm actually saying it out loud, I feel like a horrible human being."

"I know what you mean, and don't feel bad," Gigi said reassuringly. "Honestly, Jake, Jesus Christ himself could descend from heaven right now and your mom would probably pick a fight with him for being friends with a hooker. Your mom is not a nice person, plain and simple."

"Well, there's something else that happened too," Jake said slowly.

"Oh my God, you didn't kill her, did you?"

"What? No! When I was at the hospital, I ran into Colt."

"Humphrey? You've got to be kidding me! What was he doing there?"

"Working. He's a doctor and apparently lives in Newport now."

"How unfortunate. Of all the places to live, he chose to go back there?"

"I think it's kind of sweet," Jake said, but instantly regretted the words.

"Oh no. Don't even think about it, Jacob Ruiz!" Gigi said in the most authoritative motherly tone he had ever heard come out of her mouth.

"What are you talking about?" Jake asked innocently, but deep down he knew what she was reprimanding him for.

"Are you kidding me? Do you *not* remember Halloween our senior year of college? Do you *not* remember what happened?"

"Relax. It was just a nice conversation between the two of us," Jake said reassuringly.

"Mmhmm. Okay… Well, that's good, I guess." Gigi said, clearly not buying what Jake was trying to sell her.

"Besides, he said he's dating someone," Jake said, feeling inclined to share this bit of knowledge to show that even if he was hypothetically interested in Colt, he was off the table anyway.

"Oh, really? Well, all I can say is hopefully he found a girlfriend outside of town and then imported her back to Newport. Otherwise he's probably dating someone with meth teeth… You know, the ones that look like corn kernels?"

"God, Gigi! There are plenty of cute people in Newport," Jake said as he tried to convince himself of this statement as well. "I mean *we* came from Newport."

"Yeah, and we left! If there's one thing that Helen has taught me, it's that you can always find better cuts of beef in Spokane." Gigi had been on a first-name basis with her mother for as long as Jake could remember. It was odd hearing a child refer to their mother by first name when they were kids, but it was at Helen Clayton's insistence.

"Helen's single again? What about that teacher she was dating?" Jake asked.

"Oh, he was like two boyfriends ago. She'll give you the lowdown on her dating life. That much, I am sure of," Gigi said. Helen stayed casually single after Gigi's father ran away with a woman half her age. He had sent cards to Gigi on all the major occasions, like high school graduation, twenty-first birthday, or when Gigi had landed her first real job with Microsoft after college, but as far as Jake knew, Gigi had not seen him since the day he ran out on her and her mother. And it wasn't like Helen was unattractive. She had a free-spirited, hippie energy about her. Her curly blond hair was usually worn down, and she often had some sort of beaded jewelry she had just made woven into her braids. She wore only organic clothing or secondhand, because she was very much against the massive carbon footprint that new clothing and retailers made on the world. And you couldn't think of anyone more opposite Consuela Ruiz than Helen Clayton, who was a weed-smoking, pro-choice, women's rights, liberal activist, painter. Gigi inherited her biting sense of humor from Helen, and had Jake's mom known just the type of person Helen Clayton was, he knew he would have never been allowed to become as close of a friend as he had become to Gigi.

"Anyway," Gigi said, bringing him back to the matter at hand. "So, you saw Colt Humphrey. You're in love with him again, and your mom is still awful. Doesn't sound like much has changed, does it?"

"First, I'm not in love with him. Second, yes—my mom is awful. I'm going to have to call my lawyer tomorrow morning."

"You should just fly back here. Forget about them. You don't owe them anything, Jacob Ruiz!"

"I know. But it's my dad," Jake said, thinking of his father. Although the relationship with his father wasn't great, it was infinitely better than what he had with his mother. And for that reason, Jake felt obligated to stay until he could at least see his father.

"Well then, I'm hopping on a flight to Spokane. I'll be your muscle against your mother. I've been waiting almost two decades to slap that woman." As she said it, Jake knew that Gigi wasn't kidding in the slightest.

"You don't need to do that, Gigi."

"Relax. I needed to use up some of my vacation from last year anyway. Besides, Helen has been hounding for me to come over. I've been telling her I was going to wait until the Pass was clear of snow, but she learned that the DOT has cameras you can view online all along the Pass and called me on my bullshit."

"Gigi, there hasn't been snow on the Pass for a couple months. You really think Helen is going to believe there's snow at Snoqualmie Pass in June?"

"It is a VERY HIGH ALTITUDE, JACOB RUIZ!" Gigi said, screaming into her phone as she enunciated every single word.

"Well, having you back here would be fun. And maybe when we are both in town, we could get the gang together," Jake said, knowing full well Gigi would see through his veiled attempt at trying to find any excuse to hang out with Colt, and more importantly, find out more about his girlfriend.

"You are one sick puppy, Jacob Ruiz," Gigi said. "I'm calling Dragon and I'm having her light a candle for you the next time she's in church."

Jake began to slow down as he reached the driveway that led to Helen Clayton's house. Affixed to the side of her mailbox was a faded bumper sticker with a marijuana leaf on it that read: "Go green." To the right of her mailbox was a sign that read: "Meat Is Murder." Next to that sign was an "Elizabeth Warren 2020" sign just barely visible because another sign that read, "Any Competent Adult 2020" was blocking it. Jake couldn't believe it, but Helen Clayton somehow was able to show more of her personality in ten square feet around her mailbox than most people could in their autobiography. It was the middle of the night and Jake could see the warm glow of the porch light and the living room lights on. He knew that Helen would be awake and waiting for Jake because that was the kind of person she was. And if there was anyone besides Gigi that could make him feel better after the encounter with his mother, it was Helen Clayton. The woman that filled the void that Consuela Ruiz should have occupied.

CHAPTER 5 – OCTOBER 27, 2006

"Colt!" Gigi said, throwing herself into Jake's childhood crush, Colt Humphrey, who now stood in front of them at Blue Spark. To be fair, he was also technically Gigi's childhood crush as well; a fact she didn't find out until Jake finally came out to her.

"Hey, Gigi," Colt said, wrapping his arms around her and giving her a big squeeze. "And Ruiz!" Colt let go of Gigi and went to hug Jake. Jake felt a million things. First, Colt's muscular arms wrapped around Jake. It was better than he could have ever imagined. Colt had been a good six inches taller than Jake, so Jake's face pressed just against Colt's collarbone and pectorals. The last thing Jake felt was panic. Panic because he had no idea what would happen if he ended up getting aroused in his skimpy shorts. The thought caused him to quickly pull away from Colt and then cross his hands over his crotch. He was almost certain nothing was visible, but he wanted to be safe. Unfortunately, subtlety was never a strength of Jake's, and the quick jerk reaction did not go unnoticed by Gigi or Colt.

"Hey, Colt," Jake said quietly.

"Let me guess…Pebbles and… Well, the top half of you looks like Bamm-Bamm. Where'd the other half of the costume go, Ruiz?" Colt said with a big smile.

"It's Gigi's fault. She thought it would be fun to skank up these costumes," Jake said, making air quotes and speaking in the most unamused voice.

"It's a good look on you," Colt said, still smiling. Gigi shot a glance at Jake, her eyes bulging and the veins in her neck looked like they were about to burst at any minute. If she could telepathically ask Jake if his gaydar was going off with Colt in front of them, she would have been screaming this.

"Here's your drink," a waitress said, handing a beer to Colt. She stood there, rocking on her feet as she stared at Colt while he took a sip.

"Hey, not bad! See? I'm always a good judge of character." Colt said. The waitress nervously giggled before she walked away.

"So, what are you dressed as? Are you a pastor or a young Orville Redenbacher?" Jake asked, trying to change the conversation from the odd encounter he had just created. He assessed Colt, who was dressed in a three-piece suit and a tie. Had it not been for the wig, Colt would have looked like he had just gone to a funeral.

"I'm Jonas Salk," Colt said, as if the mention of Jonas Salk would be an instantaneous explanation of his costume.

"I'm sorry...who?" If there was anything that Gigi got annoyed with, it was Halloween costumes that weren't obvious and made you think.

"Dr. Jonas Salk. He helped create the polio vaccine," Colt said.

"Cool story, Colt. I'm going to go get us drinks. You want one?" Gigi asked.

"I'm good for right now," Colt said, holding up a glass.

Gigi rolled her eyes and sighed so heavily, as though she were physically exhausted from the brief interaction with Colt, before she made her way over to the bar, leaving the two of them.

"So, how's school going Ruiz? You're at GU, right?"

"Yep! School is good. Looking forward to being done though. What about you?"

"Nice! I wish I was almost done. I just got accepted into UW Medical School!"

"That's awesome! Congratulations. I bet your parents are thrilled," Jake said, thinking about Colt's parents, who were both doctors. His dad had a practice in Newport, and his mom was a psychiatrist in Coeur d'Alene, Idaho.

"Yeah, they're pretty excited. So, what are you two up to tonight?"

"Well, some of my friends from college are meeting up with us and we figured we'd just barhop. Gigi wants to go to Dempsey's later tonight."

"Dempsey's? You better be careful... You'll be the talk of the town," Colt said.

"What do you mean?" Jake asked, startled.

"Figuratively speaking, of course. I just meant with that costume… Well, I'm sure you will get a lot of attention."

Jake couldn't tell if Colt was paying him a compliment, or chastising him for the choice in costume and their eventual destination.

"Drink up, ladies!" Gigi said, rejoining Colt and Jake, holding up three drinks. "Three Mind Erasers!"

"Gigi, we're really starting this hard?" Jake said, taking a sniff of the drink that immediately stung his nostrils and made his stomach churn. Colt looked just as hesitant after smelling the drink.

"To Jozef!" Gigi called out, holding her drink.

"The Slovakian exchange student?" Colt asked before he downed the shot with Jake and Gigi. Not even the coffee liqueur could mask the vodka that burned all the way down their throat.

"That was disgusting, Gigi. You're not allowed to buy any more drinks like that," Jake said, setting the glass on the table.

"Fine, but it's going to have to be after this next round because I already ordered three more," Gigi said as she grabbed the empty glasses and made her way back to the bar.

"So did Jozef die or something?" Colt asked once Gigi was out of earshot.

"Huh? What are you—? Oh. Gigi's just being Gigi. I'm sure he's doing just fine and still pocketing panties," Jake said.

Colt burst into laughter. It was one of the best sounds that Jake had heard in a very long time. Even under his ridiculous Jonas Salk costume, Jake could see that Colt hadn't really changed. He was still the fun-loving, lighthearted guy he had always been.

"That's right! I totally forgot about that," Colt said, remembering the time that Jozef had been found in the bedroom of Stacy Morrell, stealing a pair of her underwear from her drawer.

"Hey, Colton. We're about to head down the street. You ready?" A guy from Colt's table approached the two, dressed as a banana. He looked Jake up and down and then shot him an arrogant, crooked smile. Jake had been around this guy for less than five seconds and could already tell the guy was completely full of himself. But he could look past it, considering the guy was smoking hot, Jake thought. He looked like Channing Tatum in *Step Up*, which Jake had conveniently found an excuse to go watch at the movie theaters four times in the last two months.

"Nice costume, dude," the banana said to Jake.

"Where you guys headed?" Colt asked.

"We are going to some dueling piano bar one block up."

"Is it cool if I meet up with you guys in a bit? Just catching up with old friends from high school," Colt said.

"Of course. Harrison Peake, the third," the banana said, extending his hand out to Jake in an intentionally arrogant manner.

"Bamm-Bamm Rubble, the first," Jake said, grabbing Harrison Peake, the third's hand and squeezing tightly as he shook it. His hand was soft and warm and maybe he had imagined it, but Jake could have sworn that he saw Harrison look down at Jake's exposed legs and bite his lip. Colt quietly snorted in the background at the interaction between Jake and Harrison.

"Cute," Harrison, said with a haughty sense of smugness. "We'll catch up with you later, Humphrey. Later, Bamm-Bamm." He gave Jake a smirk and left with Colt's friends.

"He seems...nice," Jake said, deciding to lie rather than insult Colt with telling him his friend seem like a grade-A douchebag. A very *hot* douchebag.

"He really isn't. He's the definition of an asshole," Colt said.

"Oh good! I wasn't sure what to say," Jake said. "How do you know him?"

"From school. All four of us were here for the premed conference. None of us are really friends. We're staying over at the Convention Center. To be honest, I may just have to ditch them and hang out with a more entertaining crowd." Colt said, winking at Jake.

How is it that Colt barely has to do anything and oozes sex appeal and charm, Jake thought.

"That would be awful," Jake said in an overly dramatic tone of sarcasm to ensure that Colt would pick up on it.

Gigi returned to the table with three drinks rather than shots, so it was already a huge improvement. They were an orangish yellow and had little umbrellas at the top, and from what Jake knew about umbrellas, they usually only came in tasty drinks.

"Did they run fresh out of that sewage juice you made us drink? What's this?" Jake asked.

"Mai tais! I figured it was a safer bet," Gigi said, taking a sip.

"Good guess, G. Thank you," Colt said, clinking his glass with the other two before taking a sip. "So, what brings you back to Spokane for the weekend?"

"Well, Jake and I made a promise back in freshman year that we would spend every Halloween together. And so far, we have. I didn't want senior year of college to be the first," Gigi said. "What about you? Aren't you in Seattle? Did you hear that the Halloween scene in Spokane was way better or something?"

"Of course. I mean…clearly," Colt said, waving his hand around at the now empty bar. "I'm actually in town for a conference for school."

"So, what I'm hearing is that you have a hotel room that we can crash in if we get too drunk then!" Gigi said excitedly.

"Well, yeah, I guess so," Colt said.

"Aw, Colton Humphrey, you always were my favorite," Gigi said, squeezing Colt's arm and resting her head against him. Jake couldn't help but feel a tinge of jealousy that Gigi could be so openly flirty with Colt and no one would think anything otherwise.

The late afternoon progressed as the three continued to catch up and by the time that evening came, downtown Spokane was finally filled with people in Halloween costumes. Also, Jake, Gigi, and Colt were now very, very drunk.

"I just want a hot dog in my mouth. RIGHT NOW!" Jake said, as the three made their way down to the next bar.

"And in your butt," Gigi whispered and then cackled in laughter, her speech a bit slurred as she poked her finger on Jake's nearly exposed butt cheek. She was practically being propped up by Colt, as she had her hands wrapped around his arms. He wasn't sure if it was the awful choice in alcohol they had consumed or the fact that Gigi and Colt looked like a real-life couple, but Jake felt sick to his stomach.

"Shut up, you drunken wench," Jake called out.

"Okay, okay. Maybe let's get some food real quick…and some water." Colt, the apparent voice of reason for the evening, guided a drunken Gigi and a somewhat sulking Jake to a diner.

"Aren't your friends wondering where you are?" Gigi asked Colt.

"Nah. I texted them and told them I'd catch up with them tomorrow. I'm sure they've already forgotten about me." The three walked into Dewey's Diner and devoured three plates that were piled high with bacon, hash browns, and fried eggs.

"Oh my God, why is bacon sooooooo good?" Jake asked as he tilted his head backward and lowered the bacon into his mouth as if he were a baby bird.

"Woah, Jake. You want to get a room with that hog?" Gigi called out.

"Huh?" Jake said through a mouthful of food.

"You're practically deep throating that bacon!" Gigi said before going back to devouring her eggs.

"That was the most delicious thing I have ever put in my mouth," Gigi moaned before sliding back in her seat. "I'm sorry we didn't get to go to the gay bar."

Jake shot her a horrified look that he only prayed Colt did not notice. Between the "deep throat" comment and now this, Gigi's words had practically slapped him back into partial sobriety. He swore that if Gigi's drunken lips were how he was outed to his former classmate and that was how his parents found out, he would literally murder his best friend.

"What time do you think it is, G? It's, like, nine," Colt said, laughing.

"WHAT?" Gigi grabbed her phone to look at it. She was clearly oblivious to her near disastrous slip-up. "Oh my God. I thought it was like two a.m.! Can we stop and grab a coffee somewhere before we go anywhere else?"

"Oh man, I could definitely go for some coffee right now," Colt said.

After ordering and downing scalding hot cups of coffee, the three made their way out of the diner and back down the street. For the first time this evening, Jake was thankful everyone was drunk. Gigi's comment was brushed over, so he was hopeful Colt had not even really heard it.

"So, were you the one wanting to go to Dempsey's?" Colt asked Jake curiously. Jake studied Colt's face, and for as long as he had known him, Jake couldn't tell what Colt was thinking. Was it curiosity? Judgment? Intrigue?

Shit, Jake thought. Any hope that the comment wasn't heard in their drunken haze was now thrown out the window. Jake realized that in this exact moment, he had two options. He could deny it and say Gigi was just being drunk. Or he could find the courage to own up to Gigi's comment and come out to one more person. But this wasn't just anyone. It was his childhood crush.

"I just thought it might be fun," Jake said, opting for a third option he came up with in that moment.

"I think it will be," Colt said. The way he looked at Jake somehow felt electric. It was as if their conversation and eye contact had somehow allowed them to connect on a different level. Nothing about this interaction felt forced. It reminded Jake of when the two had been kids. Colt had always been his best friend up until around fifth grade. Colt started doing more with sports, and Jake just found no interest in that. The two started drifting further apart, but remained friends throughout the rest of junior high and high school. However, Jake would be kidding himself if he said he hadn't missed the friendship they once had. He wondered what it would have been like to have been best friends with Colt through high school, but then Jake realized that it would have likely been one filled with heartbreak.

"What do you mean?" Jake asked.

"Well, we're still going, right? I mean, we're only a block away," Colt said, pointing the way up the street.

"YES!" Gigi squealed as she jumped up and down on the sidewalk. "Can we? Can we?"

"I'm down for it if you are, Ruiz," Colt said with his eyebrow raised.

Jake had no idea what the outcome would be, but he knew that beyond the shadow of a doubt, he would forever hate himself for the rest of his mortal life if he passed up the opportunity to go to a gay bar with Colton Humphrey. "All right, all right. Let's go."

"Hey, weren't you supposed to meet up with your friends?" Gigi asked.

"Oh no!" Jake pulled out his cell phone that was wedged between the waistband of Bamm-Bamm's shorts and his boxer briefs. Five missed phone calls and three text messages.

Colleen 10/27/06 8:14 p.m.: Where are you? Why aren't you answering your phone?

Adam 10/27/06 9:03 p.m.: Jake? Buddy? Everything okay? Colleen says you're not answering

Colleen 10/27/06 9:33 p.m.: Ok…Well, we are going to head over to Patton's. Text us if you are on your way.

"Crap." Jake scrolled through the messages before texting his friends back. Adam had been his roommate freshman year and they had become close friends, and then once he started dating Colleen, Jake accidentally grew a little closer to her. This was largely due to the fact that she reminded him so much of Gigi—a fact that whenever it was brought up always infuriated Gigi, who claimed she had been replaced. "Colleen and Adam have been trying to call me."

"Oh no," Gigi said dryly. "I hope that we haven't missed them. That would be awwwwwwwwful."

Colt chuckled and looked at Jake. "I take it she's not a fan?"

"No, not really," Jake said.

Earlier that night, there was virtually no one out, but now all the bars seemed packed. Colt was generous enough to pay for a cover charge that seemed ridiculously overpriced even by Halloween standards and especially by Spokane standards.

"I can buy the drinks," Colt offered.

"No! Let Jake," Gigi interjected. "Look at him! That costume is bound to get us some kind of discount. Your Dr. Scholl's outfit or whoever you're supposed to be is going to get us zip."

"Again…Jonas Salk, but good point. Jake, take your sexy self over there and work your magic," Colt said, wrapping his arm around Gigi. There was so much to unpackage with Colt's last comment that Jake was happy to see a long line at the bar. It let him really think about what Colt had just said. Hearing him call Jake sexy created what felt like heartburn, but Jake figured that could have also been the fried bacon and scalding hot coffee they had just devoured.

Work your magic? What kind of magic did Colt think that Jake possessed? *Maybe Colt really does find me attractive*, Jake wondered. Jake knew he was considered good looking by society standards. At one

41

point in high school, Gigi had called him the "poor man's Enrique Iglesias." She may have meant it as an insult, but Jake didn't care. To be compared to Enrique Iglesias, even as a poor man's version, was a huge compliment. Hell, he'd take being compared to a "homeless man's Enrique Iglesias" and still think of it as a huge compliment. He had a toned, swimmer's body that wasn't quite as defined as Colt's, but he was in good shape. The brown vest that helped cover Jake's chest would not stay closed, and Jake couldn't help but feel extremely exposed to the crowded bar. He stood there, pulling at the brown vest to keep it closed as he continued to obsessively dissect Colt's comments.

"Jake?" a voice from behind him said. Jake spun around and felt his heart fall into his stomach. Standing in front of Jake was a pharaoh with just about as much clothes on as Jake. And under this costume was TJ Smith—the only boy that Jake had ever dated. He was the closest thing to a boyfriend that Jake ever had, but giving that title to what transpired between Jake and TJ would have been way too generous. TJ had come on incredibly sweet in the first two weeks they had dated. Jake was excited to have met someone who seemed to be the perfect guy for him. That was until he found out that TJ was also the perfect guy for about five other guys he had been seeing simultaneously. It was a whirlwind "romance" that lasted for about three weeks, but it left Jake jaded about potentially finding love with another man. "Men are jerks. And if you're lucky enough to find one, it will only be a matter of time until you find out what kind of scumbag he is. A cheater. A misogynist. Or a panty sniffer like Jozef," Gigi told him in a phone call where Jake had cried for more than an hour and was inconsolable.

"TJ…" Jake said frostily. "Which boyfriend are you here with tonight? Thing 1, Thing 2, or Thing 3?"

"Yeah, I guess I deserve that, don't I?" TJ asked, as if it were even up for debate. As hard as he tried to maintain eye contact with Jake, TJ kept glancing down at Jake's costume, or lack thereof. "You know, I've done a lot of thinking since we stopped talking. I'm actually single. I realized I needed to do a lot of work on myself before I start dating again."

"Oh?" Jake couldn't help but find himself ever so slightly interested to hear more about this self-enlightenment that TJ had experienced.

"What can I get you?" the bartender asked Jake, who had finally made his way to the front.

"Just three Bud Lights, please," Jake said.

"Open or closed?" the bartender asked after taking hold of Jake's credit card.

"You can close it," Jake said. The bartender handed him a receipt to sign and three bottles before moving to the next customer at the other end of the bar. Jake turned around to catch TJ looking at his ass. He couldn't help but feel a little good that his ex, for lack of a better term, still found Jake attractive, and more importantly, that Jake had emotionally broken him to the point where he wanted to change himself.

I'm like a gay Dr. Phil, Jake thought. "So what kind of things have you been working on?"

"Oh, like…a lot of stuff!" TJ said unconvincingly. "I've started reading self-help books about loving yourself and just being more accepting with who I am."

"What's the name of the book?" Jake asked. Something about this story seemed illegitimate, and Jake was determined to catch TJ.

"What?"

"The book… What's the name of it?"

"Oh, it's called…*Loving Yourself.*"

"*Loving Yourself?* That sounds like a book about jerking off, TJ. You expect me to believe this?"

"All right, all right. So I haven't started reading a self-help book, but that doesn't mean I haven't changed." TJ was now bordering on sounding like he was begging. Unfortunately, it came in between two separate drag queen acts and for a brief moment, the entire bar could hear their conversation, including Colt, who looked over in the direction of Jake and TJ and locked eyes with Jake.

"Hey, babe, did you get our drinks?" Some random, mildly attractive guy dressed in drag as Cleopatra came walking up behind TJ and wrapped his arms around him.

"Yeah, here you go," TJ said, his cheeks turning red as he handed Cleopatra his drink.

"Who's this?" Cleopatra asked TJ.

"Oh, just an old friend," TJ said, realizing he had been caught.

"An old friend?" Jake repeated. He really despised drama, but given the amount of crying this scumbag had caused for such a short period of time they had dated, Jake was not about to let this conversation get away from him. "Hi, I'm Jake," he said, reaching out his hand to Cleopatra.

"Benji," he said as he took Jake's hand and shook it.

"Well, Benji, I should let you know you are here with one class act. I'm not sure what's going on between you two, but TJ here was just trying to hit on me."

"Really, TJ? Can you NOT for just one night?" Benji had nearly the entire crowd in the bar now invested in this argument that was unfolding before their eyes.

"Babe, I'm sorry."

But Benji stormed off before TJ could finish.

"Is everything okay?" Jake spun around and felt as though a panic attack was imminent when he saw Colt standing behind him.

"This doesn't concern you," TJ snapped back at Colt.

"Actually, it does," Colt said, looking at TJ. "Jake's with me."

"With you?" TJ said in disbelief. "I highly doubt that."

"Why?" Colt said. He wasn't sure if it was the alcohol, but Jake thought Colt sounded as if he were in genuine disbelief why him and Jake couldn't be together.

"Well, you scream *breeder*, for one! There's no way that you're gay," TJ said as he spiraled into this free fall of illogical thought.

"Well, I am, and I'm telling you that Jake is with me. Come on, *babe,*" Colt said as he laced his fingers into Jake's open hand as he pulled him back toward the drag queen stage and Gigi. Jake had no idea what had just transpired, but this was now, hands down, the best day of his life. They were only halfway back to Gigi when the moment was ruined by TJ yelling out across the bar.

"Good luck with that!" TJ hollered. "Like it will last!"

This time, Colt spun around and looked past Jake toward TJ. The anger in his face was unlike anything Jake had ever seen in his life. It was like he had been personally attacked. For a moment, Jake was worried Colt was going to go back and beat the living hell out of TJ, but instead, he placed both his hands on Jake's waist, leaned down and kissed him right on the lips. The complete shock of getting kissed by Colton

Humphrey shocked Jake so much that all three beers he had in the other hand fell to the ground and shattered.

Colt's lips were different than how Jake had always imagined. They were soft, yet slightly rigid on the outer edges. They were chapped, Jake realized, but he couldn't care less. Here he was kissing Colton-fucking-Humphrey and he didn't want this moment to end, chapped lips and all. But Colt pulled away, ending the moment, and smiled back at TJ. The moment felt so genuine and the kiss so electric that it left Jake with about a thousand more questions.

"All right, fellas… I think you've had enough for the night. Time to go." A bouncer placed a hand on Jake and Colt's shoulders and started to push them toward the entrance. As they were literally pushed out of the bar, Jake caught a glimpse of TJ, who stood there smirking at the spectacle as he remained in the bar, but it didn't even bother Jake. In fact, absolutely nothing else really mattered at this point.

"Oh shit…Gigi," Jake said once they were out on the street, realizing they had left her behind in the chaos. He tried calling her and no answer.

Jake: Are you still inside? We just got kicked out!

Gigi 10/27/06 11:05pm: Seriously? Where are you guys going?

"I'm really sorry," Jake said, feeling guilty that his drama caused both him and Colt to get kicked out of the bar.

"It's cool. I'm not," Colt replied.

"Gigi wants to know where we are going now."

"I don't know. Why don't we just walk and see what's still open?" Colt said.

"Okay," Jake said, putting his phone back in his costume, forgetting about Gigi.

"So…are we going to talk about that?" Colt asked Jake. "Who was that?"

"Colt, that was…my ex? I mean, I guess that's what you would call him," Jake said with extreme hesitation. "I'm…gay."

Colt stopped walking and turned to look at Jake. He grabbed Jake's hands and held both of them. "I think I've known for a while, but thank you for telling me. I know it's really hard to come out."

"You've known for a while? Like, for how long?" Jake asked, shocked.

"Like since seventh grade," Colt replied.

"WHAT! Are you kidding?"

"Jake, you stare. Like, a lot," Colt said, kind of laughing, but stopped as soon as he saw the reaction on Jake's face was more of an expression of humiliation rather than amusement. "Plus, there was homecoming night. Remember?"

"Oh yeah," Jake said, thinking back to homecoming night when Colt had decided to throw a party after the dance. Just the thought of what happened after the party made Jake embarrassed all over again.

"Relax, I don't think anyone else in high school knew. Besides, it seemed like you really only stared at me."

"Well I did like you, Colt. You weren't just my best friend when we were kids. You were my first crush. My childhood crush," Jake said. Here he was, in the middle of downtown Spokane, a lifetime of feelings now exposed. It was something that made him feel more naked and vulnerable than his skimpy costume could ever make him feel.

"Really? Jake..." Colt paused for a moment, appearing to be at a loss for words.

"I just can't believe all this time that you're gay too!" Jake said, unable to hide the excitement that trailed from his voice.

"Listen, Jake... I'm not," Colt said. Those four words made Jake feel as though someone had just kicked him from cloud nine and he was now plummeting back into reality.

"You're not? But you kissed..."

"I'm so sorry, Jake. I shouldn't have done that," Colt said. "I just saw how that dick was talking to you, and I don't know..."

"What? Say it," Jake fired back. He felt a mounting rage that was on the level of his mother. It was this anger that Jake finally felt like there may have been parts of him that made him more alike than unlike Consuela Ruiz.

"I felt sorry," Colt said quietly.

"I don't need you to feel sorry for me, Colt!" Jake said. He could feel the shakiness and unevenness in his voice and felt as though he may be on the verge of crying at any moment, but he was determined to not let Colt see him cry. "I've gotten by for this long without anyone feeling sorry for me, and I'm not about to start now!"

"I know, I know. Maybe those weren't the right words."

"No, they were. No need to sugarcoat things." Jake felt his eyes welling up. "I think maybe you should go find your premed friends, Colt."

"Jake…" Colt said. Had Jake stopped to listen and not been so angry, he would have heard the slight unevenness in Colt's voice.

"Good night, Colton. It was nice seeing you," Jake said, and then turned away from Colt and made his way back to Gigi.

Jacob Ruiz finally experienced the heartbreak he envisioned would be inevitable when he was a teen, if he were to ever have any type of romance with Colton Humphrey.

CHAPTER 6 – PRESENT DAY

"As I live and breathe!" The front door of Helen Clayton's home opened, releasing the warm smell of burning sandalwood incense that had been bottled up inside. Helen was wearing a rust-colored kaftan with about six or seven necklaces of varying lengths that went almost to her hip. Her blond hair was slightly frizzy and there were now several more streaks of gray in it than the last time that Jake had seen her. Helen had stopped coloring her hair during the Covid pandemic and decided that she would let it all go gray. She reached out and scooped Charlie from Jake's arms, allowing Jake to grab his bags.

"Hi, Helen," Jake said, smiling at the ray of sunshine that was Helen Clayton.

"Oh sweetie. I'm sorry to hear about your dad," Helen said, leaning forward and kissing Jake on the cheek and squishing Charlie between the two of them in the process. "Let's get this kiddo to a proper bed, and if you're up for it, I have two glasses of wine with our names on it!"

"Oh, I am definitely up for that!" Jake said as he followed Helen into her home. He didn't care what time of the night it was. He was in desperate need for a glass of anything after the encounter with his mom. When he stepped into Helen's home, it was evident that she had smoked a joint not too long ago and had been trying to mask the smell by overcompensating with the incense. Instead, the result was a strange and exotic smell with the subtlest hint of weed.

"Charlie can take Gigi's room, and you can have the guest bedroom. There's clean towels on both the beds," Helen said. She must have also noticed the lingering smell of weed as she hurried over to her coffee table and began to light another incense stick.

"Thanks," Jake said. He walked into Gigi's room. Helen must have had a penchant for nostalgia as she hadn't touched Gigi's room. There were still posters on one wall of NSYNC, 98 Degrees, LFO, and for some reason still unknown to Jake—a poster of Worf from *Star Trek: The Next Generation*. Jake had made fun of the poster and asked if Gigi had a crush on Worf one time, which resulted in Gigi not talking to him for a solid week. He never brought up the poster again. Jake slipped Charlie's shoes off and tucked him into the bed before sneaking back out into the living room.

"So, I have a really cheap red that I got at the grocery store or whiskey," Helen called out from the kitchen. "But I guess the question I should be asking is, have you seen your mom already?"

"I have," Jake said, walking into the kitchen.

"Whiskey it is," Helen said. She wasted no time placing a large, spherical ball of ice into two glasses and then pouring a liberal hand of whiskey from a decanter into two glasses.

"You know, I'm probably the only person who took one of those DNA home kits and hoped for the type of scandal that reveals you have different parents," Jake said, taking a sip of the whiskey. It burned at first and then made him feel warm. Helen smiled faintly as she pulled out a jar of Kalamata olives and what Jake already knew was a block of vegan cheese. "Does someone have the late-night munchies?"

"Oh damn, I was sure I burned enough incense to hide it. I promise I won't smoke in the house while you two are here." Helen's face had begun to flush slightly from embarrassment.

"Oh Helen, this is your house! But thank you. I wouldn't ask that of you if Charlie weren't here," Jake said. He felt slightly guilty but knew that Helen loved Jake and Charlie and would do anything for them.

"You know, families are a lot like those boxes of mixed chocolates you get from awful people who don't really know you at Christmastime," Helen said.

"I'm sorry, I don't understand," Jake said. Helen went over to her breadbox and grabbed a chocolate box that had been sitting on top.

"Gladys Hopper," Helen said, looking at the gift tag affixed to the box as she rolled her eyes in disgust and dropped the box forcefully on the counter in front of Jake. She lifted it, revealing an untouched box of chocolates.

"Families may all look the same on the outside, but you don't really know what's going on in the inside." Helen ran her finger up and down the rows of chocolate before stopping at one and squinting her eyes. She picked it up and took a bite and spit it back into her hand. "Coconut raspberry. But you see, they all look similar on the surface, but some of them… Well, they're truly awful. The thing is, Jacob, no family is perfect, and for some of us, we forge our true family much later in life. It doesn't make it any less special than a real biological relationship. You'll always be my boy, and you'll always have my love."

"Cheers to that," Jake said quietly. He wiped his eyes that had begun to tear up the second Helen turned to put the chocolates back on top of the breadbox.

"Are those chocolates vegan?" Jake asked.

"Jacob, I'm still human, and chocolate just happens to be my weakness. Even if it's disgusting chocolate," Helen said as if that cleared things up.

"Can I ask you something that may be too personal?" Jake asked.

"Of course," Helen said, placing her elbows on the counter and leaning forward excitedly. "Those are always the best questions to answer."

"It's been fifteen months since…" Jake paused. It was still difficult for him to talk about it but he knew that Helen already knew where he was going. After all, Helen was the one who flew to Seattle to sit with Jake at the funeral, where his parents should have sat. She was the one who stayed an extra month to help take care of Charlie after the funeral. "When did you want to start dating after…?"

"After Gigi's dad decided to run off with a tramp?" Helen chuckled and swirled the whiskey around in the glass. "Well, as you are well aware, things are different when you have a child. Gigi still doesn't know this, but I actually went on a date about three months later. It was pretty bad, but it at least gave me the confidence and self-awareness that I didn't need a man to be happy."

Jake wondered if Helen's date had been as disastrous as Jake's first date after his husband's death. But something told him that Helen probably was a lot stronger than he was.

"I saw someone tonight that kind of reminded me of how I used to feel when you get those butterflies. You know? I guess I'm afraid. What if we only get one truly remarkable love in our life and that's it?"

"Jacob Ruiz, I poured this whiskey because I thought you were recovering from a conversation with your mother. A matter of the heart requires an entirely different drink." Helen tossed back the remnants of the whiskey into her mouth, emptying the glass. She walked over to her antique Tibetan cabinet, opened the doors, and pulled out a dusty bottle of cognac.

"I'm still working on the first," Jake said, holding up the whiskey.

"Well, you best hurry up! This is what you actually need," Helen said. And if there was ever a point in time that Helen and Gigi sounded like the same exact person, it was that comment. "I poured myself a glass from this bottle the night Gigi's father left and I haven't touched it since. I figured I would save it for another night when I knew I would need it. I think, my dear, that is tonight. You want to tell me about him?"

The fact that a maternal figure was taking an active interest in hearing about Jake's boy troubles had the instant effect of Jake unpacking everything. He started with the history he shared with Colt and ended with the conversation tonight where he learned that Colt was now dating someone, which produced the tiniest sliver of what Jake believed to either be jealousy or disappointment. But more importantly, Jake was angry. Angry that so many years could pass and Colton Humphrey still had the power to elicit any type of feelings in Jake.

"*Even love unreturned has its rainbow.* J.M. Barrie," Helen said. For as long as he had known her, Helen always seemed to have a fitting quote for the situation at hand. And it only made sense that a children's book illustrator would be able to quote the author of *Peter Pan.* "You know, being back home after being gone for so many years can create a lot of emotions. And couple that with your father and seeing Colt, well…I'm not surprised you feel a bit confused. But have you thought that maybe feeling anything like this may be a gift?"

"How so?" Jake asked.

"Well, perhaps it's your heart telling you that it's close to putting all of its broken pieces back together."

CHAPTER 7 – JULY 20, 2018

"Thank you so much for agreeing to do this interview, Jake," Jaime Mayer said over the phone. Earlier in June, she had sent an email to Jake Ruiz, asking him if he would be interested in doing an interview for Pacific Northwest Airlines. Jaime Mayer had been someone Jake had gone to college with during his undergraduate studies. One time, Jaime agreed to stand in line for student tickets to a Gonzaga basketball game for three hours at Jake's request. He had promised that one day he would repay the favor and then they graduated. He had forgotten about that until he had randomly received an email from Jaime, who had now become the communications director at Pacific Northwest Airlines, and it was now time to repay the favor.

"Hey, the way I see it is we're even now, right?" Jake said, chuckling.

"Jake, are you kidding? It was downpouring that day and I got soaked, which then turned into a cold and nearly the flu. I guess you could say I nearly died by getting you your basketball tickets," Jaime said in an overly dramatic fashion. "Besides, I'm really doing *you* a favor by publishing this story for thousands of readers to see. I'm thinking that maybe I'm due one more favor."

"Getting greedy there, Mayer," Jake said jokingly. "All right, fire away. Just make sure that you make me look good."

"Deal!" Jaime said and then started asking Jake questions about his love for food. When did he first realize he had a passion for cooking? He talked about how he grew up in the kitchen. When his friends were out playing basketball or baseball, he was helping his parents with their small restaurant in the tiny town of Newport, Washington. He talked about his family making tamales on Christmas Day and seeing the love that was put into these meals. He spoke about his mother fondly in a way that he hadn't talked about her in years. It was enough to ensure that the reader would have no idea just how fractured the relationship between him and his parents had become.

"It sounds like you have a really amazing relationship with your parents that is connected through food," Jaime said. She and Jake had run in similar circles in college and had taken several classes together, but she had no idea the nerve she had touched upon with her last comment.

"I guess you could say food is the one thing that still keeps us connected," Jake said. He knew it would be a good quote for the story, but it was also the truth. His mother and father had made no attempt to reach out to him or be a part of his life. In fact, he had been the one who had reached out some time ago to speak with his father. He was trying to recreate an enchilada recipe his father had made years ago, but couldn't remember all of the ingredients. And to his surprise, Carlos answered the phone and talked with him for hours. It was the best conversation he had had with his father in years, and all they talked about was food. Carlos made no mention nor asked about Jake's personal life, but as they sat there talking and laughing about a memory from eating hot peppers on a drive down to California, Jake felt like he had his father back if only for a moment. So, as he sat there in the chair of his office telling Jaime that food was the one thing that kept him connected to his parents, it wasn't a lie.

"Can we talk about your family for a minute?" Jaime asked.

"I thought we already were," Jake replied.

"I mean your husband and son," Jaime said.

"Um, sure," Jake said hesitantly.

"You said in a previous interview with *The Seattle Times* that your husband was largely the inspiration for your French-inspired restaurant, Forchette. I'm just wondering if your son played inspiration to any of your restaurants as well."

Jake felt a wave a relief rush over him after Jaime had asked the question. For some reason, he expected some sort of hard-hitting journalist question when she broached the topic of his family. But it was all softball questions from Jaime Mayer.

"Well, Charlie's palette really only consists of dinosaur-shaped chicken nuggets and apple granola bars right now. I'm pretty sure that if

I were to open a restaurant right now on the eating habits of my three-year-old, I would be in business for about one day."

A knock on the door and Jake's restaurant manager, Diane, peeked through the opening. "There's someone at the bar to see you," she whispered. Jake held up his finger and Diane slipped back out of the door and quietly shut it.

"Do you have any plans to open additional restaurants in the near future?" Jaime asked.

"Well, when I first opened Viva la Vida Cocina, it was really meant to be a love letter to my parents and the cooking I grew up with," Jake said with absolute honesty. "The dishes at the restaurant are inspired by the food my mother made for our family. They were the meals we prepared for special occasions. That's why that restaurant has an incredibly special place in my heart.

"But, as you know, I went to cooking school. I was able to learn about so many different cuisines, styles of food and flavors. I always had a love for barbeque, but knew that I would not be able to do what I had envisioned with additions to the Viva menu. That's when I opened Beacon Hill Barbeque. And then came my Capitol Hill tequila bar, Blue Agave, because who doesn't love tequila? Then came Maple Point Bakery. And finally, Forchette. I guess what I'm trying to say is that I never set out to open something new with each of these businesses. They came to me organically, and I saw potential for them in the Puget Sound area. I'm not ruling out opening another restaurant, but I want to make sure I see there's potential for it to be successful and stand the test of time before I make that commitment."

"Oh wow," Jaime said as Jake could hear the furious typing on her keyboard in the background. "What a beautiful sentiment! Well, I think I should have all that I need for this article. I'll call you if I'm missing anything, but thank you so much. I'll call you when I'm ready to cash in on that favor."

"Nice, Jaime," Jake said, laughing. "It was good talking with you. Take care."

"You too, Jake."

As he made his way to the bar, Jake wondered if he had shared too much with Jaime to the point where he sounded insincere. After his mother, Jake had always been his toughest critic and he tended to focus on even the most minute of details and then dissect it. When he finally made it to the restaurant bar, he felt his chest tighten and his heart rate pick up. There, at the end of the bar, sat his father. He took a deep breath and walked over to the open seat next to his father and sat down.

"Jacob!" his father said, turning on the stool and leaned over to give Jake a hug. He couldn't remember how long it had been since he had actually seen his father in person, so Jake was surprised to find his father more than 300 miles away from Newport.

"Dad? What are you doing here?"

"Well, I just came in for the day to catch the Mariners game against Chicago. And I figured since I was in town, I'd stop by your restaurants."

"Restaurants?"

"Well, I went to your bakery first. Delicious conchas, by the way! They said you weren't there and that I'd probably find you here, but I wanted to stop by Viva la Vida first. You know, scope out the competition," Carlos said with a smile.

"Dad, my restaurant is almost five hours away from you. I'd hardly consider myself a competitor to your restaurant." Jake was happy to see his father. He didn't quite care that Carlos's main motivation for coming to Seattle was for a baseball game. He was just happy that his father appeared to making some level of effort and was potentially extending an olive branch. At the same time, he was curious about his father's opinion. "So, what did you think then?"

"Of what, *mijo*?"

"The restaurant?"

"Oh! It was amazing. You're an artist in the kitchen, just like your moth—" Carlos stopped dead in his tracks, but Jake already knew where that comment was heading. Saying he cooked like his mother, though, was a compliment. If his father had said he was acting like his mother, however, Jake would have voluntarily committed himself.

"It's good to see you, *mijo*," Carlos said, patting his son on the back.

"And where's Mom?" Jake asked, fully expecting this pleasant moment to be hit with a nuclear warhead that was Consuela Ruiz.

"She stayed back in Newport. She…wasn't feeling well," Carlos said. His father was an awful liar. Jake knew she didn't want to come because she was probably expecting Jake's father would want to make a visit like this.

"Do you want something to drink, Jake?" the bartender asked, coming over to the two of them.

"Just a club soda, please." Jake looked up at the bartender. "Oh, and Roxie? Can you put his stuff on my tab?"

"Sure thing," Roxie said.

"You don't need to do that," Carlos said. "I'm happy to pay full price at my son's restaurant. Ha! Who thought I'd be saying that?"

"Dad, what are you doing here?"

Carlos shifted in his seat. It was obvious something was either bothering him or just seeing his son after such a long period of time was hard for him. "It's Los Ruiz, *mijo*. We are having some trouble."

"What kind of trouble?" Jake asked, already understanding what his father was saying and now fully comprehending the nature of his father's visit.

"The money kind, *mijo*," Carlos said. "We had to fix the roof, and then the walk-in refrigerator had to be replaced. People just aren't visiting as much as they used to."

"Do you need money?" Jake asked. The happiness Jake had felt to see his father had faded as he realized that had it not been for the financial issues and the fact that his son was very successful, Jake's father may not have been sitting in front of him right now.

"Well, yes...and no," Carlos said. "I have a business proposal."

"What is it?"

"Well, ever since you were a kid, our plan was to always pass the restaurant down to you. The plan was that when either your mother or I passed away, you would inherit fifty percent equity in the business and help the surviving parent continue to own the restaurant. But then..."

"But then I married a man and you guys stopped talking to me and essentially cut me completely out of your lives?"

"*Ay*, you really are like your mother," Carlos said, and Jake knew that was not meant as a compliment. "Look, Jacob, I'm sorry we don't talk like we used to. This whole ordeal has been hard on your *mamita*. She's only ever wanted the best for you."

"Well, Dad, I would hardly call who I've married and decided to raise a son with an 'ordeal.' And if Mom has only wanted the best for me, she's certainly not acting like it."

"*Mijo*, sometimes your mother takes longer to realize things. She doesn't realize that what she sees as 'best for you' is actually what is convenient for her. She'll come around. She's incredibly stubborn…but she'll come around."

In all his years of being around his mother, Consuela Ruiz was not one to "come around" or apologize for being in the wrong. In fact, Jake didn't believe he had ever heard an apology come out of his mother's mouth. At least not a sincere one.

"I guess we will just have to wait and see. And what about you?" Jake asked, looking at his father.

"What about me?" Carlos said.

"You're here. I mean, you're here to ask for money, but…are you here for anything else?"

"Jacob, of course I'm here for other things besides money. Did you hear me earlier? I'm also seeing a Mariners game." This was classic Carlos. In even the most serious of times, Carlos would crack jokes as if it were his own wall of defense to help hide and protect his true feelings. "I'm kidding. You are my only child. Even when you didn't know it, I've been following your career and rooting you on from the sidelines. I may not agree with who you've married, but it isn't my life to judge.

"You know, Abuelita Cervantes didn't like me much when your mother and I first got married. She called me a lowlife drunk. And she was kind of right; I was. But I worked hard to provide a good life for your mother and for you and in the end, Abuelita still doesn't like me, but I think she respects me. Besides, I was happy. I've had a rewarding life.

"I see you are happy, and…I think that's all I'd want for you. I grew up in a different time, *mijo*. I think it's time I…maybe get with the program."

Jake sat there frozen and slightly numb. He felt tears running down his cheeks, but didn't care who saw. This was all he had ever really wanted to hear from his parents. It may have taken several years for one of them to say it, but it was progress.

"And what about Mom?"

"*Ay*, she'll need time. She'll get there. I'm not sure when, but she will."

"Thanks, Dad. So…this business arrangement?"

"You'll still get the fifty percent ownership when one of us passes. But I'd also give you a thirty percent stake in the company right now…for an investment into Los Ruiz Restaurant and Karaoke Lounge. And in the future, that would add up to eighty percent if one of us were to pass."

"Will my thirty percent stake give me authority to suggest taking 'Karaoke Lounge' out of the restaurant name?" Jake asked.

"You're such a jokester," Carlos said, laughing for the briefest of moments and then going deadpan and silent. "No. Besides, I just had the neon replaced on the sign, so it stays."

"Okay, so how much would this thirty percent stake cost?"

"Well, I figured with the building and the restaurant, she is worth about five hundred thousand. So, a thirty percent stake would be a hundred and fifty thousand. But you're my son, so I'd give you a thirty percent stake in Los Ruiz for thirty thousand. There's just one catch."

"And that is?" Jake asked.

"That we don't discuss this with your mother," Carlos said, finishing up his beer.

"She doesn't know about the money trouble, does she?"

"She does the books, Jacob."

"So that's a no." Jake thought about how disorganized his mother had been when they were growing up. She may have been the restaurant's accountant, but an accountant she was not. Their "financial records" that Consuela kept for filing taxes had usually been kept in a large paper grocery bag next to the desk at their house. There was no sort of organization to the contents of the paper bag and if anyone didn't know what it was, it would have looked like a bag full of old receipts. Jake realized that his parents' financial issues were likely a direct consequence of Consuela's accounting practices.

"Pretty much." Carlos laughed quietly in amusement, while his face told a different story. One filled with embarrassment of having to ask for money from his estranged son in the first place.

"Let me go get my checkbook and I'll be right back," Jake said. He made his way back to his office. He knew that even at the "family discount," his father was asking for quite a bit of money, but Jake knew that for his father, this was more than about money. It was a way to bring Jake back into the family. This was at least his hope.

"Thank you, Jacob. I really appreciate this," Carlos said, tucking the check Jake had just wrote into his wallet. "Hey, I don't suppose you'd want to catch a Mariners game with your old man, would you? My treat!" Carlos pulled out two tickets and showed them to Jake. "LeBlanc's the starting pitcher and I have a good feeling about the game…"

"Sure, Dad. Let me wrap up a couple things and then we can head out," Jake said. He figured that when your father, who you haven't spoken with in several years, shows up at the restaurant you own on the other side of the state and asks you to a baseball game, you say yes. And he was glad he did. It was the best night Jacob Ruiz had in years. And for the first time in a long time, he felt optimistic about a future with his parents.

CHAPTER 8 – PRESENT DAY

"Good morning, sweetie!" Helen called out as Jake walked into the kitchen the next morning. It wasn't even seven yet and Helen was already serving a small stack of pancakes to Charlie, who was sitting at the kitchen island.

"Coffee. Must have coffee to function," Jake said, mimicking a robotic voice. Charlie began to giggle between mouthfuls of pancake he had already shoveled into his mouth. Jake made some beeping sounds as he walked rigidly over to Charlie and kissed him on the top of the head. "Good morning, buddy!"

"Morning, Dad! You didn't tell me we were coming to see Grandma Helen," Charlie said excitedly. Charlie was the only one who referred to Helen as a "mom" or "grandma." And as much as she had encouraged Gigi to call her by her first name when Gigi was a child, Helen never corrected Charlie. She would never admit it, but Gigi and Jake both knew that Helen secretly loved the name.

"I didn't? Well…surprise!" Jake said as he went over to the coffee maker to pour himself a cup. "How on earth are you awake this early and making breakfast after being up so late?"

"It's the curse of artists," Helen said, handing a plate of pancakes to Jake. "After you went to bed, I started painting a page for a book I'm working on. Creativity comes alive at the times you least expect it, and you find the time to sleep where you can. There's syrup next to Charlie. That is, there was."

Jake looked at Charlie's plate, which now looked like a giant lake of syrup. Charlie looked up at Jake with a wide grin. Syrup was smeared around his lips and Jake could have sworn that Charlie's eyes were the slightest bit dilated from the sugar intake.

"So, I received a call this morning from the hospital," Helen began. "From a certain doctor friend."

Just the mention of Colt created a twisting feeling in Jake's stomach. He looked over at Charlie, out of fear that Helen's abstruseness would create suspicion. Jake realized how ridiculous a thought that was as he watched Charlie continue to shovel pancakes into his mouth and then begin to lick the plate clean of its syrup.

"Charlie, really?" Jake asked, disgusted with how Charlie was eating.

"Huckleberry," Charlie said dreamily as he slumped back into the chair and patted his belly. "Can I have some more pancakes?"

"Of course, dear!" Helen said. She walked over to the table and plopped two more pancakes onto Charlie's plate, leaving the syrup pouring to him. Charlie let out an overexaggerated panicked sound just as Jake watched the remaining contents of the syrup bottle empty out onto Charlie's plate, which was being held vertically.

"Okay, okay. I don't think so. If you eat all of that, you're going to go into a sugar meltdown." Jake pulled the plate away from Charlie and set his pancakes on a clean plate that was on the counter. Charlie sat back in his chair and huffed with disappointment. "What did he say?"

"Apparently, he received word of what happened last night between you and your mother. My guess is with how the rumor mill works in Newport, he heard about it before you probably even left the hospital. Anyway, he spoke with your mother and wanted me to tell you that it's okay to go see your father. She won't be there until after one p.m. today. He said she will be spending the morning at church, praying for your father."

"Well, that was nice of him," Jake said, thinking about how unnecessary it was for Colt to get involved, and yet he did. It was very "on brand" for Colt Humphrey. Jake's mind lingered on Colt's action and then he starting to think about last night. *He really hasn't changed,* Jake thought to himself.

"Jake?" Helen stood on the other side of the kitchen island, and Jake knew she had been talking about something, but his mind had been elsewhere, focusing on a certain doctor.

"Hmm? I'm sorry. What did you say?" Jake replied.

"I said that I'd be happy to keep Charlie here if you'd like," Helen said.

"Are you sure? I mean, that would be great if you could."

"Of course! I'd be happy to. Besides, I could use a five-year-old's professional opinion on a book about a mouse and an enchanted toilet plunger."

"That's a joke, right?" Jake asked.

"I wish it were. It's for a Hungarian children's book. The mouse becomes friends with a toilet plunger that talks and they go on adventures together. You don't need to tell me – the plot sounds like utter garbage."

"Well, if there's anyone that can make the story of a toilet plunger beautiful, it's you," Jake said. Helen had won countless awards for the work she had done over the years, so it was strange to hear that someone who was the recipient of so many prestigious accolades was now illustrating animated toilet plungers.

After breakfast, Jake made his way to the hospital and he couldn't help but think about Colt. What did Colt say to his mother that made her agree to let Jake see his father? For as long as he knew her, Consuela was a stubborn woman, so to get her to change her mind was no small feat for Colt to accomplish. Jake's thoughts were interrupted when his phone buzzed. The name of his marketing and social media manager for the restaurant group, Marcia Schrader, scrolled across the on-screen display of the rental car.

"Hi, Marcia," Jake said after pushing the answer button on the steering wheel.

"Jacob, have I got some news for you! Can you come by the office tomorrow?"

"Well, I'm actually not in Seattle. I had to take a flight to Spokane last night. What's up?"

"Oh, shoot. I was hoping to share this with you in person, but I got a call from the team at *Wake Up With Us*. They are apparently on the hunt for a permanent replacement to their morning show chef, and guess who they'd like to fly out for a guest segment, which is actually an audition?"

"You're kidding!" Jake said in disbelief. Aside from a few appearances on the locally broadcast show *The Puget Taste*, Jake had never been in front of a camera. He didn't even realize he was on a radar of any sort for this kind of opportunity. "What did you tell them?"

"I told them to send over the details. I'm having a friend who is a lawyer in L.A. take a look at it."

"How would this even work if I ended up getting the job? Would I film my segment inside of a news station studio here in Seattle?" Jake asked, already anticipating a very different answer.

"Well, you'd need to move to New York. But Jacob, this is a once-in-a-lifetime opportunity," Marcia said.

"What about the restaurant group?" Jake asked.

"It would still run. You would just need to hire more people on the team to run the operations side of things. But Jacob, let's be very real with each other. You need this," Marcia said.

And there it was. Marcia knew the exact state of Ruiz Kitchens. Jake's business had been flourishing and then once the Covid pandemic hit, it destroyed everything. The capital that Jake had reserved was now non-existent and two of his restaurants were teetering on shuttering for good. None of the restaurants had fully recovered, and there were still plenty of empty tables even on the busiest of nights. Accepting a spot as the chef on the #1 morning show program that was broadcast to millions of homes around the country could get Ruiz Kitchens an injection of life and publicity they all so desperately needed. This was a golden opportunity and Jake knew that Marcia was fully aware he couldn't turn it down.

"When do they want an answer?" Jake asked.

"Soon. They apparently have a few other chefs they are going to rotate, so they'll get back to me in the next day or so for scheduling."

"Thanks, Marcia."

"This is good news, Jacob. I'll talk with you tomorrow."

On top of everything that was already running through Jake's head, he now had to begin thinking about a major career change and move that most certainly assured Ruiz Kitchens would be able to recover. He knew he would need to say yes. Besides, the thought of living in New York City kind of excited him. He knew that Gigi would kill him for leaving Seattle, and Helen would be upset he was moving so far away, but what else was keeping him in Washington besides his restaurants? He had an operations team that was able to help his company survive a global pandemic, so he knew they would be just fine if he moved to New York.

When he arrived at the hospital, Jake was greeted once again by Stacy Morrell and all her last names. Jake wondered if Stacy ever left the place.

"Jake!" Stacy said, leaping to her feet. "Do you have a minute?"

"Is it my father?" Jake felt a surge of panic and worry as he rushed over to the nurse's station.

"Oh no. God, I'm sorry to scare you like that. He's still in stable condition. I just wanted to apologize about last night," Stacy began. "I think you misunderstood me. I meant no harm or insult when I mentioned the wife thing. I shouldn't have made assumptions. I'm a total ally for the LGBTQ community!"

"It's fine, Stacy, really. I mean, it was really late. Besides, it was literally the least dramatic thing that happened in this hospital last night," Jake said, referring to Consuela's outburst in the hall.

"Yeah, your mother is still as…fiery as ever," Stacy said slowly. "Anyway, I just wanted to tell you that. OH…and also, I love *Will & Grace*!" Stacy said with a proud smile.

And she had been doing so well right up to the end, Jake thought as he walked into his father's room. To his relief, his mother was nowhere in sight.

"Hey, Dad," Jake said as he sat down next to the bed. His father's eyes were closed and he still had tubes running into his nose and an IV in his arm. There was no response from his father, and Jake found himself staring at the patient monitor that was bouncing to the beat of his father's heart. It was still showing signs of life, even though his father remained motionless, with the exception of the gradual rise and fall of his chest.

"I'm sorry if you heard me and mom last night," Jake began. "I'm trying, Dad, but sometimes Mom… Well, she just makes things so difficult."

Jake wondered if his father could hear his words. He realized that if he could, maybe talking about the fight that he and his mother had wouldn't be the best way to get on the road to recovery. He needed to talk about something more positive.

"You know…I had run into one of my restaurants the other day when I wasn't planning on working. The employees were laughing at what I was wearing and they asked why I would still be wearing a Wade LeBlanc jersey since he's not even on the team anymore. I told them that I bought that overpriced jersey during the best Mariners game I had ever been to. That was a great day.

"I remember you said you had a good feeling about that game when you were at my restaurant, and you were right. They beat Chicago three to one. And then Chicago kicked our asses the next day, but that's beside the point. You said you had a good feeling about that game and you were right. Well, I have a good feeling too. I know you're going to pull through this. You've got to. Your grandson is here in town and I'd love for him to…get to know you." Jake wiped away his tears as he talked to his father, who still remained asleep.

"That was your father's favorite day too," a quiet voice said. Jake spun around to see his mother standing in the doorway of the hospital room. She held a vase of flowers and walked in slowly to set them down on the table next to his father. He wondered how long she had been standing there and if she had heard him complain about her. He could see Stacy run up behind her mother with a complete look of terror on her face that Consuela was in the hospital room where Jake was. But when there didn't seem to be any type of argument like last night, Stacy practically moon-walked back to the nurse's station.

"Your father… He came back from Seattle and he wouldn't stop talking about that silly game. He said it was unbelievable… He said you were unbelievable. He saw your restaurants, and you know what he did? He came back here and was trying to make conchas to put on the menu. *Pendejo*," Jake's mom said, rolling her eyes as she sat the vase at his father's bedside. She reached into her purse and set a *TV Guide* onto the table. Jake had so many questions. Like, for starters, does a man in a medically induced coma really need reading material, and if so, why would she bring a *TV Guide*? It wasn't like Carlos was going to pop up out of bed and think to himself, "Gee, I'm glad this *TV Guide* is here so I can see what is on the hospital's CCTV." Also, Jake wondered why his mother had brought a *TV Guide* with a cover that read "Summer 2019 TV Preview."

God, she didn't even bring a recent copy, Jake thought as he looked at the two-year-old issue. If a *TV Guide* really was the thing to bring his father out of his coma after suffering a stroke, he was going to be sorely disappointed when he found that the copy Consuela brought wasn't even recent.

"He did?"

"*Ay.* Your father...he's a good chef, but he's a shit baker," Jake's mom said. He had to bite his tongue from laughing. In his entire life, he had heard his mother curse maybe once or twice in English, so to hear her curse so freely, Jake's natural instinct was to laugh. "I swear the things were hockey pucks. I told him to not tell people they were food...tell them we were selling doorstops."

Jake started laughing. This was the version of his mother he had loved, but it wasn't the one he had seen in a very long time.

"You think your coworkers thought you were crazy when you were wearing a Wade LeBlanc jersey? Well, imagine how crazy people thought I was about a month ago when I was going to every sports store trying to find his jersey. The stupid employees kept trying to give me a Felix jersey and I told them it had to be LeBlanc. Your father wore that other one to the threads. I don't know how there are seven days in the week and your dad...he wore it eight. But I had to go and find a new one for him. That's how special that day was to him."

Jake felt his eyes begin to well up and was determined not to let his mother see him cry. His mother's emotions and temper ran hot and cold so sporadically, Jake worried the pleasant version of his mother would flip so quickly Jake wouldn't have time to get out of the way from the freight train that was Consuela Ruiz.

"Mom..." Jake began, but his mom held up her hand. This time, she didn't say anything to silence him though.

"I just came by to apologize for my behavior last night," Consuela said. The fact that an apology was coming out of his mother's mouth so freely, without any indication it was being forced out of her, left Jake speechless. Apologizing was just not something Consuela did. "It was uncalled for. You have never stopped being your father's pride and joy. But you have also always been his disappointment."

As easily as she giveth, Consuela just as quickly tooketh away. Jake never knew anyone in his life besides his mother who could send his blood boiling in a hot second. He felt his hands instinctively slide under his legs in the hospital chair, restricting them from possibly jumping out and strangling his mother.

"If you'd like to see your father, you can come to visit before one p.m., and I'll come after one. That way we can stay out of each other's way. I think that will be best. *Comprende?*"

"Sure," Jake said flatly. His mother made her way past him and left the hospital room, leaving Jake once again with his father. The gesture was a huge milestone for Consuela, Jake acknowledged, but he still was in complete disbelief with how cold and transactional Consuela's offer was. Her capacity to love was not large, and Jake wondered how someone could justify this behavior toward their own child. Jake couldn't imagine anything that Charlie could ever do that would make Jake treat him the way Consuela treated him. And she did this all in the name of her religion that stated the second most important commandment was to love your neighbor as yourself. The rejection from his parents so long ago had sent Jake on a path that people usually only experience when their parents die. And now Jake found himself back in his hometown—back near his parents—and he began to wonder if he was truly willing to put himself through that kind of heartbreak a second time.

"Knock, knock," a voice said at the entrance to the hospital room. Jake turned around to find Colt standing there. "I got a panicked call from Stacy that your mom was here. Is everything okay?"

"I don't know if I'd say things are okay, but nothing was thrown, so I guess that's a good thing, right?" Jake said, half laughing even though he wasn't kidding at all.

"I'm so sorry. When I spoke with her, she said she wouldn't come until the afternoon," Colt said. He appeared to be distraught that he had somehow caused this to happen.

"There's no need to apologize. Consuela Ruiz may tell you one thing, but if it isn't what she wants, don't set your expectations very high," Jake said.

"Look, Stacy and I are wrapping up our shift here in the next couple hours. We were thinking about going to Jersey's for a couple drinks. You wanna join?"

"Sure," Jake said without realizing the response had already escaped his mouth. *So much for playing it aloof,* he thought. And then it dawned on him—could Stacy and Colt be dating? They had been close friends in high school and maybe Stacy had her eyes set on Colt being her third, fourth, or whatever number husband she was on at this point. The thought of the two of them dating sat like a pit in Jake's stomach.

"Well, that certainly paints a visual that can't be unseen, doesn't it?" Gigi said on the phone later that afternoon once Jake left the hospital and shared his suspicions that Colt might be dating Stacy. "I seriously doubt that those two are dating. It wouldn't even make sense if they were the last two people on Earth, right?"

The way Gigi said it, though, Jake could tell that even she wasn't quite sure herself.

"Can you imagine? Nope... I just can't!" Gigi said, as though she were having a conversation with herself on the phone.

"I guess I'll let you know in a little bit." Jake said. He had just pulled into Jersey's, which was some weird combination of a sports bar and biker bar on certain nights. It was one of just a couple bars in Newport, so it attracted a variety of the different crowds and groups that lived in the county. "I'll call you later."

Colt and Stacy were sitting in the back area of the bar. Colt had on an old Seattle Supersonics hoodie and gym shorts. If Jake didn't know better, it would have looked like Colt was a college frat bro in Newport and not a successful doctor with a well-established practice.

"Jake!" Stacy popped up out of the booth and ran over to Jake to give him a hug. "I'm so glad you came. It's like a mini-reunion!"

"I guess it is. I just got off the phone with Gigi and she'll be here next week too," Jake said. He had hoped news of Gigi's imminent arrival would assure him of a second outing with Colt. He still wasn't sure what he was doing, but he didn't want to waste an opportunity to see his childhood crush, even if it was just for a couple days again.

"Oh my God! When's the last time the three of us were together? I think it was Halloween night!" Stacy said. Jake looked over at Colt, who nervously shifted in the booth at the mention of Halloween. "Anyway,

I'm glad we are all back together again. Hey, why don't you go catch up with Colt and I'll get us some drinks?"

Jake had not anticipated this would have been an awkward encounter, but Stacy had innocently brought up a memory that Jake knew Colt would rather sooner forget. There was no way she could have known that the mere mention of Halloween would create this tense moment Jake now found himself in.

"It's kind of weird being at a bar in Newport," Jake said. He would kill for a drink in his hands right now, but Stacy hadn't returned yet.

"Just wait," Colt said. "It gets even weirder when people see us here and try to practically get their physical taken in the middle of the bar."

Jake laughed so hard he let out a small snort and felt his face turn red. Maybe this wasn't going to be as awkward as he had thought.

"Serious. It's why Stacy and I hide out in the back now," Colt said.

"Well, I hope they at least buy you a drink before they pull their pants down in the bar," Jake said, chuckling at his joke that seemed to fall flat on Colt, who just kind of stared blankly back at him and then winced a little.

"So many visuals with that, Ruiz," Colt said before he smiled.

"Sorry it took so long," Stacy said, arriving back at the booth with three drinks in hand. "I asked Art to make something sophisticated for our city friend here, and you would have thought I asked him the meaning of life. I gave up and he gave us three rum and Cokes. Cheers!"

The three held up their drinks and tapped the edges of the glasses together before taking a sip. Before long, they were rehashing stories from their youth and growing up in Newport. In true Stacy fashion, she brought up some of her drunkest memories, including homecoming night. Jake found this ironic, considering she didn't even remember the entire night. As she ordered another round of drinks, Jake wasn't sure if he was more impressed that Stacy had been able to hide half the stuff she was sharing with him or that he could finally recall all three of her surnames now.

"Colt, do you remember Bradley's party in the woods when we were sophomores–? Oh God. Jake, I'm sorry. I completely forgot." Stacy said. She obviously had just remembered the aftermath of how Jake had to confess his sins at Consuela's Bible study group.

"Don't worry about it. My mom is, well…I'm sure she means well in her own head. Unfortunately to everyone else, she's…" He had no idea how to finish that sentence.

"Too much?"

"Exactly. Thank you, Stacy." Jake said.

"Well, that was hands down one of the funniest nights of my life. We were all playing strip poker when someone dared Bradley to pee on the electric fence to see if anything would happen. And of course, something happened and he said he almost shit himself. I don't think I've laughed harder in my life, until the sheriff pulled up. And there we all were, running through the woods after Bradley had peed on the electric fence," Stacy said in hysterics. The story made Jake begin to wonder what kind of trouble Colt had possibly been involved in.

"Who would have thought you two would end up together?" Jake said, laughing as he took a sip of his drink. He heard Stacy shriek in laughter.

"Oh my God, we aren't together!" Stacy giggled. "Colt is dating Eli."

Jake felt as though the entire bench had been pulled out from beneath him. *Could Eli possibly be a girl's name?* Jake wondered. *Maybe it was short for Elizabeth…or Eliza…or Ellie.*

"And there he is now!" Stacy slid out of the booth and made her way to the entrance.

"You're…gay?" It was the only words Jake found leaving his mouth.

"What? I told you. You knew this," Colt said quietly.

"Nope, you definitely didn't," Jake said. He wasn't sure what he was feeling exactly, but if he had to give it a name, it would be close to anger. Colt certainly didn't share he was gay and that he had a boyfriend. He did say he was dating, but Jake knew there was no way the detail of the gender of Colt's partner would just slip past him. He felt his pulse begin to slightly race as he thought about Halloween night in college and how things were last left with Colt.

"Hey there," a voice said, approaching from behind Jake and the moment Stacy and Eli slid into the booth, Jake made an audible groan. Not only was Jake just learning that Colton Humphrey was gay; he was also dating a man that was equally as gorgeous as him.

This is going to be a long happy hour, Jake thought.

CHAPTER 9 – SEPTEMBER 30, 2002

"And the student body council would like me to remind everyone that tickets are still on sale for the homecoming dance that will be on October eleventh, after our football game. We would also like to say a special thanks for this year's sponsor of the dance, Los Ruiz Restaurant and Karaoke Lounge…" Several of the students in Jake Ruiz's class started hooting and hollering at the mention of Los Ruiz, tuning out Principal Sloane's announcements. "Lastly, the maintenance team has requested that I inform everyone that they are installing cameras on the baseball field and that whoever is…defecating… Is that right, Margaret? … You're kidding," Principal Sloane said, forgetting he was still speaking into the microphone system. "All right, whoever is vandalizing the baseball fields with their…bodily waste will not only be caught on camera. They will be severely punished and charges will be pressed. And on that note, today's inspirational quote is 'You learn more from failure than from success. Don't let it stop you. Failure builds character.'" Principal Sloane liked to end every morning announcement with a motivational quote, because that was just the person he was. He was likely the reason that the company that made those stock image posters with one inspirational word below were able to stay in business. Half of his office was plastered with posters that said things like *Persevere*, with the picture of a fishing boat right as it was about to get capsized by a tsunami.

"Are your parents still planning on coming to the dance?" Gigi asked, leaning over the aisle to whisper in Jake's ear.

"Yeah, Dad wants to promote the restaurant and thought sponsoring the dance would be a good idea. I had to talk him out of coming with the coupons he wanted to print to give to all the students. Mom wants to go because… Well, she thinks dances are evil and the devil will try and tempt me into getting a girl pregnant or something," Jake said. He wished he had been joking, but his mother had actually said the night before how Peter from the Bible warned that dancing led to sinful thoughts that darkened your soul. Jake knew he would never be able to explain to his mother that in no way, shape, or form would dancing with a girl lead to any sort of sinful desire or inclination.

"Oh my God. Sounds like Consuela's fallen a bit further down the rabbit hole," Gigi said.

"Virginia?" Mrs. Smythwick called out to Gigi. "*Pouvez-vous traduire ce qui est écrit au tableau?*"

"*Oui*," Gigi said reluctantly. She leaned just slightly out of her chair and whispered out the side of her mouth to Jake. "SOS."

"*Arrêtez, Monsieur Ruiz*," Mrs. Smythwick said before Jake could help Gigi, who looked like a fish out of water. Her face was now bright red.

"There's a quiz tomorrow," Colt Humphrey whispered on the other side of Gigi.

"There is a quiz tomorrow?" Gigi said.

"Incorrect," Mrs. Smythwick said. "Thanks to Mr. Humphrey, there is a quiz right now."

There was a collective groan in the classroom as Mrs. Smythwick passed the quizzes down the rows of the classroom. Jake took one look at the quiz and smiled. Fortunately for him, French came easily and he was going to breeze right through this quiz. Gigi, on the other hand, looked like she was about to have an aneurysm at any moment from stress. Jake had finished up his test before Gigi had even turned the page and was forced to watch his friend, who looked like she was writhing in agony. He looked past Gigi and watched Colt turn his mechanical pencil in his hands. He looked like he had strong hands that Jake imagined were soft. He wondered what it might be like to hold Colt's hand—to feel his fingers intertwined with Colt's. Colt bit his lower lip as he struggled to get through the rest of the quiz. He looked up and locked eyes with Jake, who he had caught staring at him. Paralyzed that he had been caught staring at Colt, Jake wanted to quickly look away, but couldn't. Colt just stared back at him and smiled before looking back down at his quiz.

Why does he have to be so cute, Jake thought.

Gigi and Colt scrambled to get the last few of their answers in just as the bell rang. By the way they walked to Mrs. Smythwick's desk at the front of the class, neither seemed confident in a passing grade on the quiz.

"You know you didn't have to help me," Gigi said to Colt as they made their way down the hall.

"Are you kidding? You looked like the vein in your head was going to burst from panic. I was throwing you a life line," Colt said defensively.

"Well, thanks to your lifeline, you probably sank my GPA for French," Gigi said.

"Let me make it up to you," Colt began. "Come to my party after homecoming next Friday."

"At the 'Hump House'? Are you sure we are cool enough to attend a social gathering at such a sophisticated place called the 'Hump House'?" Gigi said in a mocking tone, referring to the nickname Bradley Jones gave to Colt's house. All Jake wanted Gigi to do at this point was to say yes and shut up. With his luck, she would blow this opportunity for him to spend more time with Colt.

"Come on, I don't call it that. The basketball team does," Colt said. "Jake, you want to come?"

"Yeah, that would—"

"Are you freaking kidding? You really think your mom is going to let you go to a party after homecoming?" Gigi said, interrupting Jake. "Consuela's probably going to make you leave homecoming the second a slow dance starts. And forget a party!"

"Oh yeah...I forgot," Colt said. And just like that, Jake could see the window of opportunity to spend time with Colt slipping out of his fingers. Jake wondered how his mom was still able to ruin his life from afar. Consuela's reputation was known in his class and pretty much the entire town at this point. "Hey, do you think she'd let you come over if you told her you were sleeping over and not mention the party?"

"If I what?" Jake couldn't believe what he was hearing. Colt was inviting him to a sleepover? He hadn't had a sleepover at Colt's house since they were in fourth grade. Now he was inviting him over?

"I mean, you don't have to if you don't want—"

"No!" Jake said a little too eagerly. "That sounds good!"

"Cool, we can't wait for the Hump House Gala," Gigi said dryly as she pulled Jake away from Colt and back down the hall. Jake turned around as he walked away from Colt. He ran his fingers through his dirty blond hair, pushing it out of his eyes, and smiled at Jake as he walked away. Something about Colt made him feel like he was interested in Jake and attracted to him. But for all he knew, Jake was the only gay kid in his school. In fact, Jake had never met another gay teen, so he had no idea if he was reading too much into a simple invitation. His gut told him he wasn't though.

"What was that?" Gigi asked. "I thought you and Colt weren't really friends anymore."

"I mean, we aren't *not* friends," Jake tried to say convincingly.

"Well, I hope you two have fun braiding each other's hair and having a pillow fight in your underwear." The sudden image of Colt in his underwear made Jake's heart begin to race excitedly. Gigi was clearly irritated and he had no idea why.

"What's the matter with you?" Jake asked.

"It's nothing," Gigi said, leaving Jake in the hallway as she pushed through the other students. It was clearly something, and Jake had a feeling it was the fact that he knew Gigi had a crush on Colt. He felt so awkward that they had a crush on the same guy, and Jake hated that he could never tell Gigi this. But that was no excuse for how she was acting now, which was a bit bratty over the whole invitation. It wasn't like Jake even had a chance with Colt. But Jake quickly began to focus on other things. Like how homecoming night could not come soon enough.

CHAPTER 10 – PRESENT DAY

"Eli…" Colt began, pausing momentarily, as he spoke to his boyfriend who just arrived at Jersey's. "This is one of our oldest friends and classmates, Jake."

"Hi," Jake said in a voice that was unfamiliar to him. It was about an octave deeper than he normally spoke and he found himself reaching his hand out and forcefully shaking Eli's.

"Nice to meet you," Eli said. His eyes lingered longer than necessary, which made Jake feel even more awkward than he already had been. His only saving grace at this point would be Stacy sharing another story about how she lost her underwear in the woods. "So, what are we talking about?"

"Oh, just some of my more scandalous stories," Stacy said with a cackle before taking another drink.

"And there's plenty of those, you crazy slut!" Eli said loudly and high-fived Stacy. Jake looked over at Colt. His face was smiling but his body seemed to be saying something entirely different as he took a deep breath and then let out an audible sigh. "What about you, Jake? Any scandalous or salacious stories?"

"No, not really," Jake said.

"What about Halloween night?" Stacy asked. It made Jake realize that Colt had told Stacy about Jake's most humiliating memory, and depending on when he had told her, he also outed Jake to one of their former classmates. The fact that Colt would share something so personal with Stacy infuriated him. "You know when you and Co—AHHH!"

Colt had conveniently spilled the remainder of his rum and Coke all over the table and into Stacy's lap, immediately silencing her. "I'm sorry, Stacy! Here, let me help you with that."

Eli shifted to allow for Colt to get past him. The second Colt was standing, he pulled at Stacy's arm. She slid out of the booth while she continued to dab her legs with a wad of napkins she just grabbed from the dispenser. The two disappeared, leaving Jake and Eli alone at the table.

"So, you're going to have to give me the dirt," Eli said. "Like, was Colt always this hot? You're gay, right?"

"I am," Jake said slowly.

"I knew it. I have, like, bionic gaydar," Eli said as he grabbed Colt's drink and sipped from it. "So…what was Colt like?"

"He was…" Jake wasn't sure what to say. What could he say? Clearly, Eli didn't know every story from Colt's past. That was evident by the rum and Coke that was now soaking Stacy's clothes. "He was one of my best friends."

"Oh my God… You guys had sex, didn't you?" Eli asked. His tone was both disgusted and intrigued.

"What? No. No, we didn't," Jake said, but now he had a visual he didn't want to go away anytime soon. "So, how long have you two been dating?"

"Almost four months. Stacy introduced us. I'm her ex-husband's cousin," Eli said.

"Which husband?" Jake said dryly, looking around for Colt and Stacy, who were nowhere to be seen.

"Oh, I like you!" Eli said, playfully slapping Jake's hand. "Anyway, I was totally over all of the dating and hookup apps. Well, I run into Stacy, who tells me about how this cute guy she works with in Newport is now on the market after finally recovering from a four-year relationship and she thought we'd hit it off. I mean, I wasn't really interested until she told me he was a doctor and then I was like, *Yes, please!* Who doesn't want to date a rich doctor?"

Eli let out an obnoxious cackle and then took another sip of Colt's drink. Jake had no idea what kind of impression he gave Eli, but it took all his strength to not show his disgust. The more Eli talked, the more repulsed Jake grew. He didn't think it was possible to dislike someone so much in less than five minutes, but Eli proved that it actually was. Jake had no idea what Colt saw in him other than the physical attributes. Eli was about six feet tall with jet-black hair and almond-shaped eyes and by the looks of his body, he went to the gym regularly.

Sure, he's cute, Jake thought. That was, until he talked and his dumpster of a personality showed. It was obvious to Jake that what Colt saw in Eli was most likely everything on the surface.

"So, you're from this town too?"

"Yeah, born and raised. So…Colt was in a four-year relationship?"

"Hmm? Oh yeah…Harrison," Eli said as he rolled his eyes. "Apparently he cheated on Colt. Like…a lot. Made Colt 'broken goods' for, like, forever. Anyway, I'm so sorry. I can't imagine growing up in a town like this. What a dump!"

"I actually really enjoyed growing up in Newport. Some of my best memories come from this town and the people who live here," Jake said defensively. If Jake had to sit there any longer and listen to this jerk, he told himself he was going to leave. "Where are you from?"

"Mercer Island. That's over in Seattle," Eli said, as if Jake was completely clueless and had never seen a map or driven to Seattle.

"I know Mercer Island. I live in Phinney Ridge and work in Seattle," Jake said.

"Oh nice! What do you do?" Eli asked the same way a nosy neighbor who is trying to pry information out of you asks.

"I'm a chef and operate a few restaurants," Jake said.

"Nice! How much does that pay?" Eli asked intrusively.

"Enough," Jake said flatly. He looked around for Colt and Stacy, who were still nowhere in sight. Based on the person sitting in front of him and the fact that Colt had just been outed by Stacy, Jake assumed the two were having some level of "damage control" conversation.

"I wish there was some good food in this town. Colt keeps taking me to this run-down Mexican restaurant that I swear should be condemned. It's a real dump. Los Ruiz… Have you heard of it?"

"I have. You know what? I just realized the time, and I need to get going," Jake said. He looked around and Colt and Stacy were still nowhere to be seen. "Could you let Colt and Stacy know that I'm sorry I couldn't stay."

"One second," Eli said. "What's your Insta? We can follow each other."

"It was nice meeting you, Eli," Jake said and turned to leave Jersey's. He heard Eli mutter not so quietly *bitch* as Jake made his way to the exit as quickly as possible. People like Eli and Consuela seemed to somehow drain Jake of energy the longer he had to be around them. But there was one good thing that actually came of this horrible happy hour. Jake now knew that Colton Humphrey was actually gay, despite what he had said on Halloween night. Unfortunately, he was also now in a relationship with one of the most horrid human beings Jake had ever met.

CHAPTER 11 – OCTOBER 11, 2002

It was the night of the homecoming dance, and it had felt like the entire week had dragged to get to this day. By some stroke of luck, not only had Jake's dad agreed to let him go over to Colt's house after homecoming and spend the night, but his mom was also not going to the dance. Consuela Ruiz had embarrassed Jake so many other times that Jake thought that perhaps Jesus felt sorry for him and answered his prayers of being able to have one night off from his mom's constant watch and Biblical parenting. Despite her obvious absence from tonight's dance, Jake was fully preparing himself for the talk of a lifetime by the looks of how his mom was squeezing her rosary beads. Jake kept looking out the window, waiting for the moment that Gigi had arrived. They had agreed to meet and go together to the dance as "individuals" and Jake was praying Gigi arrived before his mom began her "talk." At least having Gigi there would perhaps make it somehow less awkward.

"*Mijito*, we need to talk before you head off tonight," Jake's mom said as she approached him from the kitchen. Apparently, her prayer for courage to have one awkward conversation had been answered as she still clutched her rosary beads.

"Mom, I know," Jake said, practically begging her not to put them both through the agony of this conversation by acknowledging he already knew what she was going to say.

"Ttt, ttt, ttt," Jake's mom said, pointing to the couch next to his dad, who was focused on the TV. Jake looked over and saw his dad watching the home shopping channel. He knew his dad had no interest in a women's handbag collection for three easy payments of $49.99, but was most likely pretending to be anywhere other than sitting in the middle of this conversation. As Carlos sat there as still as a statue, Jake couldn't help but have some semblance of admiration for his dad, who had enough common sense to mentally check out right before Consuela dove right into some Old Testament parenting. "*Mijito*, I can't stop you from going to this dance and this sleepover. Believe me, I already tried and your dad said no."

"Mom," Jake said in a tone that almost mirrored a three-year-old whining.

"What I'm trying to say is to have fun," Jake's mom said reluctantly. Whatever Consuela Ruiz was selling, Jake wasn't buying it. There was no way in hell she would just cave like this. She looked over her shoulder at Jake's dad, who began to cough loudly and unnaturally. Jake realized his dad had either had a conversation with his mom about not guilting Jake into going to the dance, or he put a shock collar on Consuela and had his finger on the activate button if she got unruly. "Come here and give your *mamita* a hug."

"Thanks, Mom," Jake said as he hugged her.

"And don't forget…" Jake's mom squeezed him just a little bit tighter and moved her face closer to his hear and then whispered, "Jesus is watching you. All. The. Time. Like all the time, *mijo*. He knows your heart and sees everything!"

"Consuela…" Jake's father said, his voice growing louder, without even pulling his attention from the TV.

"Dad, thanks again for helping the school with the homecoming fund," Jake said.

"Sure thing, *mijo*. Go have fun and please stay safe. *Comprende?*"

"*Sí.*"

"And Jacob? Call us when you get to Colton's, so we know you got there safely."

"Sounds good." Just then, the door swung open and Gigi walked into their house. It would have been nicer had she shown up maybe three minutes earlier, but Jake was happy to see her. Hopefully she would save him from any other conversations with his mom.

"Well, if it isn't my favorite second family!" Gigi exclaimed.

"Virginia!" Jake's dad spun around in his recliner and waved excitedly at Gigi. "How's your mom?"

"Helen's good. She just landed a big illustration job," Gigi said.

"Well, you tell her to come by the restaurant and we'll celebrate. The next meal's on me," Carlos said happily.

"That's a deal, Mr. Ruiz," Gigi said. "Hello, Mrs. Ruiz."

"Virginia," Jake's mom said coldly. She still hadn't forgiven Gigi for being such a "bad influence" on her son and getting him to drink at a party in the woods last summer. "Jacob, please be safe. And please don't make any bad decisions." The moment Consuela had said the word "bad," her eyes drifted over to Gigi.

"I won't, Mom. I'll see you tomorrow…and I'll call you when I get to Colt's!" Jake said, as he was already being pulled by the arm to the door by Gigi.

"*Adiós mi amor!* Be safe!" Jake's mom called out. And right before Jake shut the door, he could hear his mom yell, "And don't forget Jesus is always watching!"

"Do you think that's true?" Gigi asked.

"What?" Jake replied.

"That Jesus is always watching? The way your mom says it, she makes him seem like a bit of a perv, right? I mean, you think he's watching you when you're taking a shower? Or when you're masturbating?"

"Gigi!" Jake yelled in embarrassment.

"Oh, come on. You are a teenage boy, Jacob Ruiz. I'm not stupid," Gigi said flatly. The two didn't say another word until they got into Gigi's car. Once they were a safe enough distance from the house, the conversation continued. "Okay, so why do you think Colt really invited us tonight?"

"What do you mean?" Jake asked. It wasn't like the thought hadn't crossed Jake's mind. He talked with Colt all the time, but the last time he had been to his house was in seventh grade for a summer barbeque. Before that, it was around fourth or fifth grade.

"I mean, do you think he likes me? Maybe that's why he invited us," Gigi said all too eagerly. Jake looked at her and couldn't help but feel annoyed, realizing that out of the two of them, Gigi was the only one who stood a chance with Colt on the count of her having a vagina.

"Jeez, I don't know, Gigi," Jake said. His annoyance was all too clear in his response. "Maybe he just invited us because he wanted us to come to his house with the rest of the class."

"What's up your butt?" Gigi shot back at Jake. "Sorry, I thought this was a safe space to talk about my thoughts."

"Well, I'm not your therapist," Jake said. He found himself getting very angry. It was like his emotions were now on cruise control and he had no ability to stop them. It was the curse of being Consuela's son; he inherited everything, including his mother's temper.

"Wow, this is starting to be a *REALLY* fun night," Gigi said sarcastically. "Shall I take you back to your house so you can hang out with your mom? I mean, she is the life of the party, after all."

"Gigi, I'm sorry," Jake said. "Can we just forget about the last few minutes and start over? Let's have a good night."

"I'd like nothing more than that. Is everything okay with you? You seem extra..." Gigi paused, looking for the right words. "I can't sugarcoat this, Jake Ruiz. You seem like your mother right now."

"Yeah, I know," Jake said.

"What's going on?"

"I mean, I don't know," Jake said. He kept thinking about going over to Colt's tonight. It felt like an eternity to get to this night from when Colt had invited them both after the surprise French quiz. And now that it was here, Jake felt like it was going to be another eternity before he was able to actually hang out with Colt. He still had to get through a football game, where the only thing that interested him was being able to see Colt in his tight football pants and then the dance. If Colt were a girl, he could easily just talk openly about him to Gigi and how he felt. But instead, he had to remain silent. He had to keep that part of him tucked away and sequestered in the deepest parts of himself. Even from Gigi.

"Well, there is something clearly bothering you. And as your oldest and dearest friend, if you can't talk about it with me, who can you?"

"Gigi..." Jake had felt like saying she wasn't his oldest and dearest friend. That was Colt. But he had enough common sense from saying a petty response that would devolve into a much larger argument. He wanted to tell her to forget about it and just get to the school, but instead the next words that came out of his mouth were, "I'm gay."

The brakes to Gigi's car slammed and her car came to a screeching halt, throwing Jake forward far enough for the seatbelt's emergency locking mechanism to catch him and make him feel like someone had just swung a baseball bat right into his collarbone.

"OH MY GOD!" they said in unison.

"What is your problem?" Jake screamed. "You could have killed us."

"Jacob Ruiz, you're gay?" Gigi said, unfazed by the fact their car was still at a standstill on the highway.

"Come on Gigi, at least pull over to the shoulder," Jake pleaded.

"So, you lied to me!" Gigi screamed at Jake.

"What? When?"

"When you said you didn't know if I looked better with bangs last summer!" Gigi was seething. Jake wanted to laugh at her response, but something about her seemed feral and genuinely angry.

"Are you kidding me, Gigi? That's what you're concerned about?"

"What? You lied to me!"

"You're seriously mad at me because of your stupid bangs?"

Gigi sat there quietly for a minute. She was clearly processing a lot…perhaps their entire friendship as she put all the pieces together that would have led her to realizing that Jake was gay much earlier in their friendship. Without saying another word, she put her foot back on the gas pedal and pulled to the side of the road, putting the car into park and turning off the engine.

"Have you told anyone else?" she asked quietly.

"No. You're the first person I've ever told. I haven't even ever said the words out loud to myself," Jake said honestly. He had known he was gay for a few years now, but had never said the words.

"Jacob Ruiz, come here." Gigi turned to face Jake. She leaned across the armrest and wrapped her arms around him. It was a roller coaster of emotions he had just experienced from Gigi, but as she had her arms around him, Jake couldn't help but feel a giant sense of relief that at least he still had Gigi as a friend.

"Gigi, I can't breathe," Jake struggled to say as his friend continued to squeeze him tightly.

"I'm sorry," Gigi said, letting go of Jake. "I'm so sorry that you didn't feel like you could say this earlier to me."

"I did. It's not that. I just…wasn't sure myself. Not until tonight."

"Why tonight?" Gigi asked.

"Because I'm spending the night at Colt's," Jake said. He looked at Gigi, and he could have sworn he could see the gears actually moving in Gigi's brain as she finally began putting things together.

"You…like him?" Gigi asked quietly.

"Yeah, since, like, fifth grade," Jake replied.

"God. You do realize that one of the reasons I'm such close friends with you was because I never thought that we'd be interested in the same person. And now you're telling me that I have to compete with you now for Colt?"

"You're incredible. Only you would be able to find a way to make my coming out about you," Jake said incredulously.

"I'm sorry! This is all new for me too," Gigi said. "But in the very best of ways."

"Yeah? Thanks, Gigi. And relax… There's no way that Colt is gay. So, you're good," Jake said reassuringly.

"So…are there any other boys who you like?" Gigi asked curiously.

"Nope. It's always been just Colt," Jake replied. He thought about how as a kid he had loved hanging out with Colt. The two, at one point, in their early childhood were inseparable. During the summer, Jake would spend days at a time at Colt's house, and his parents thought of him as a second child. It would be years later when Jake was working at his family's restaurant that Mark and Beth Humphrey would come into the restaurant and tell Jake how much they missed him and how much they wished Colt was still friends with him. Mark and Beth were the "anti-Consuela Ruiz." They were outspoken liberals in an extremely conservative town; they weren't religious at all. When Jake's mom found out, she nearly threw a fit and when the two began to spend less time together, Consuela couldn't have been more pleased. Jake was determined to take this to his grave without telling another soul, but losing Colt as a friend had been the first heartbreak he had ever experienced.

"Well, dammit," Gigi said. She put the car in drive and pulled back onto the road.

"What are you doing?" Jake asked.

"We need to get you to that dance and then to Colt's party," Gigi said confidently.

"Really? You sure you're okay with all of this?"

"Jacob Ruiz. Of course I'm okay with this. I've always loved you, and you sharing that you are gay doesn't change that. If anything, it makes me love you more. Now I can appreciate your true self! And I can just find a new guy to get a crush on other than Colt. Besides, he's a little too flawless."

"He is, isn't he?" Jake said. He couldn't hold back the smile on his face as he thought about Colt.

"Yeah. I think I need to find a guy who has some issues. Those seem to be the ones who are only ever interested in me anyway," Gigi said.

That evening, the Newport Grizzlies lost at their own homecoming game by seven points. Jake would have been kidding himself if he said the loss was disappointing. His mind was elsewhere, and he honestly couldn't care less about his high school football team losing. Instead, he couldn't stop thinking about where tonight was headed: Colt's party. While everyone danced the night away inside the gymnasium, Jake stood outside the atrium staring at the giant stuffed grizzly bear inside a glass case.

"You know, if you look at him long enough, his little glass eyes will follow you wherever you move," a voice said. Jake spun around to see Colt behind him. "Ruiz, what are you doing out here when everyone is in there?"

"I don't know," Jake said quietly. "Guess I wanted to get away for a moment to marvel at a fine piece of taxidermy."

"I hate to disappoint, but I think this bear's seen better days," Colt said, pointing to a part of the bear that looked like its fur was falling off. "Either that bear has alopecia or our big stuffed bruin may need to be replaced soon."

"Sorry you guys lost," Jake said. Although he was indifferent about his school losing, he wasn't sure how Colt had taken the loss, considering he was the captain of the team.

"It's cool. You win some, you lose some," Colt said. "Riverside played a good game and we tried our hardest. Thanks for coming, by the way."

"Well, it's not like I went there for you," Jake said and then nervously laughed. The second the words left his mouth, he wanted to punch his own face.

Who says something like that? he thought. *Jake, you are a world-class idiot.* He glanced at Colt, who just kind of stood there, staring at him. He looked as though he were trying to unpackage the comment and make out what Jake was trying to say. Colt's fixated stare just made Jake feel even more awkward. He felt like he was a slug and Colt had just sprinkled salt on him and just watched now as Jake mentally shriveled up.

"Yeah, I know that," Colt said somewhat defensively. Jake felt the interaction shift from somewhat casual to what now felt like an extremely awkward encounter. "So, you and Gigi still coming over tonight?"

"Yeah. I mean, if that's still cool," Jake said.

"Of course, dude," Colt said. "It'll be pretty fun. You gonna crash at my place?"

"Absolutely!" Jake said, biting his lip and cringing as though he had just heard someone scrape nails on a chalkboard while pulling cotton balls apart at the same time.

Play it cool, you big giant, jackass, he told himself.

"Cool. I'll see you out on the dance floor then," Colt said with a raised eyebrow and made his way back into the gymnasium. Jake didn't need to be some sort of expert at facial expressions to tell that Colt found the interaction with Jake odd, to say the least.

"GOD! There you are!" Gigi said, brushing past Colt. She smiled at him as he walked past her. When she got closer to Jake, she began to talk so quietly she was almost whispering. "So...did you talk to him? What happened?"

"Nothing. I mean – I don't know," Jake said. "I was kind of acting like a freak. I'm pretty sure he thinks I'm a psycho right now."

"What did you say?" Gigi asked.

In great detail, Jake recounted the entire experience with such accuracy, he could have been a court stenographer describing their interaction. If there was any doubt that maybe he was blowing things out of proportion, that was completely thrown out the window by the facial expression on Gigi's face when he told her what he had said.

"You know these high school dances," she began to say. "Someone is ALWAYS spiking the punch. Maybe you can tell him you're hammered."

"Really? You think that would work?" Jake asked hopefully.

"Oh, it definitely would! Except there's no punch bowl here."

"God, Gigi. Why would you do that?"

"I don't know, but you need to come out to the dance floor with me. That weird exchange student Jozef was trying to dance with me, and I could have sworn he asked me in a whisper if I was wearing any underwear," Gigi said, scrunching her nose in disgust. "Hot In Herre" by Nelly came on over the speakers and Gigi screamed. "Okay, come on, Jacob Ruiz. We are going to go out there and have fun. And then we're going to Colt's party, okay?"

"All right, all right," Jake said, allowing Gigi to pull him into the gymnasium where they joined the rest of their classmates who had already started dancing in a manner that would have sent Consuela Ruiz to an early grave. No amount of rosary beads could pray away the debauchery that was happening on the dance floor right now.

Jake had found himself having so much fun that there were moments throughout the night that he forgot about Colt's party later that evening. Instead, Jake continued to dance with Gigi until Stacy Morrell wedged herself between Gigi and Jake.

"Do you mind if I cut in?" Stacy asked as Christina Aguilera's "Dirrty" started playing. Before Gigi could even respond, Stacy had already started pushing her butt against Jake's crotch. Jake heard catcalls from others around them, and against his better judgement, decided to go along with the hot train wreck that was Stacy Morrell. Gigi looked at him and threw her hands up in either approval or surrender, realizing Jake had to dance with Stacy. After all, what kind of hormonal, "heterosexual" male teenager would refuse?

"So what's the deal with you two?" Stacy asked as she turned around and wrapped her leg around him while she bobbed up and down as if Jake's body were a stripper pole.

"Ummm..." Jake said nervously. He had never been in this situation and felt as though someone had lit his entire face on fire. Sure, Stacy was cute, but it was obvious she was not the person Jake was interested in. Or the gender. Knowing he could never tell Stacy this, Jake panicked with how to respond to her question.

"Ahhhh, I see," Stacy said with a knowing nod. "Jacob Ruiz, you little sneak."

"WHAT? No, it's not that," Jake said in a panic.

"Oh, so you're single then?" Stacy asked eagerly. Jake regretted his response as he felt Stacy pull his neck closer to her mouth. She smelled like a couple Tic Tacs masking a more overpowering scent of cigarettes that made Jake gag. He could have easily said Gigi and him were an item and Stacy would have likely uncoiled and slithered over to her next prey, but instead, Jake found himself in a situation of his own making.

"I mean, yeah," Jake said reluctantly.

"Jacob Ruiz, are you a man yet?" Stacy asked, whispering into his ear. It was that very moment that not only did Jake's heart begin to race uncontrollably, but he also recognized a third scent coming from Stacy. Tequila.

"Stacy, are you drunk?" Jake asked.

"Whaaaaaaa?" Stacy asked, but halfway through her response, she clearly forgot the question she was responding to.

"Why don't we get you some water," Jake said, pulling Stacy by the hand to the other side of the gym where the vending machines were. He put in a dollar and then selected a bottle of water he handed to Stacy. "Here, drink this."

"Jacob Ruiz, already buying me things? Better watch out, I may marry you," Stacy said as she swayed, most likely from the alcohol and less from the music.

"Where'd you get the tequila, Stacy?" Jake asked.

"Why? Do you want some?"

"No. I want to make sure you don't get any more," Jake said.

"I got it from Bradley."

"Jones? Okay, you stay here and drink the rest of this," Jake said. He looked around the gym and saw Bradley Jones talking with his girlfriend, Jenny Watson and Colt on the other side of the room. He made his way through the gym until he reached Bradley, Jenny, and Colt.

"Yo, did you give Stacy tequila?" Jake asked.

"Hey, Ruiz. Yeah, why? You want some?" Bradley asked, pulling a flask out of the pocket of his letterman jacket only slightly so Jake could see.

"No. But don't give her any more, okay? She's completely out of it," Jake said.

88

"Not my problem," Bradley said.

Bradley looked over at a couple of the other football players and they all started to laugh. Jake wanted to throat-punch the dickhead. Jake and Bradley had been "frenemies" at best. It was Bradley that Jake had blamed for losing his friendship with Colt. Colt started hanging out with Bradley more and the shared mutual interests the two had in sports made Jake begin to fade out of Colt's life. It was because of this that Jake never really warmed up to Bradley. And the older they got, Bradley became less likeable, which made it easier for Jake to justify his animosity toward him.

"Well, if you give her any more, you better make it your problem," Jake said, thrusting both his hands into Bradley's chest. He spun around and made his way back toward the vending machines where Stacy was. Jake felt like he should probably run after what he had just done and he refused to turn around to see Bradley's reaction. He wouldn't be surprised if at any point he felt Bradley's fist slam against the back of his head, but to his surprise, nothing happened. When he made his way back to Stacy, who was tracing the grout lines between the cinder block walls of the gymnasium, Jake realized he may have just blown his invite to Colt's for the evening.

"It's weird how this is kind of like a maze, right? It's like my finger is a little mouse trying to find some cheese," Stacy said, continuing to trace the cinder block grout lines.

"Did you drink all that water?" Jake asked.

"Ta-da!" Stacy held up an empty water bottle and began to shake it. Jake put another dollar into the machine for another bottle of water and handed it to her.

"There, drink all of this one too," Jake said.

"Are you kidding? I'll explode," Stacy said, but before Jake could respond, she had already removed the cap of the water bottle and started downing it.

"Hey, lover," Gigi said as she approached Jake and Stacy.

"I KNEW IT," Stacy said, practically spitting out the water in her mouth. "Jacob Ruiz, you *are* a man."

"Huh?" Jake asked.

"Gigi, your man is cheating on you. He was trying to get with all of this," Stacy said, her speech now completely slurred, as she rubbed the water bottle around her face. She lost her grip and dropped it, soaking her dress. "Ah, dammit!"

"Is she okay? Sorry, I didn't know about Bradley's flask," Colt said, who had just walked up behind Gigi. Although he was talking to the entire group, he seemed to be focusing on Jake.

"She'll be okay. Colt, do you think Jake can ride with you to your house? I'm going to take Stacy home, and I can head over there after," Gigi said. The look of concern on her face was only vaguely visible behind the expression someone makes right before they are about to say "checkmate." Jake felt flustered at Gigi's spur-of-the-moment ploy.

"Yeah...of course," Colt said, looking over at Jake. Had the gym been any brighter, he may have noticed the warm shade of red that now covered Jake's entire face.

"You guys want to help me get Stacy out the back door so the teachers don't see? Otherwise, she's suspended," Gigi asked.

"Where are we going?" Stacy asked as Jake and Colt helped Stacy to her feet and started making a swift exit to the back door.

"You, my dear, are going home. Your carriage has turned back into a pumpkin, and unfortunately, you've made a spodie of it," Gigi said, opening the passenger door of her car and buckling Stacy into the seat.

"I don't know what any of that means, but it sounds like a fairy tale," Stacy said in a really whiny voice before closing her eyes and seemingly passing out. Colt started making his way back toward the high school and stopped at the sidewalk to wait for Jake.

"Sorry about this, Jake! I just saw a golden opportunity for you and decided to take it," Gigi said. "Are you going to be okay?"

"Of course! You're a good friend, Gigi. And not just to me," Jake said, looking in the direction of Stacy, who was definitely passed out.

"No one's driving drunk on my watch," Gigi said in her most parentlike voice, and Jake knew how serious Gigi was. When they were in second grade, Gigi's grandpa was killed by a drunk driver, and her mom moved Gigi from Spokane to Newport so they could be closer to her grandma. "Have fun! I'll see you in a little bit."

Gigi drove off and Jake made his way back to Colt on the sidewalk. Jake felt somewhat alone now that Gigi wasn't with him. He looked at Colt, who looked like some sort of sexy teen spy in his black suit jacket, white shirt, and black tie. Even though it was homecoming, hardly anyone dressed as nicely as Colt looked right now. Most of his classmates showed up to the dance in a polo at best for homecoming. But Colt wasn't like the rest of Jake's classmates. He always put his best foot forward, whether it was in class, school, or dances. It was one of the qualities that made Colt stand out from the rest of the class.

"Damn, Gigi's a saint for dealing with Stacy," Colt said.

"Well, she wouldn't have had to if Bradley hadn't got her so drunk," Jake said. He wasn't mad at Colt, but the way he responded did not make that entirely clear.

"Sorry, Jake. I honestly didn't know about the flask," Colt said. Knowing Colt, he probably didn't, and Jake realized he may need to reel in his frustration so Colt didn't feel attacked.

"I know, sorry if I'm sounding pissed at you," Jake replied.

"Hey, it's all cool," Colt said, placing his hand on Jake's shoulder and patting it. "Let's get back inside."

When Jake and Colt made it to the back door they had snuck Stacy out of, the two realized the universe had no desire of having them return to their homecoming dance. The door, which Colt had propped ever so slightly open with the doorstop, was now sealed shut and locked.

"Shit," Colt said, pulling at the door.

"Um, does that mean…?" Jake began.

"That we can't get back into the dance? Yeah," Colt replied. When they had arrived at the dance, the teachers who were chaperoning the dance reminded every student that there were no in-and-out privileges. Once they had entered the school, they weren't allowed to leave and come back in during the dance.

"Well, this night just keeps getting better and better," Jake said as he leaned against the wall and slid down to the ground.

"Hang on a sec. Let me try something," Colt said. He pulled out a cell phone, flipped it open, and began dialing.

"You have a cell phone?" Jake said, impressed. Not many people he knew had a cell phone, and no matter how many times Jake had asked his parents to get one, he was constantly shot down. His mother would tell him he was either at home with them, at the restaurant with them, or at school with his teachers. There was no need for a cell phone, she would state before abruptly ending the conversation.

"Yeah, my parents gave it to me for emergencies. And this is an emergency," Colt said with a smile. He stood there silently with the phone pressed to his ear for a few moments before shutting the phone. Jake studied Colt's profile and the sharp jawline that made Colt appear so much older than everyone else their age. "Dammit," he said.

"What?" Jake asked, pulling himself out of his lingering gaze at Colt.

"I thought I'd call Bradley and see if he could come open the door, but he's not answering," Colt said.

"Can you call anyone else?" Jake asked.

"No. Jenny's the only other person I know with a phone, and she was complaining earlier that she left it in her car."

"Well, it was a good idea," Jake said. "What are we going to do?"

"Well, the dance is really only going on for another hour or so. You want to just head over to my place now?"

"Sure!" Jake said a little too eagerly and then had to consciously remind himself to not sound so excited. He could care less about the dance. The only thing he had been looking forward to was going to Colt's, and now Colt was offering to head over there earlier.

"Ha! Don't sound too excited," Colt said jokingly as he stood up and reached out his hand to Jake. He took Colt's hand. Just like he had imagined in French class as he watched Colt turn the pencil around in his hand, Colt's hand felt exactly like Jake had imagined—soft and somehow strong at the same time. The moment his hand was wrapped in Colt's, Jake felt his heart begin to race.

"Thanks," Jake said once he was on his feet. He silently prayed that his face wasn't flush from holding Colt's hand.

"No worries. Come on, let's get out of here," Colt said. Jake didn't need to be asked twice and followed Colt back out to the parking lot and to his red Jeep he had seen him in all the time. And just like that, the part of the night that Jake had been waiting days for was finally about to begin.

CHAPTER 12 – OCTOBER 11, 2002

Jake worried briefly that the ride out to Colt's house might be slightly awkward. After all, this was really the first time that he had been alone with Colt in a very long time. He worried that the time they spent apart might make the time that they were now together weird.

"Bradley's kind of an idiot, right?" Colt said as he drove on the highway. It was the acknowledgment from Colt about Jake's "frenemy" that he needed to hear. It helped to confirm Jake's hope that Bradley's cocky attitude and behavior had not passed over to Colt in the time he had become friends with him.

"I mean, he's certainly not smart," Jake said, not wanting to insult Colt's best friend. "It's a good thing he's good at sports."

"And he has a nice face," Colt said with a distinguishable sense of sarcasm, but the comment lingered on Jake's mind long after Colt had said it.

Could there be a chance that Colt is gay? Jake thought. *Bradley is certainly cute, and he would certainly be Colt's type. After all, he is tall, athletic, muscular and his butt looks fantastic in his football uniform. Hell, he would have been my type—if only he never talked.* Jake had to stop himself after he realized he was thinking about Bradley Jones while he was in the car with Colton Humphrey.

"Oh, he has the best," Jake said, matching Colt's tone of sarcasm, and the two started laughing.

"When's the last time we were in a car together?" Colt asked, looking upward as he attempted to recall.

"I think it was maybe four years ago when your parents took us to Sam Nelson's birthday in Spokane at the paintball course," Jake said.

"Oh yeah. Damn, that was a while ago."

"It was. So, your parents are okay with you having a party?"

"I mean, it's not like it's going to be some sort of rager. Just some of our class, and I was going to set up a bonfire. Besides, my parents are over in Seattle right now. Dad's at a medical conference."

The thought of spending the night at his crush's house with no parents present would have naturally caused excitement for anyone, except when your crush also happens to be a boy who was very straight. That didn't mean that Jake's mind didn't wander into ideas of what could possibly happen tonight if there was a God. The thought of Jake kissing Colt and all the things that this could possibly lead to caused Jake's mouth to go dry and his heart begin to race.

When they had finally arrived to Colt's house, it was exactly as Jake had remembered. Not much had seemed to change at the giant mansion that had been dubbed "Hump House" for no apparent reason other than Colt's last name. Jake thought it was disgusting, but it had never stopped him and Gigi from jokingly talking about all the sordid things that might have happened in the house to give it that nickname.

"I bet it has a sex dungeon," Gigi once said as they talked about a party Colt had that they had not been invited to.

"Gross, Gigi," Jake replied.

"I mean, why would you call it that?" Gigi asked.

"Humphrey? It's his last name," Jake said.

"Simple minds come up with the simplest of nicknames," Gigi said, unamused.

"You want to help me set up the bonfire?" Colt asked as they jumped out of his Jeep.

"Ah, I see. This was all a secret plot to get me here to help you with the setup," Jake said, catching up to Colt, who was already making his way down the hill that led to the back of the house.

"Oh no! I'm sorry," Colt said, a look of panic appeared on his face.

"Relax. I'm just kidding. So, where we setting up this bonfire?"

"I figured right here," Colt said to an open dirt clearing that overlooked Sacheen Lake.

"You sure? This seems kind of close to the house for a bonfire," Jake said. It couldn't have been more than fifteen feet away from the house.

"Nah, it's cool. We had a fire here last year and it was fine. Besides, I don't think my parents would really like if I burned another hole into the grass. You want to get the chairs and I'll go grab some wood?"

"If you say so." Jake walked over to a pile of chairs under the balcony and started unstacking them. Something about the proximity of the bonfire to the house gave Jake a horrible gut feeling, but if Colt had already built a fire this close to the house before and the house was still standing, he figured he'd just go along with it.

After they had set up a small stack of logs, Colt started the small fire and plopped back onto the chair next to Jake.

"Beer?" Colt said, handing Jake a bottle of Bud Light.

"Umm, sure," Jake said hesitantly and grabbed the bottle from Colt. The last time he drank alcohol, his mother unleashed the seven realms of Hell on Jake and then made him confess his sins in front of their church Bible study. This led to Jake having to seek alcohol counseling from the church and community service. Jake didn't even like the taste of alcohol and hadn't planned to ever drink again, and after his mother's wrath and everything that had ensued, he definitely didn't want to. It was far too much work than what it was worth, but the prospect of sitting alone with Colt in front of a fire seemed worth it. Jake knew there was likely going to be a price to pay for this, but he didn't care. He took a drink and nearly gagged from the taste.

"Not a fan?" Colt asked.

"I'm more a fan of...eyepuhs," Jake said. To be honest, he knew nothing really about beer. Other than a few brand names and the fact that there were apparently a lot of different kinds of beer.

"Eyepuh?" Colt asked, confused.

"Yeah, you know. I-P-A?" Jake replied. The response sent Colt into a fit of laughter so hard he nearly fell into the bonfire.

"Oh my God, Ruiz. I forgot how funny you were," Colt said before collecting himself and taking another sip of his beer. Jake had no idea what he had said that was so funny, but he made a mental note to discuss this with Gigi so they could figure it out.

"Cheers!" Colt tipped his bottle toward Jake, who clinked his glass with Colt and took another sip. He had no idea how people consumed this on a regular basis, as he pushed his body not to gag from the sip.

"So, have you started applying for any colleges?" Jake asked.

"Yeah, a few. I don't know." Colt started. "Dad wants me to go to U Dub and get into medicine."

"Well, do you?"

"I don't know. It's such a huge choice," Colt said. "The thought of making the wrong decision for a career kind of paralyzes me. I don't know what I'm doing ninety percent of the time, and I'm just making it up as I go. And now I have to make this choice that will carve out the entire direction for the rest of my life?"

"I know what you mean," Jake said, taking another sip of beer. This time he didn't gag. "I haven't told anyone this yet, but I've only applied to Gonzaga. My parents want me to go to school for business and I kind of feel obligated to do that."

"Yeah?" Colt said, looking at Jake for what seemed to be a longer-than-normal period of time. "And if it were up to you, what would Jake Ruiz do?"

"I don't know. I've always loved cooking. Maybe go to culinary school?" Jake said. It was the first time he had ever said it aloud. Here he was, talking to a doctor's son, who was likely going to college for medicine, and he was sitting here talking about going to cooking school. He knew he had no reason to feel this way and should be proud of what his goals were, but in that moment, Jake couldn't help but feel uncomfortable.

"I think that's a great idea," Colt said.

"You do?" Jake asked, beginning to feel less embarrassed.

"Of course! You're an amazing cook. I mean, I can only speak to the few times you helped your mom make dinner when we were in grade school, but it was literally some of my favorite dinners I've ever had," Colt said. There was no trace of sarcasm in his voice. He was genuine.

"Thanks. That means a lot," Jake said. "And what about Colt? What would you want to do?"

"I mean, I really love this area. It's home to me. Seattle is…it's so far away," Colt said. "Maybe I should just go to Gonzaga and we can be roomies."

"Yeah…" Jake said, laughing. Just thinking of being Colt's dorm mate made Jake feel like he was about to have a heart attack from the mere thought. Then he realized how torturous it would be to watch Colt night in and night out eventually bring girls back to their dorm. "I figured you and Bradley had some grand plan to go to college together."

"Nah. He's pretty dead set on not going to college for a couple years. Said he wants to go work construction with his dad until he figures out what he wants to do," Colt said. He leaned back in the chair and looked up at the stars. "It's crazy to think that a year from now we are all going to be in different places."

The two sat there silently. Colt continued to look up into the sky, and Jake couldn't help but get lost as he gazed at him. He had known Colt for nearly his entire life and on the days he was able to see Colt, those were often better than the days he didn't. Jake had no idea if this was the same way that others felt about their unrequited love, but Jake hated it. It was painful to see the object of your affection within arm's reach and have no possibility in conveying how you felt and get rejected to at least get some sense of closure. His eyes followed the wispy silhouette of Colt's dirty blond hair down to his chin.

I wish love didn't hurt this bad, Jake thought.

"So, what's the deal with you and Gigi?" Colt asked, pulling his gaze from the night sky and refocused on Jake.

"Huh?" Jake asked, caught off guard. "What do you mean?"

"I mean…" Whatever he was about to ask, he seemed to be dancing around the question and hesitated to ask it. "Are you two, like, dating?"

"What? No!" Jake said. He answered a little too quickly and also sounded slightly insulted, he thought. "We're just friends."

"Good," Colt said. The two continued to sit there without saying a word, but the silence somehow wasn't awkward at all. Jake had to hand it to Colt to be able to have the ability to leave someone analyzing and wracking their brain over a singular word. Why would Colt ask that and then follow it with "good"? Any sane person who was trying to get Jake to grasp the reins of reality would tell him that Colt just said "good" because maybe he was interested in Gigi and wanted to make sure she was available. But something about how Colt had said it made Jake feel differently. Why else would Colt be happy that him and Gigi weren't dating? The optimist in Jake was trying to convince himself that it was because Colt was interested in Jake, but the realist was doing a better job at convincing Jake that was nowhere near the case. Either way, Jake had no chance at being able to learn why Colt felt this way, because his thoughts were interrupted when a herd of his classmates came barreling down the hill, holding giant forty-ounce bottles of beer.

"The party's arrived," Bradley Jones hollered as Jenny Watson and more of Jake's classmates appeared at the bonfire. "Wuttup, Ruiz? We cool?"

Jake looked at Bradley Jones and wanted to punch him square in the nuts. He could have sat under the stars with Colt by the fire for hours, but of course it had to be ruined by this human taint of a person. Rather than saying about a hundred things that Jake would have loved to say to Bradley, he replied, "Yeah, man, we're cool."

"All right, all right! Here, my dude…a peace offering," Bradley said, bowing and handing Jake the bottle of Olde English in his hands as though he were the Queen of England at an investiture.

"Um, thanks," Jake said, looking at the bottle. He had no idea whether this was liquor or beer and was very afraid of finding out.

"Well, come on, man. Let's cheers!" Bradley pulled out a second bottle from a backpack and held it up to Jake.

For better or worse, Jake was about to find out what this tasted like, and he was certain this was the very first time in his life that he was truly afraid of something. Jake twisted the cap off and clinked the bottle next to Bradley and took a sip. It tasted just about as good as the beer that Colt had gave him, but Jake knew that if he drank this entire bottle, the only thing he would do tonight is vomit.

"Here, let me try," Colt said, grabbing the bottle and taking a sip. He didn't even wipe the top. Jake was slightly repulsed, but mostly enamored.

Jake grabbed the bottle from Colt and without giving it a second thought, he took a sip. The moment the bottle made contact with his mouth, he thought about it touching Colt's lips. He wasn't sure what he would gain from drinking right after Colt. Maybe he would get some kind of indication of what Colt's lips tasted like. But instead, he just got more malt liquor and was disappointed. He looked over at Colt, who shook his head and started to laugh at Jake's disappointed reaction, which he likely interpreted as Jake's disappointment in the taste of the alcohol.

"You call this a bonfire, Hump?" Bradley said, taunting Colt. The fact that he called Colt "Hump" made Jake loathe Bradley just a little bit more.

Who does that? Jake wondered.

"Let's get some more wood on this thing," Bradley said, grabbing his crotch. Instinctively, Jake hated that his eyes looked at where Bradley was grabbing before he quickly looked away.

"I'll be right back," Colt said, patting Jake on the back and following Bradley over to the stack of wood on the other side of the yard.

"Where's Gigi?" Jenny Watson, who had walked over to Jake, asked once Colt and Bradley were a safe distance away.

"Um, she should be here soon. She was taking Stacy home and then was going to head over after," Jake said.

"I know you got mad at Bradley about Stacy, but you should know she drank nearly a fifth of vodka in her car before she went into the gym," Jenny said. "He shouldn't have given her any more, but it's not entirely his fault."

A fifth of vodka *and* whatever was in Bradley's flask? Jake was beginning to wonder how Stacy had even managed to stand on her own two feet.

"I didn't know that," Jake said. He had started to feel guilty for berating Bradley like he had, but then he looked over at him, standing behind Colt, who was grabbing wood for the fire. Bradley was pretending to hump Colt like a dog in heat, and Jake realized that Bradley might have turned into a better human being if more people had put him in his place like Jake did. Jake also hated that as he watched Bradley thrust himself into Colt that he couldn't help but feel jealous at their relationship. The fact that he was envious of Bradley, at least in that moment, was enough to make Jake want to jump straight into the bonfire.

"Hey, party poopers!" Gigi appeared out of nowhere and threw her arms around Jenny and Jake. "What did I miss?"

"Nothing! We just got here," Jenny said. "How's Stacy?"

"Well," Gigi said, slumping down and grabbing the bottle of malt liquor out of Jake's hand. She glanced at it, then gave Jake a suspicious look before taking a drink herself. "I got her home, but only after she demanded I stop at McDonald's and buy her a fish filet sandwich. She told me that is the only thing she orders at McDonald's because she likes 'fresh Alaska-caught salmon.' The girl is clearly out of her mind. Anyway, I had to help hoist her through her bedroom window so her parents wouldn't find out just how drunk their Bible-study-leader daughter is."

"Good God," Jenny said. She looked down at her empty bottle and quietly made an exit to likely go find someone with alcohol.

"What are you doing?" Jake asked Gigi as she took another drink of his malt liquor. He knew that Gigi had a strict rule of not drinking if she had plans on driving, so the question had to be asked where Gigi thought she was staying tonight.

"Relax," Gigi whispered. "Jozef isn't drinking and offered to drive me home in my car. And since he lives with Bradley, who lives just down the road from me, it works out!"

"The exchange student?" Jake asked, shooting a look over at Jozef, who was busy telling a very animated story with his hand gestures. He was either talking about shaking a soda can until it exploded…or masturbation, by the looks of it. Jake couldn't tell who was more repulsive—Bradley or Jozef, but considering that Bradley was pretend-humping what Jake considered to be the love of his life at that moment, he decided that honor went to Bradley. "Gigi, you can't be serious. Does Jozef even have a license?"

"He does," Gigi said quietly. She looked over at Jozef and his captivated audience, who was listening to his story and watching his vulgar hand gestures. "I told you I need to find a guy with issues. And I think that Jozef has plenty! Besides, his unibrow is kind of growing on me."

"That's disgusting. Don't ever tell me what happens between you two," Jake warned her.

"Speaking of forbidden love, what's going on with you two?" Gigi asked. "It looked like Bradley's getting to him before you."

"We need to talk. Gigi, I don't know if I'm reading too much into things, but there's something about him that makes me think he may actually be into me."

"Are you serious?" Gigi asked, grabbing the bottle of malt liquor from Jake and taking another sip.

"I mean...maybe? I don't know," Jake said, more confused than ever. "What am I doing here? He clearly is not gay. The universe just does not work that way."

"Jake, your mother is Consuela Ruiz." Gigi pointed to Colt, who was walking back over to the bonfire. "Maybe the universe realizes the cards you were dealt with your mom and is rewarding you now with Colt!"

"Gigi, come on," Jake said. As crazy and overbearing as his mother was, Jake still loved her and felt guilty whenever Gigi spoke ill of her.

"Look, I'm just saying maybe the universe *does* work that way. You always hear of high school sweethearts. No one said that two boys can't be each other's!"

"The law does, Gigi. The law does," Jake told her. This topic of conversation was entirely new to the both of them, considering he had only just come out to his best friend a few hours ago. But being able to talk to someone so openly about this made Jake wonder why he hadn't come out to her sooner.

"What am I missing?" Colt had snuck up behind Jake and placed his hands on Jake's shoulders. Hearing his voice and feeling his touch nearly made Jake jump several feet in the air. He had begun to panic, wondering if Colt had heard any part of their conversation.

"Uh..." Jake spun around and looked at Colt with a dumbfounded stare. He couldn't even think of a bad lie to tell.

"We were just talking about how it looks like Bradley just got you pregnant," Gigi said casually.

"Yeah, he's a little out of control. Can I?" Colt looked down at Jake's bottle of malt liquor, and Jake handed the bottle to Colt, watching him take a large sip. Without hesitation, Jake took another sip when Colt handed it back to him, but unfortunately, all he still tasted was the cheap alcohol and nothing else. Jake also started to realize Colt was making him turn into an insane person.

"Is that, like, a communal drink?" Gigi said in a tone that suggested she was disgusted she drank from it. "Goddammit, Jacob Ruiz. You could have told me!"

"Hey, can you come with me a second?" Colt asked, looking at Jake.

"Yeah, sure!" Jake said. He glanced at Gigi, who raised an eyebrow. He followed Colt out toward the lake, and when he turned around, he saw creepy Jozef sit down next to Gigi. Jake thought Gigi had no interest in Jozef, but was more interested in Bradley, who was Jozef's host family, but he wasn't really sure. Gigi was starting to feel like a loose cannon.

Colt walked down a sloped hill until he stopped at a clump of trees. The bank of land appeared to have had receded at some point and some of the roots were now exposed for several of the trees.

"I totally forgot about this until my dad pointed it out a while ago," Colt said, pointing at the tree. "You remember this?"

Jake looked at the tree and the memory of a summer so many years ago resurfaced. Jake and Colt must have been in third or fourth grade when they took one of the steak knives out of the kitchen and decided to take it outside. There, on the surface of the trunk read:

JR + CH

"Oh my God," Jake said, looking at their initials. He couldn't help but laugh at the sight.

Colt seemed to laugh hesitantly, but then genuinely started laughing along with Jake. The two stood there, looking at their initials.

"My mom was so pissed that we ruined that steak knife," Colt said, shaking his head.

"You know, they came into the restaurant not too long ago and I waited on their table. She told me she'd be keeping an eye on her steak knife, and I had no idea what she was talking about. I forgot," Jake said, laughing.

"Dad jokes that it looks like we were in love," Colt said. He sat down on the bank, swinging his feet.

If only he knew, Jake thought. And as Jake sat down beside Colt, continuing to look at their initials carved into the tree, Jake realized just how long he'd loved Colt. It was nearly his entire life. He remembered the day they had carved their initials into the tree. They had meant it as a friendship pact, unaware of how it could be interpreted by others.

"WOOOOOOOO!" In true Bradley Jones fashion, the moment between Jake and Colt was interrupted as he came screaming down the hill. Jake turned around and saw a naked Bradley heading toward them. "We're going skinny-dipping."

102

And just like that, about three more of Jake's classmates, including Gigi, trailed after Bradley, peeling off their clothes as they ran out toward the dock. He had emotionally exposed himself to Gigi earlier in the night, and now she had physically exposed herself to Jake, and he couldn't help think they were somehow even. He watched his classmates all jump into the lake, which had to be freezing. It wasn't like it was summer. It was October and in Newport, that sometimes meant snow on Halloween.

"Whaddaya say?" Colt said, jumping up. He started taking off his shirt. The sight of Colt's toned chest was enough for Jake to pass out. "Come on, Ruiz. Race you there!"

Colt pulled down his pants, and before Jake realized it, Colt's ass was exposed. He turned to face Jake, and there it was. Jake had sleepless nights thinking about what was now right in front of his face. Jake knew if he spent any longer looking at anything other than Colt's face, he would be outed, so it took all his energy to pull his fixated gaze up to Colt's eyes.

"You're losing..." Colt said almost playfully, pulling off his socks.

Jake stood, realizing there was a problem. There was no way he would be able to get naked in front of Colt right now and not have Colt know Jake liked what he saw. He started thinking of anything that would make his erection go away. He took off his shirt and the moment he did, he definitely saw Colt look down at his chest. Colt laughed playfully and then raced toward the dock.

It was dark enough down at the dock that Jake figured whatever was still there might not be as noticeable. The others were already in the water, and it wasn't like they were staring, Jake assured himself. And so with that, he peeled off the rest of his clothes and ran toward the lake. Without giving it another thought, he jumped right in. The moment he broke the lake's surface, it felt like a million needles had stabbed him. That water wasn't just cold. It was freezing cold. He looked around and had no idea where Colt was and then was grossed out with the realization he was skinny-dipping in a lake with a bunch of his classmates. Just then, a clothed boy ran out onto the dock, his arms flailing in the air.

"COLTON! COLTON!" It was Jozef. He looked like he had seen a ghost.

"Come on, Jozef, get in!" several people shouted, trying to coerce the exchange student into the cold lake.

"Colton! Your house! It's on fire!" Jozef screamed. If there was one thing Jozef could have said that would create enough panic in everyone to get out of the lake, it was that.

Jake looked around and saw one specific person in the distance flail their arms and begin to swim back to the dock. Jake watched as Colt emerged from the lake and by some blessing from God, he caught another glimpse of *it*. And then as Colt ran past Jozef, he watched his beautiful ass disappear into the darkness.

"JOZEF! Are those my panties?" some girl on the other side of the dock screamed, and Jozef shoved something into his pocket.

"Come here, you little perv," the girl shouted, and one by one, everyone started getting out of the lake to follow Colt.

When he finally got to his pile of clothes, Jake threw on his underwear and ran up to the house. The bonfire—the one that Jake had warned Colt about setting too close to the house—had erupted into a high flame that had begun to warp and melt the vinyl siding on the side of Colt's parents' house. Parts of the siding started to look like drooping taffy.

"Help me put the fire out," Jake screamed to the onlookers, who watched the siding melt in awe as if it were some sort of fireworks display on the Fourth of July.

Bradley ran up the hill and reappeared a few moments later with a hose and began to douse the bonfire. At one point, Jake watched Steve Hawthorn pour his alcoholic beverage on the flames, which caused a small pillar of fire to shoot up and then make Steve scream and stumble backward. After what seemed like hours but was probably more like three minutes, Bradley was able to get the fire down to almost nothing. In all the chaos, Jake looked over at Colt standing near the side of the house and realized he was still naked. Most of his classmates had redressed to some extent, but not Colt. He stood there in all his glory. Jake walked back over to the tree where their carved names were and picked up their clothes. He went over to Colt and handed him his pile of clothes, which he let fall to his feet.

"Thanks," Colt said quietly. "My parents are going to kill me."

Jake looked at the side of the house. Where the siding once was in a uniform parallel placement, it now drooped. Part of the siding resembled more of a weird, creepy smiley face than actual siding. Jake knew Colt's parents weren't as terrifying as his own, but he couldn't help but think that Colt was right. His parents *were* going to kill him.

"I think you need to end this party, Colt," Jake said. "Tell everyone to go home. I'll help you clean up."

"Yeah…" Colt said, still in shock.

"And…maybe you should at least put your underwear back on," Jake said, picking up Colt's boxers and handing them to him again. Jake didn't have to say anything and could have just stood there, staring at Colt in all his glory, but something felt so wrong about this moment to Jake.

"Thanks, Jake," Colt said. He slipped on his boxers and looked around. It was as if Colt and Jake were on stage. The entire party was quiet, looking at the two of them. "Hey, guys, I think I'm going to call it a night. Thanks for coming, but we should probably wrap this up."

There were a few groans amongst the crowd, but one by one, people started making their way up the hill.

"I'll talk with you tomorrow?" Gigi whispered to Jake. She was standing there in her underwear shivering.

"Yeah," Jake whispered back and watched as she walked over to Bradley, Jozef, and Jenny, who were making their way up the hill. Within ten minutes, Jake and Colt were alone once again, but this time, it felt different.

"I'll put the chairs away," Jake said, and started pulling the chairs away from the bonfire.

"Hey, Jake?" Colt asked.

"Yeah?" Jake said.

"You're still staying here tonight, right?" Colt asked.

Jake couldn't tell if it was a request or a question, but either way, he had no intention of leaving after hearing the distress in Colt's voice.

It was well after two in the morning when Colt and Jake had cleaned up everything around the backyard and had made any trace of a party disappear. The siding on Colt's parents' house was toast. There was no way it could go unnoticed, and Jake thought Colt was lucky Jozef was courteous enough to stop doing whatever he was doing with his classmates' panties to come and warn Colt about the fire. There wasn't much conversation for the rest of the night, and once they finally made it in the house, the two were asleep in a matter of minutes.

CHAPTER 13 – PRESENT DAY

"Well there's a plot twist that you didn't see coming," Gigi said, after Jake had told her about the happy hour and meeting Eli. Helen had her tablet propped up on the kitchen counter for a video call with Gigi. "How did we not hear that Colt is gay? Helen, the Newport gossip chain's infrastructure really seems to be crumbling."

"I mean, Colt's only been dating this guy for a few months," Jake reasoned with Gigi.

"Yeah, but didn't you say he was dating someone else for a few years? How did that slip right past the rumor mill?"

"Maybe he's really private with his personal life," Helen said, who had been busy painting a bisque vase that looked like it was made entirely of women's breasts. Charlie was preoccupied watching a cartoon in the other room, and Jake was fervently praying that he would not come into the kitchen to see Helen's latest piece of art. "If he's smart, which it sounds like he is, Colt knows how to keep his life private from the prying eyes of this town. I've been able to."

"Helen, your life is an open book," Gigi said.

"That this town is not allowed to read," Helen replied. "But I think we are missing the more important question here, Gigi. Sure, he may have lied to you one night in college, but maybe he wasn't ready to accept himself and share who he is with others at the time. You've made a remarkable life for yourself that some can only dream of, and unfortunately my dear, Colt is dating this man. He may be horrid, but that is who Colt has decided to be with. But Jacob, why does this even bother you so much?"

Jake looked at Helen, who had started painting the nipples on her vase a dark blue. She had a point. Helen Clayton always had a point. She was like some sort of sage mentor—like a hip female Yoda who frequently smoked marijuana. Jake thought about the question, and Helen was right. Why did this bother him so much? He had come back into town to see his father, who was at the hospital in a medically induced coma, and now he was allowing some vapid and shallow person to make him jealous over the first love of his life. And there it was—*the first love of his life*. Jake thought about those words and remembered that Colt had not been just some childhood crush. He had been the person who made Jake realize what love meant. He was also the one who taught Jake what heartbreak felt like. And although he grew from those moments in his life and found love, seeing Colt and learning the truth felt like those scars had been pulled wide open once again. Between Consuela and now Colt, Jake knew he had to get out of this town. He felt the emotional stability he stood on just two days ago being pulled out from underneath him like a tablecloth trick. He worried what might happen if he stayed in Newport any longer.

"Would you excuse me? I have to make a call," Jake said.

"You're on a call right now!" Gigi waved her hands on the video screen, but Jake was already on his way to the guest bedroom. He pulled out his phone and scrolled through his contacts until he found the number and dialed.

"Hello?"

"Hi, Marcia," Jake said to his marketing manager. "That opportunity with *Wake Up With Us*? Can you let them know I'm interested?"

"It's a smart move, Jacob. This is going to be just what Ruiz Kitchens needs! You won't regret this. I'll get back in touch with you after I have all the details," Marcia said.

"Sounds good. I'll talk with you later." Jake ended the call, thinking about what he had just done. He wasn't one to make rash decisions, and this was one of the biggest decisions of his life that he made in a matter of seconds. Jake sat there on the bed wondering what he was doing, and the fact that he had no idea how to answer that question terrified him.

PART II

COLTON HUMPHREY

CHAPTER 14 – PRESENT DAY

Colt Humphrey adjusted his rearview mirror as he pulled out onto the highway and made his way into Newport. The drive into town was sometimes a lengthy one, but Colt loved watching the scenery zoom past him as he drove through the wooded roads of northeastern Washington. He was listening to an NPR podcast when his phone rang.

"Hi, Mom," Colt said.

"Hi, honey," Beth Humphrey said in a tone that Colt understood as *I haven't heard from you in a few days so I wanted to check in*. It was a rare occasion when Colt went more than a day without at least calling or texting his parents to say hi, but with his parents traveling across Europe this summer, their communication had been less frequent.

"Hey, Mom. What's up?" Colt said. He started to slow his car down as soon as he spotted several deer standing on the side of the road. The last thing he wanted was a deer deciding at the last minute to jump right into the road and get hit by his car, which happened all too often.

"Well, I just figured I'd check to make sure you were alive. Your father and I haven't heard from you since Saturday." Beth Humphrey was joking of course but she had a way of making Colt feel guilty, even in humor.

"I'm sorry. It's been kind of a busy week at work. What time is it over there?" Colt said, lying. It had actually been pretty slow the entire week, but Colt figured telling his mom he was busy at work would be a solid excuse. Colt reasoned he was at least being somewhat honest, considering that for the last few days all he did was really go into work and then go home where he would eat dinner and then promptly go to sleep. It had been a very mundane week for Colt Humphrey.

"It's five p.m. We just checked into our vacation rental in Mykonos," his mom said. "I tricked your father into going on the *Mamma Mia* tour across the island!"

"Oh yeah? What's that?" Colt asked.

"Oh, it's really just your mother singing ABBA songs off-key really loudly as we travel through the island tomorrow. It's an unofficial and unsanctioned part of the tour."

"I wish I was there to see," Colt said, laughing at his mom. He loved that about Beth Humphrey. She was never afraid to be herself. If she wanted to sing off-key, Beth Humphrey would sing with the confidence of a platinum record-selling artist.

"Oh honey, we wish you were too. Maybe we can look into all going to South America or Japan next summer! Whaddaya say?"

"Only if I can sing with you. Eli would probably like South America," Colt said. Every summer since he had graduated high school, he had gone on a summer vacation with his parents.

"I bet he would," Beth said dryly. She was not a fan of Eli or Colt's previous boyfriend, Harrison. And it wasn't because they were men. It was because they were assholes. Of course, she would never use these specific words with Colt, but she would put her own Beth Humphrey translation when sharing her feelings with her son. "Are you sure you're happy? I just don't hear that spark in your voice when you talk about Eli."

"It's still early, Mom," Colt said, restraining a sigh. Eli had a big personality, much larger than Colt's, and the more Colt spent time with him, that personality continued to grow. It was a bit overwhelming for Colt, to be honest, but the fact that Eli lived in Spokane and only came up to Newport a couple times a week allowed Colt time to recover from Eli's domineering personality. He knew that needing time to recover from your boyfriend, who was somewhat exhausting, was definitely not a sign for a lasting relationship. If he was still dating Eli by next summer, it would be a surprise to him as well. But he couldn't tell his mom that. He had only been seeing Eli for a few months and he felt obligated to give it a chance since his friend Stacy was the one who set the two of them up.

"It is. Well, all right then, let's try and find some time to plan this out when we get back, all right? I love you to the moon, peanut," Beth said.

"And back, Mom," Colt said. For as long as he could remember, it was how they always ended conversations. Even in his thirties, Colt's mom never stopped saying it. Colt ended the call just as he entered

Newport. He was amazed whenever he entered Newport at how it was something like a time capsule. Newport had hardly changed during the course of his entire life living in it. Sure, the facades of most of the buildings had faded somewhat and were overdue for a new coat of paint, but for the most part, everything was as it had been for decades. He turned the corner and the familiar exterior of Los Ruiz Restaurant and Karaoke Lounge came into view. For a long time, Colt would look at the restaurant, expecting to see one familiar face. But after a while, Colt realized he needed to get past that part of his life and move on. He even started taking a different route to the hospital so he would miss driving past Los Ruiz altogether. He had taken Eli there a couple times during the last couple months, and Eli was so loud that Colt realized that perhaps it wasn't a good idea. He may have been out to his parents and very close friends, but it was something he did not openly share. Colt could appreciate what could only be described as irony of being outed at Los Ruiz, of all places, by Eli. But today, whether it was because he was distracted by talking to his mom or some other subconscious reason, he found himself driving past the restaurant. And as if it were by instinct, Colt looked into the windows of the restaurant. Nothing.

Colt pulled into the parking lot of the hospital when his phone began to ring again.

"Hey, Mom, I actually just got to work…"

"Colt, it's me, Stacy," the voice said on the other line.

"Oh, sorry, Stacy. I just got off the phone with my mom, and—"

"Colt, you need to get in quick. They just brought in Carlos Ruiz. He's had a stroke," Stacy said quietly.

Just the name Ruiz made Colt's heart sink, and he knew whether he liked it or not, he would likely be face to face with Jacob Ruiz again very soon.

CHAPTER 15 – OCTOBER 27, 2006

"So, what do you think?" Colt walked out of the hotel bathroom in a three-piece suit, showing off his costume to Harry, who he was sharing a hotel room with for the Pacific Northwest Medical School Conference. Harry, who was lying in his bed in his boxers, looked up from the book he had been casually reading.

"Where are you going? A funeral? I thought we were going out for drinks," Harry said as he rolled his eyes and looked back down at his book.

"I mean, we are, but it's Halloween weekend. You mean to tell me you didn't bring a costume?"

"You mean to tell me that what you're wearing is supposed to be a costume?" Harry asked dryly.

"Oh!" Colt walked over to his suitcase and placed a black wig over his dirty blond hair. "How's this? You want to take a guess at who I am?"

"Oh God, I don't know. Lee Harvey Oswald?"

"You think I'm dressing as the man who killed JFK?" Colt asked. "I'm Jonas Salk."

"Clever," Harry said unamused, rolling onto his back and holding the book over his head.

"Come on, you've got to do something. It's Halloween," Colt said, poking Harry in the ribs.

"Oh, I *was* planning on doing something tonight for Halloween," Harry said, setting down his book and focusing all of his attention on Colt.

If there was one person more conflicted with their sexuality than Colt, it was Harrison Peake. Colt met Harrison at University of Washington during their premed program and the competitive nature of

114

both men inevitably caused Colt and Harrison to become friendly rivals, constantly trying to outdo the other in their grades. And over the course of time, they had somehow formed a friendship of sorts. Harrison became the chairman for the College Conservatives Group and had canvased and worked fervently for the last gubernatorial election, in a state that hadn't elected a Republican for governor in more than two decades. Just a few months ago, Harrison had started dating Claire Farling, who was planning to go to law school right after graduating. The couple made little sense to just about everyone for a number of reasons, one of them being that for a long time, many of Colt's classmates, including himself, had thought that Claire was a lesbian. It made even less sense to Colt, who had drunkenly had sex with Harrison the year before. It was his first experience he ever had with a guy, and it was incredibly awkward. Harrison refused to kiss him but freely did everything else. Colt told himself over and over that it could never happen again, but after hooking up with Harrison at least four more times, every time without kissing, he had stopped telling himself that. And then Harrison started dating Claire and pretended as though nothing had ever happened. It was the most awkward Colt had ever felt.

"Are you kidding, dude? What about Claire?" Colt asked furiously.

"Oh relax, Claire and I aren't constrained to the societal constructs of a relationship, and we don't practice monogamy. And it's like they say, 'What happens in Spokane...'" Harrison began to say.

"Harry, no one says that. Literally no one. Besides, I'm not cool with that, and like I said before, *that* cannot happen again." As much as he wanted to stand his ground, Colt looked at Harrison lying there in his boxers. If only his personality was a fraction as attractive as his body, Colt thought.

"Yeah, I've heard that song and dance before," Harrison said, popping up out of the bed. "If it makes you feel better, I brought a banana costume that I can throw on."

"Thank you. Now hurry up! The girls are going to be here soon," Colt said.

Unlike Harrison, Colt really enjoyed the two girls he had traveled with from Seattle. He had rarely interacted with either of them prior to the trip, aside from a few study groups here and there, but now that they were outside of an academic setting, Carmela Rodriguez and Sweeney Jorgensen's personalities started to shine. Colt had no idea how he would have been able to survive the trip with Harrison had it not been for the girls.

"So let me get this straight," Carmela, who was dressed as Sailor Moon, said as the group made their way out of the lobby of the hotel. "Of all the nights where you can literally be anything you want and dress as wild as you want, you chose to go as Jonas Salk?"

"I mean, I thought it would be kind of funny. You know, because of the conference," Colt said. He was beginning to feel embarrassed about a costume he was certain would have been a hit.

"Oh, don't get me wrong, it's a fantastic outfit and wickedly clever. It's just…very formal?" Carmela clearly wasn't sure how to end that sentence and instead, she made it sound more like a question than a statement.

"What Carm is saying is that it's not skimpy enough and we aren't seeing enough skin," This was ironic coming from Sweeney, who was dressed as the Hamburglar. "But I love it! I am a little concerned though. Are we the only ones dressed up?"

"We probably look like fools." Harrison looked around and pulled up his costume. The end of the banana had started to drag on the sidewalk as they made their way downtown. "Here, can we just go in here? It's open, and it's empty. Looks like a good place for four jackasses to hide until at least more people are downtown in costume."

"Sounds good to me," Colt said, walking into a bar called Blue Spark. He followed the girls and Harrison over to a booth in the distance.

"Can I see your IDs?" A waitress approached the table and looked at the four of them. One by one, the group pulled out their licenses and handed them over to the girl, who looked like she was younger than all four of them. "What can I get you?"

"Can I get a Corona with a lime?" Sweeney asked.

"I'll have the same," Carmela seconded.

"I'll have a Tito's tonic, or whatever top-shelf vodka your bar has. And are your limes organic?" Harrison asked. The waitress shot a glance at the others as if she were telepathically asking them if this guy was for real. The smugness in his voice sounded as if this bar was beneath Harrison and they were lucky to be graced by his presence.

"They are definitely not organic," the waitress said.

"Fine. Just the Tito's tonic and hold the lime," Harrison said. The waitress rolled her eyes and then turned to Colt.

"Uh, what IPAs do you have?" Colt asked.

"A couple of local ones. Do you want me to bring you a sample?" the waitress asked. Her facial expression seemed to perk up once she was no longer interacting with Harrison.

"Nah, just bring me one you like. I trust your judgment," Colt said, smiling at the waitress, who blushed and walked off.

"By the looks of this dump, that lime would probably give me a foodborne illness anyway," Harrison said.

"Harry, let's be civil now," Carmela said, reprimanding Harrison as if she were a mother trying to scold her spoiled child. "Besides, I think this place is cute."

"Is it like that wherever you go?" Sweeney asked Colt. Apparently, Colt wasn't the only one who noticed the waitress's reaction.

"What do you mean?" Colt asked, pretending as though he had no idea what Sweeney was talking about.

"You just seem to ooze charm. Must be your superpower," Carmela asked, smiling at Colt.

"I just want to know what's with you and IPAs," Harrison said, wanting to shift the subject. "That's all this guy ever orders when it comes to beer."

"I like the taste, and it makes me think of good memories," Colt said. He didn't feel like he owed it to any of these three to give the real reason he only ever ordered IPAs, which he had come to love. He couldn't help but think of homecoming night that now felt like a lifetime ago. And from that night on, he always heard "eyepuh" in his head whenever he ordered the beer, and the memory of Jake Ruiz sitting next to him at a bonfire would resurface. Thinking about the smile on Jake's face always made Colt happy, which his friends would assume was a buzz from the beer. The last time he had seen Jake was at their graduation ceremony, and he often thought about memories from when the two still lived in the same city and went to the same school. Moments that didn't quite pan out the way that Colt had wanted them to. *What if they had?* Colt often wondered.

"So, what was your favorite part of the conference?" Carmela asked the group. "I really liked the keynote address on pediatric medicine."

"It was okay," Harrison responded.

"Oh Harry, you really are a hard one to please," Sweeney said curtly.

"Woah! Take a look at that dude's costume," Harrison said, cutting off the conversation and causing the entire table to look toward the entrance. A Pebbles Flintstone and one scantily clad Bamm-Bamm had just entered Blue Spark and looked as though both of them had lost half their costume. It was as if a horse had kicked Colt in the chest the moment he looked over at the door. Had the universe listened to his thoughts and delivered his wish in record time, Colt wondered.

"Dude must be queer," Harrison said before taking another sip of his beer.

"Harry!" Carmela said in a shocked and disapproving manner. "That's completely uncalled for."

"Seriously!" Colt said. "Besides, you aren't really one to talk."

Colt wanted to punch Harrison square between the eyes for the comment, but he slid out of the booth before he did anything he would regret. He couldn't believe Harrison had the nerve to make a comment like that, given his own sextracurricular activities outside of his "open" relationship. But as he made his way over to Jake and Gigi, Colt forgot all about Harrison, Sweeney, and Carmela. Instead, he couldn't help but look at the beautifully toned brown calves of Jacob Ruiz. He had bulked up. He couldn't believe how short Jake's costume was. Bamm-Bamm's shorts appeared to be only a few inches long, exposing Jake's thighs as well. Colt had to force himself to not stare once he was standing behind Jake and Gigi.

"Well, well, well. Look who it is," Colt said. Gigi turned around and then for a moment, time stood still. Jake slowly turned around, and when he finally locked eyes with him, Colt realized how much he'd missed Jacob Ruiz.

"Colt!" Gigi said and catapulted herself into him. The mere force of Gigi made Colt take a step back and brace himself so he wouldn't topple over.

"Hey, Gigi," Colt said, squeezing her tightly and getting part of her red Pebbles wig in his mouth. And even through the red ponytail and dinosaur-bone scrunchie, Colt never stopped looking at Jake, who looked away. He wasn't sure what it was about Jake, but he seemed different.

"And Ruiz!" Colt turned and went to wrap his arms around Jake. The moment he felt their chests touch, Colt experienced a million things. He swore he could feel Jake's heartbeat through both their costumes, and it seemed to be racing. Jake's head seemed to linger on Colt's collarbone and for a minute, nothing around them mattered. He didn't want to pull away, and he held his arms around Jake for as long as he could before it seemed too awkward. When he finally let go, Colt subtly ran his hand down Jake's arm. Jake jerked back from Colt, and Colt was embarrassed.

Good going, moron. You just freaked him out, Colt thought.

"Hey, Colt." Jake seemed a bit quieter than he remembered.

Colt started to panic and began to think about how to fix this situation as he said, "Let me guess…Pebbles and…Well, the top half of you looks like Bamm-Bamm. Where'd the other half of the costume go, Ruiz?"

That had done it, Colt thought, as Jake's demeanor seemed to relax and revert back to the Jake he remembered.

"It's Gigi's fault," Jake said. "She thought it would be fun to skank up these costumes."

"It's a good look on you," Colt said, smiling.

It's a good look on you? IT'S A GOOD LOOK ON YOU? Colt began to cringe internally as the words that left his mouth played over and over in his head. *If they didn't think you were gay in high school, they certainly do now!*

"Here's your drink," the waitress said, handing a beer to Colt. Carmela and Sweeney called it. The waitress was putting down some serious flirtatious vibes as she stood there waiting for Colt to take a sip.

"Hey, not bad! See? I'm always a good judge of character," Colt said. She began to laugh and then went back to the bar.

"So, what are you dressed as? Are you a pastor or a young Orville Redenbacher?" A wry grin stretched across Jake's face as he asked Colt the question. If Colt hadn't been mistaken, it almost felt like flirty banter, but maybe he was reading too much into everything. *Orville*

Redenbacher? Colt thought. *Jake really thinks I decided to dress as the popcorn man?*

"I'm Jonas Salk," Colt said, believing that would clear things up, and then realized his choice of costume really was a piss-poor decision. *Shit,* he thought. *Everyone is dressed as a banana, the Hamburglar, a really sexy Bamm-Bamm, and I choose to come out as Orville-fucking-Redenbacher.*

"I'm sorry...who?" Gigi always seemed to speak her mind without a filter. It was a trait that was endearing, humorous, and at times a little off-putting when they were growing up. He had to admit he had missed her too, but definitely not as much as he missed Jake.

"Dr. Jonas Salk. He helped create the polio vaccine," Colt said.

"Cool story, Colt. I'm going to go get us drinks. You want one?" Gigi asked. It was obvious she was itching to get away from this conversation and Colt.

"I'm good for right now," Colt said, holding up his glass of beer before Gigi made an overly dramatic sigh of exhaustion and walked to the bar.

"So, how's school going, Ruiz? You're at GU, right?" Colt already knew that Jake was at Gonzaga, but he didn't want to sound like he was some sort of stalker.

"Yep! School is good. Looking forward to being done though. What about you?"

"Nice! I wish I was almost done. I just got accepted into UW Medical School."

"That's awesome! Congratulations. I bet your parents are thrilled," Jake said.

He had no idea what Jake and Gigi were up to tonight, and he didn't care. He looked back at the booth he had exited. Harrison looked like he was telling a story that Carmela and Sweeney were exhausted from listening to. The universe had just presented Colt with a golden parachute, he thought. He didn't care where Jake and Gigi were going tonight. They could be going to a midnight mass in costume and Colt realized he would rather spend his night with these two than the nightmare that was Harrison.

"Yeah, they're pretty excited. So, what are you two up to tonight?" Colt asked.

"Well, some of my friends from college are meeting up with us, and we figured we'd just barhop. Gigi wants to go to Dempsey's later tonight."

DEMPSEY'S? Colt had wondered about Jake. Growing up in Newport, Colt thought that maybe he wasn't the only gay kid. He had always felt a strong connection to Jake, but Jake started pulling away from Colt when he started hanging out more with Gigi. He had no idea why Jake didn't really want to hang out with him and the loss of their friendship emotionally hurt him. But then, once they were in high school, the two started to talk a bit more and Colt could feel the reconnection of a friendship. But nothing came of it. Colt had all the friends, all the popularity, and had felt more alone than ever in high school. But here he was now. And Jacob Ruiz—Colton Humphrey's childhood crush—was talking about going to a gay bar?

Maybe he is gay. Maybe I was right… Maybe I have a chance, Colt thought.

"Dempsey's? You better be careful… You'll be the talk of the town," Colt said.

"What do you mean?" Jake seemed taken aback by the comment. The knee-jerk reaction by Jake made Colt realize that maybe he was being overly optimistic and once again reading too much into things.

"Figuratively speaking, of course. I just meant with that costume… Well, I'm sure you will get a lot of attention," Colt said. He had already lost count of how many times he had to recover from the words coming out of his mouth. But he was being honest. Jake looked hot in the costume, and Colt was pretty sure Jake knew it.

"Drink up, ladies! Three Mind Erasers!" Gigi arrived back at the table, holding three drinks.

Gigi somehow managed to show up at the most inopportune times, Colt thought. She had managed to wedge herself between Colt and Jake when they were kids. And as she stood there with three drinks in her hands, Colt couldn't help but feel angry. She had stolen his best friend and someone he viewed as his childhood crush. But Colt realized that tonight would be different. Perhaps tonight he could find a way to reopen that door with Jake.

"Gigi, we're really starting this hard?" Jake took a sniff of the drink and seemed repulsed. Colt had no idea what a Mind Eraser was, but the moment he leaned down to sniff it, he nearly vomited.

"To Jozef!" Gigi said, holding up her drink.

The three stood there as they managed to choke down Gigi's idea of a "good drink." In the few moments he had spent with Jake and Gigi, Colt knew two things. First, they were infinitely more fun than the three he was just with and second, it was just like old times. For some reason, Gigi brought up Jozef, the exchange student that lived with Bradley when they were in high school, and Colt had somehow managed to purge Jozef from his memory bank until she brought him back up again.

"Hey, Colton. We're about to head down the street. You ready?" Harrison had made his way over to Colt, Jake, and Gigi. Colt knew the reason Harrison likely came over was to find out who Jake was. Something seemed so awkward about Harrison standing next to Gigi and Jake. He didn't want Harrison to get to see this part of his life. It wasn't because he was embarrassed of Jake and Gigi. He was embarrassed Jake and Gigi would see who he decided to associate himself with. "Nice costume, dude."

"Where you guys headed?" Colt asked Harrison.

"We are going to some dueling piano bar one block up."

"Is it cool if I meet up with you guys in a bit? Just catching up with old friends from high school," Colt said, lying. He had no intention whatsoever of meeting up with Harrison.

"Of course," Harrison said. He turned to face Jake, who looked at Harrison blankly. Harrison extended his hand to Jake and then said, in the most condescending voice Colt had ever heard Harrison speak in, "Harrison Peake, the third."

The third? Really? Colt thought. *Could you be any more of a prick in adding "the third" when introducing yourself?*

"Bamm-Bamm Rubble, the first," Jake said dryly. As much as he tried, Colt couldn't contain his laughter. That was why he liked Jake.

"Cute. We'll catch up with you later, Humphrey. Later, Bamm-Bamm." Harrison waved at Carmela and Sweeney, who joined Harrison and made their way out of Blue Spark. Neither Carmela or Sweeney said anything. If Colt had to guess, they were pissed Colt had left the two of them to have to get through the entire night listening to Harrison's exhausting stories about himself.

"He seems…nice." Jake Ruiz may have been a lot of things, but he was a terrible liar. There was no way anyone in their right mind believed that Harrison could be remotely nice. Colt had met Harrison's mom and dad during Parents' Weekend at University of Washington, and even they seemed to think their son was a real dick.

"He really isn't. He's the definition of an asshole." Colt didn't hold anything back. He couldn't with Jake.

"Oh good! I wasn't sure what to say. How do you know him?" Jake asked.

"From school. All four of us were here for the premed conference. None of us are really friends. We're staying over at the Convention Center. To be honest, I may just have to ditch them and hang out with a more entertaining crowd." He knew he was kind of forcing an invite from Jake, but when opportunity presented itself to hang out with your childhood crush, Colt felt compelled to take it.

"That would be awful," Jake said. Colt was relieved when he saw the smile on Jake's face and knew he was more than welcome.

Gigi returned with three drinks in hand. To Colt's relief, this time they were an orangish color with little umbrellas on top.

"Did they run fresh out of that sewage juice you made us drink? What's this?" Jake asked.

"Mai tais! I figured it was a safer bet," Gigi said. She moved the umbrella to the side and took a sip.

"Good guess, G. Thank you," Colt said. The three tapped their glasses together and he took a sip. "So, what brings you back to Spokane for the weekend?"

"Well, Jake and I made a promise back in freshman year that we would spend every Halloween together. And so far, we have. I didn't want senior year of college to be the first.

"What about you? Aren't you in Seattle? Did you hear that the Halloween scene in Spokane was way better or something?"

"Of course. I mean…clearly," Colt said. He looked around at the bar, which was still empty, and waved his hands. "I'm actually in town for a conference for school."

"So, what I'm hearing is that you have a hotel room that we can crash in if we get too drunk then!"

"Well, yeah, I guess so," Colt said.

"Aw, Colton Humphrey, you always were my favorite," Gigi said. Colt didn't have it in him to tell Gigi that if she wanted to crash in his hotel room, she'd have to share a room with his closeted, polyamorous, Republican, self-hating roommate. He looked over at Jake, who was amused with Gigi's antics.

He hasn't changed at all, Colt thought as he looked at Jake. The small dimple on his cheek right by the tiny mole was just as cute as ever. As far as Colt was concerned, there was only one person he ever had feelings for that he would consider love. Jacob Ruiz. Over time, those feelings had dwindled, but now that he was standing in front of Colt in the skimpiest costume he had ever seen and showing that he had never changed, it was as if the dam that had been holding back all those old feelings had burst.

Colt, Jake, and Gigi stayed at Blue Spark for a while longer, talking about memories of the past and what they had been up to since they had all parted ways. In true Gigi fashion, she seemed to monopolize most of the conversation, but Colt didn't care. He would periodically look at Jake and every time he did, Jake was staring back at him before he'd quickly look away. Colt didn't know if it was coincidence or something else. He felt that it was something else. After all, he always found himself locking eyes with Jake in high school when he would look over at him in class. Everything in Colt's gut told him that Jake was gay. Deep down, something told Colt that Jake felt the same way about him. But that wasn't healthy, Colt thought. Jake wasn't gay, and even if he was, how would they be able to make it work? They were now on opposite sides of the state and from what Colt heard about long-distance relationships, they didn't work.

Are you seriously contemplating the complexities of a long-distance relationship with someone who is straight? Colt thought, and immediately wanted to slap himself back into reality. He had no idea what he was thinking or doing, but whatever it was, Colt knew it wasn't healthy.

"So, you guys do the matching costume every year?" Colt asked.

"Pretty much," Gigi said. "We wore these ones during senior year. Except...there was maybe a bit more fabric the last time."

"Gigi, there's more fabric in a bikini," Jake said, pulling down at his shorts, exposing his flat, toned stomach. And even then, the shorts didn't even get to the midpoint of Jake's thigh. Colt watched the entire reaction by Jake in amusement...and a little bit in desire.

"Okay, maybe I got a little liberal with the scissors. But come on, man! We have to find you a..." Gigi froze mid-sentence. It was as if someone had pressed the pause button on her speaking. Her eyes darted from Colt to Jake and then back to Colt. It looked like she had just caught herself from saying something she wasn't supposed to, but she also looked like she was about to throw up. Because they weren't entirely sure either, both Colt and Jake took a step back from her.

"GIGI!" Jake whispered.

"Sorry, sorry, sorry!" Gigi said. "You guys, I think I'm a bit drunk."

"You think?" Jake said loftily.

"Let's keep this night going. Let's go to the next place!" Gigi screamed as if she were inviting the entire bar.

"All right, all right," Colt said. "Let's head out!"

The three made their way down the street. Colt had felt as though he had picked a pretty fun costume when he first decided on being Jonas Salk, but now that there were more people downtown drinking, Colt felt horribly out of place. Everyone else was dressed just like Jake and Gigi, and here he was, being mistaken for Orville Redenbacher or attending a funeral.

"I just want a hot dog in my mouth. RIGHT NOW!" Jake said as the three made their way down the street.

Colt was in the middle of criticizing his poor choice of a costume when he nearly stopped dead in his tracks. He could have sworn that Gigi had just said that Jake had also wanted a hot dog in his butt. He had no idea why she would say something like that if Jake weren't gay, but Colt realized that perhaps he had consumed too much alcohol and was hearing what his subconsciousness wanted to hear.

The three stumbled into a diner called Dewey's and every booth was packed. Colt didn't think he was very drunk until he inhaled the sweet smell of greasy bacon, which made his mouth water.

"How many?" the host asked as he looked Jake up and down and then smiled. Colt felt his jaw clench and the familiar feeling of jealousy begin to creep up.

"Three," Colt said curtly, and the host nodded as he beckoned for the three to follow him. He took Colt, Jake, and Gigi to the very last booth in the diner. They were about three feet away from the bathroom door and the entrance to the kitchen, but Colt didn't care. He was drunk, he was hungry, and the longer he looked at Jake's bare thighs and skimpy costume, he started to realize he was also horny. Jake slid into the booth, and before Gigi even had budged, Colt practically lunged to slide into the same side as Jake. But the moment he did, he second-guessed himself.

Dammit. I should have sat across from him so I could see him, Colt thought.

"I'll bring over some water and menus," the waiter said. He was cute. He was just shy of six feet and had a nose piercing and a sleeve tattoo. He was grungy, Colt thought, but a cute kind of grungy. It wasn't lost on Colt that the waiter seemed to keep staring at Jake, but Colt couldn't blame him. Jake wasn't just cute. Jake was the most beautiful thing that Colt had ever seen in his life.

"Do you guys have beerfles?" Gigi asked.

"Beerfles?" the waiter asked, confused.

"Someone told me about a place here that made waffles, but they made them with beer instead of water," Gigi said, and the waiter gagged.

"No, is that a thing?" the waiter asked, sounding both mortified and disgusted.

"It can be…" Gigi said in her most seductive voice as she flashed a one-dollar bill at the waiter.

"The water is fine," Jake said, and the waiter walked off. "Gigi! You're going to get us kicked out! Besides, is that really something you heard?"

"Nah," Gigi said. "I just figured maybe I could get some food and alcohol at the same time."

"I'm pretty sure that would not only be disgusting, but that the alcohol would burn out of it anyway," Colt said.

"Well, I guess we'll never know now, will we?" Gigi drunkenly snapped back. "So, Humphrey, what's new with you? Anything exciting with your love life?"

Colt shifted in the booth. His love life was something he didn't even like talking about with the closest of his friends, much less Gigi. Aside from whatever his thing with Harrison was considered, Colt had been mostly single since graduating high school. His parents, friends and extended family just attributed this to him being very focused with school. And now that he was about to start medical school, Colt figured this would at least buy him a few more years. What could he tell Gigi? *Nope, still single. There have only been a couple people I've been interested in my entire life, and one of them is sitting across from me right now in the most scandalous costume I've ever seen.*

"Nah, too busy with school," Colt said, realizing that sometimes the best excuse was the one that was most convenient.

"So, what sounds good?" the waiter said, returning to their table with three waters in hand.

Jake...Jake sounds good, Colt thought. As much as he wanted to push it out of his head, he couldn't.

"Can I get the Big Breakfast with my eggs over medium?" Jake asked.

Colt realized he hadn't really even looked at the menu. "I'll have the same."

"Where do we stand with those beerfles?" Gigi asked the waiter.

"We don't stand anywhere with them," the waiter said, incensed.

"Well then, let's make that three of whatever they ordered," Gigi said. As soon as the waiter disappeared into the kitchen, Gigi gasped. "Oh my God! You don't think he thought I asked for three orders just for me, right?"

"No, I think he understood," Colt said reassuringly. "So Gigi, what are you getting your degree in?"

"Computer science and mathematics," Gigi said, taking a sip of her water.

"Really? You are?" Colt felt bad for how shocked it sounded coming out of his mouth.

"Yeah, is that hard to believe or something?" Gigi said, her tone and demeanor seemed to change and stiffen.

"No! Sorry..." Colt said, trying to figure out a way to recover from this. "I guess I'm just surprised. You never seemed to be that into computers in high school."

"I wasn't," Gigi explained. "But you know what I am into? Money. Besides, I realized that I'm kind of amazing at coding and development. And it's kind of fun."

"Gigi's already lined up a job with Microsoft after she graduates," Jake said excitedly.

"Oh wow! That's awesome, G," Colt said.

"Thank you!" Gigi said.

Once the waiter brought their food, the three began to devour it. Colt knew he was drunk, but he swore that if he were sober, this still would have been the best breakfast he ever had.

"Oh my God, why is bacon sooooooo good?" Jake asked. He tilted his head back and started lowering the bacon into his mouth. Colt couldn't help but chuckle at a drunk Jake Ruiz, who was just as cute, if not cuter, than a sober Jake Ruiz.

"Woah, Jake. You want to get a room with that hog" Gigi said, clearly not feeling the same way as Colt.

"Huh?" Jake said through a mouthful of bacon.

"You're practically deep throating that bacon!" Gigi squealed before shoving another pile of eggs into her mouth, and then leaned back into the booth. "That was the most delicious thing I have ever put in my mouth. I'm sorry we didn't get to go to the gay bar."

And just like that, Gigi had alluded to something that Colt had long wondered and hoped for.

Why would she apologize to Jake for not being able to go to the gay bar? Colt wondered. Unless Jake was the one who wanted to go in the first place. What if Colt was right? What if Jake Ruiz was gay? The thought began to consume Colt's mind, and then he started to wonder if Jake was, did he know in high school? Did he know at the time of the homecoming dance? Colt realized he had to know this answer, even if it was the only other piece of information he learned tonight. He wasn't sure if it would make him feel better or worse, but he had to know.

"What time do you think it is, G? It's, like, nine." Colt said.

"WHAT?" Gigi shot up in her seat and grabbed her phone to inspect it. "Oh my God. I thought it was like two a.m.! Can we stop and grab a coffee somewhere before we go anywhere else?"

"Oh man, I could definitely go for some coffee right now," Colt said.

Before paying their bill, the three ordered a round of coffee that they drank quickly.

"What do they say about liquor, fried food, and coffee?" Gigi asked between sips. "I feel like this is a horrible decision and I'm going to be sitting on the toilet."

"Probably," Jake said. "I guess we'll find out."

Once they made it out to the street, Jake let out an exaggerated sigh of relief. "Oh thank God! Look! We aren't the only ones anymore."

Jake pointed to a pair of nurses with fishnet stockings talking to a pair of overweight men with beer guts dressed as Chippendales dancers.

Colt leaned a little closer to Jake and then bumped him on the shoulder. "So, were you the one wanting to go to Dempsey's?"

"I just thought it might be fun," Jake said unconvincingly to Colt, who smiled at him.

"I think it will be," Colt said. He had no idea what he meant by it, and the fact that he was about to go to a gay bar with two people from his hometown and he was still in the closet should have terrified him. But it didn't. Instead, Colt felt more excited than he had ever felt in his life. Everything about this night was pointing to the fact that Jacob Ruiz was gay. He looked at Jake, who stared into Colt's eyes, and they didn't break their gaze. Something about the moment felt electric to Colt.

"What do you mean?" Jake asked, sounding confused.

"Well, we're still going right? I mean, we're only a block away."

"YES! Can we? Can we?" Gigi nearly knocked the two of them down with excitement. Colt knew this would not be a hard sell with Gigi clearly on board.

"I'm down for it if you are, Ruiz," Colt said.

"All right, all right. Let's go," Jake said a little hesitantly.

"Hey, weren't you supposed to meet up with your friends?" Gigi asked.

"Oh no! Crap..." Jake looked at his phone and what Colt assumed must have been several missed messages. After a couple moments, Jake shut his phone and put it back in his pocket. "Colleen and Adam have been trying to call me."

"Oh no. I hope that we haven't missed them. That would be awwwwwwwwful." It was apparent that whoever Colleen and Adam were, Gigi was not hiding her true feelings about the two.

"I take it she's not a fan?" Colt said, laughing.

"No, not really," Jake replied.

Dempsey's was a two-story gay bar in Spokane on the outer corner of the downtown district. The first floor had a bar area and a stage where drag queens performed, while the upstairs had another bar and a dance floor where the crowd eventually migrated to. They would stay there until four a.m. once they had danced all of the booze out of their system. After getting past the bouncer, Colt couldn't help but feel excited. This was his first time in a gay bar this close to his hometown. He had gone once before with a group of friends for someone's birthday party, but this time felt different. He looked around and felt out of place now that he was surrounded with a bunch of guys wearing Halloween costumes as skimpy as Jake's.

"I can buy the drinks," Colt said. He figured this would give him enough time to figure out what the hell he needed to do now that he was here with Jake.

"No! Let Jake," Gigi said adamantly. "Look at him! That costume is bound to get us some kind of discount. Your Dr. Scholl's outfit or whoever you're supposed to be is going to get us nothing."

"Again…Jonas Salk, but good point. Jake, take your sexy self over there and work your magic," Colt said. *Work your magic? Take your sexy self over there?* Colt winced internally as he thought about what he said and instantly threw his arm around Gigi, as though that would magically wipe away every gay word that flew out of his mouth and the world would once again believe that Colton Humphrey was 100% straight. Jake made his way over to the bar but did a double take at Colt, probably thinking about what Colt had just said.

"Take your sexy self over there?" Gigi said, looking up at Colt. She stared at him for a moment, as though she were examining him. They had a lot of alcohol to drink leading up to coming here, but something about Gigi in this moment made her seem very, very sober. "What was that?"

"Come on," Colt said, unaware of how he was going to finish that sentence as he paused. "I mean, look at those beautiful brown legs! They're bound to get us at least some top-shelf booze, right?"

Gigi started laughing and then nodded before turning her attention to the stage where a drag queen named Tipsy Bottom started lip-synching "London Bridge" by Fergie. Meanwhile, Colt couldn't help but glance back at Jake, and when he did, he saw him talking to some cute guy dressed as a pharaoh. He didn't know or recognize the guy, but whoever he was, Jake clearly looked like he was in a state of shock.

"Hey, G? Who is that?" Colt asked, pulling on Gigi's shoulder to turn around.

"Talking to Jake? I think that's the guy that chased Brendan Fraser in *The Mummy*," Gigi said. She lifted her finger and pointed at a guy dressed as Cleopatra who had approached Pharaoh and Jake. "And I think he is supposed to be a pyramid woman."

"A pyramid woman…nice. Gigi, I think you're on water for the rest of the night," Colt said. "I mean do you know who he is?"

Gigi took a long hard look and squinted her eyes. Her head was swaying back and forth and Colt began to worry that the increased focus on Gigi's drunken head would make her pass out.

"OH NO," Gigi shrieked, looking terrified, like she'd said something she shouldn't have. "I'll be right back."

"Why don't you wait here?" Colt said, pulling her back. "I can go."

"But…"

"Don't worry. I got it," Colt said, reassuring her. She looked a little panicked, and Colt had no idea why. He pushed his way through the crowd that had now swelled to a size that Colt assumed the fire marshal would not appreciate.

"Babe, I'm sorry," Pharaoh said, just as the guy dressed as Cleopatra pushed his way through the crowd.

"Is everything okay?" Colt said. Jake spun around, and his sudden appearance somehow made Jake looked like he was about to freak out.

"This doesn't concern you," Pharaoh said aggressively. He looked at Colt, and the man's expression of anger, desperation, and constant craning of his head down at Jake's legs made Colt understand what was going on. This guy was at some point romantically involved with Jake. There was no doubt about that.

"Actually, it does," Colt said, looking back at him. "Jake's with me."

"With you? I highly doubt that."

"Why?" Colt asked. He hadn't intended to make it sound like Jake and him were a couple, but he knew that was what Pharaoh understood Colt's comment to be. And Colt was shocked at the guy's response.

"Well, you scream *breeder*, for one! There's no way that you're gay," Pharaoh said.

Colt looked around and realized people were staring in awe as though this altercation were some sort of dinner theater being put on for their amusement.

"Well, I am, and I'm telling you that Jake is with me. Come on, *babe*." It was the first time Colt had ever even come close to saying the words that would finally let the world see his true self. He'd inadvertently shoved himself out of the closet, and he couldn't help but feel like he was somehow exposed and naked for the entire world to see. He felt his heart begin to race, and he wanted to throw up. Not from the alcohol, but from the sheer terror that people knew he was gay. Now there was no turning back. He began to feel like he was about to have a panic attack and reached for Jake's hands, intertwining his fingers between his. Wherever this night was initially going, Colt knew he had now veered it off course onto a bumpy and unknown road.

"Good luck with that! Like that will last!" Pharaoh called out.

Colt turned around and saw the smug look on the dickhead's face. He may have looked cute from far away when he first saw him talking to Jake, but now Colt thought he looked like an incredibly ugly human being. He had never hated anyone in his entire life. And now, Colt hated a person whose name he didn't even know. Who was this guy to say that a relationship between Colt and Jake couldn't last? And before Colt realized what he was doing, he turned toward Jake, placed both of his hands on Jake's cheeks, and pulled him close to him until their lips touched.

BOOM!

Colt felt fireworks shooting in his stomach as the softness of Jake's lips pressed against his. First, it was fireworks, and then it was glass shattering as Colt pulled away to see that Jake had dropped all the beers from the shock of kissing him. *Oh shit*, Colt thought. *What have I done?*

"All right, fellas. I think you've had enough for the night. Time to go." A bouncer about twice Colt's size came up and started pulling both Colt and Jake toward the doorway.

The moment they were on the street, Colt began to panic. He had no idea what he was going to say or how he would explain away the best kiss with the person he had been waiting half his life to share that with. Colt kept his eyes trained on the sidewalk, afraid to look up at Jake. *Say something!*

"Oh shit...Gigi," Jake said, breaking the awkward silence between the two of them. He opened his phone and started dialing her number. After she didn't answer, he began to text her.

"I'm really sorry," Jake said, looking at Colt. It took Colt a moment to realize that Jake was apologizing for getting the two of them kicked out of the bar. At least that was what Colt had hoped that was what Jake was apologizing for.

"It's cool. I'm not," Colt said.

"Gigi wants to know where we are going now," Jake said, looking at a text message that he received.

"I don't know. Why don't we just walk and see what's still open?" Colt said.

"Okay," Jake said. He put his phone back in his pocket and started to walk down the sidewalk with Colt.

"So, are we going to talk about that? Who was that?" Colt asked.

"Colt, that was...my ex? I mean, I guess that's what you would call him." Jake paused. Given how skimpy Jake's costume was and how cold it was outside, Colt wasn't surprised that Jake appeared to be shivering a little. But Colt realized that maybe it was this conversation that was causing Jake to tremble. "I'm...gay."

Colt felt terrible. Had he pushed Jake to come out of the closet? Jake looked like it was torture, but Colt had nothing but respect for Jake, who had the courage to tell him something so personal. He reached out and grabbed Jake's hands.

"I think I've known for a while," Colt said. "But thank you for telling me. I know it's really hard to come out."

"You've known for a while? Like, for how long?" Jake seemed shocked Colt already had an idea that Jake was gay.

"Like since seventh grade," Colt said.

"WHAT! Are you kidding?" Jake's eyes began to tear up and Colt knew that he probably felt mortified that Colt had always known.

"Jake, you stare. Like, a lot," Colt said. He couldn't help but chuckle as he thought about all the times in school he would look up only to see

Jake staring right at him. He always wondered why Jake was staring and would smile back in an unconscious way of flirting with Jake. "Plus, there was homecoming night. Remember?"

"Oh yeah," Jake said, clearly recalling the memory Colt was thinking of. After helping him clean up all evidence of a party, the two had fallen asleep back inside the house. And halfway through the night, Colt awoke to an arm wrapped around him and Jake spooning him. It was a fantastic feeling, but Colt panicked and had no idea what to do and pulled Jake's arm off him, waking up Jake, who looked as if he were going to cry from embarrassment. They both had blamed it on the alcohol and never spoke of it again, but now those same watery eyes reappeared with the realization that Colt had always known about him.

"Relax, I don't think anyone else knew in high school. Besides, it seemed like you really only stared at me."

"Well I did like you, Colt. You weren't just my best friend when we were kids. You were my first crush. My childhood crush," Jake said.

"Really? Jake…" Colt paused. Shit was starting to get real, and Colt felt everything begin to spiral. Jake was saying all the things that Colt felt about him. He had once loved Jake Ruiz and was beginning to realize that maybe he never quite fell out of love with him. Even after high school. But now this felt like Colt had now reached the point of no return. He couldn't go back. He would forever be known as gay. His entire hometown would know. He hadn't even told his parents. What would they say? Would they still treat him the same way? Was this just the alcohol speaking? Colt could feel his chest growing tighter as a hundred questions began to fill his head and it felt like all of the air had been sucked out of his lungs as he took a deep breath. *I'm not ready for this.*

"I just can't believe all this time that you're gay too!" Jake said. The expression on Jake's face was enough to make Colt realize that Jake's heart was smiling.

"Listen, Jake… I'm not," Colt said. Colt knew this was an absolute lie, and he hated himself for saying it. Especially to the only boy Colt had truly loved, but he had to. All the questions and feelings he was having right now caused his heart to race. And because he had a sufficient amount of alcohol in his body, he knew he had to wait until he was sober. If he told Jake anything that he'd regret in the morning when he was sober, especially after seeing the joy on Jake's face, Colt knew he would never be able to forgive himself.

"You're not? But you kissed…" The smile on Jake's face shattered into a million pieces.

"I'm so sorry, Jake. I shouldn't have done that," Colt said. "I just saw how that dick was talking to you, and I don't know…"

"What? Say it," Jake said angrily.

"I felt sorry," Colt said. It was the truth, but Colt knew there was certainly more to that truth than perhaps he was ready to share right now.

"I don't need you to feel sorry for me, Colt!" Jake said. His eyes began to well up and Colt watched as a single tear fell from his right eye and slowly made its way down Jake's cheek. "I've gotten by for this long without anyone feeling sorry for me, and I'm not about to start now!"

"I know, I know. Maybe those weren't the right words," Colt said, realizing this was not at all how he thought the conversation would go. Jake's tears were sobering to Colt, and he began to realize his feelings would not change once he was sober.

"No, they were. No need to sugarcoat things. I think maybe you should go find your premed friends, Colt." Jake said. His eyes were cold and expressionless as he looked at Colt.

"Jake," Colt said, realizing he needed to tell Jake the truth.

"Good night, Colton. It was nice seeing you," Jake said, and then turned away from Colt and walked back toward Dempsey's, leaving him alone on the sidewalk.

CHAPTER 16 – PRESENT DAY

From: Beth Humphrey

Subject: Dancing Queen

    Now I know what you're thinking…Is my
mother really sending an email to her gay
son with the subject "Dancing Queen"? But
before you read too much into it, I'll leave
you with this (see photo).

Colt read from his laptop in the office he shared with another doctor
whenever he was at the hospital and not his practice. He had opened an
email his mother had sent to him about three hours after he got off the
phone with her. He opened the photo attachment to the email and
couldn't help but laugh at the image he saw. His mother and father were
standing against a balcony overlooking the white stucco buildings and
vibrant blue roofs of the buildings that made up the Greek island of
Santorini. The picture of his parents could have easily been a photo for
a travel advertisement for Greece, had it not been for an obnoxiously
pink feathered boa that Beth Humphrey had wrapped around her neck.
His father had an equally offending blue feathered boa that at least
seemed to fit with the buildings of Santorini.

    I told your father that I absolutely
refused to go on a Mamma Mia! walking tour
without a feathered boa. And would you
believe he had the nerve to say that I
couldn't make demands for a walking tour
that I have made myself? And second, he
asked why I needed a feather boa. How is

136

Beth Humphrey possibly going to channel her inner "Donna Sheridan" without a boa for the *Dancing Queen* number? It's like he doesn't know me at all or how much I love Meryl Streep. Anyway, thought the photo might cheer you up. Love you, honey!

-Mom

P.S. If this email and/or photo scare you in any way from taking a South American or Japan trip with the coolest mom and dad ever next summer, please disregard this email and treat it like spam. Also, feathered boas are somewhat difficult to find in Greece. Who knew?

Colt continued to look at the photo and couldn't believe his mom had actually talked his dad into buying a feathered boa for himself. The two of them had been married for nearly four decades and you could still see how lucky his dad felt being married to his mom just in his eyes. He thought about a conversation he had with his father after his ex, Harrison, had broken up with him.

"You need to find someone who doesn't just push you, son," Mark Humphrey had said. "You need to find someone who inspires you and is willing to take on the world with you. Because that person, Colt...they're your 'ride or die.' Your mother...she's eccentric and somewhat crazy, but she's my crazy. You gotta get out there and find your crazy too. Also...please don't tell your mother I said she was crazy."

The photo of Mark and Beth Humphrey showed all the silliness of their marriage that had been the root of their happiness. He wondered what a photo of him and Eli would show. What would someone see? When he began to date Eli, Colt had succeeded on finding the eccentricity but fell far short of the authenticity.

"Oh my God, Colt!" Stacy threw the door of Colt's office open. Colt nearly fell out of his chair at Stacy's alarming arrival. "You've got to come out here. They are going to kill each other."

"Who?" Colt said, pushing the chair aside and following after Stacy, but he already knew who she was talking about.

"The Ruiz family. Consuela is…" Stacy was at a loss for words as she ran down the hall with Colt following right behind her.

"Yeah, I know," Colt said. She didn't need to finish her comment. Colt knew the type of woman Consuela Ruiz was. When the two finally got to the nurse's station, it was silent in the hall, and neither Consuela Ruiz nor Jake Ruiz were in sight.

"Oh God, do you think we're too late?" Stacy asked in panic.

"Too late for what?" Colt asked.

"Do you think they killed each—? MRS. RUIZ!" Stacy's eyes were about to shoot out of her head the moment Consuela Ruiz stepped out into the hallway with her purse and jacket. Stacy looked like she was about to throw up from what Colt could only assume were unhealthy amounts of adrenaline and paranoia that Consuela heard what she was talking about and was now about to kill the only witnesses to her crime.

"I'm leaving for the night," Consuela said, looking at both Colt and Stacy. "If Jacob tries to come back at all, I expect that you will instruct anyone who is here to contact the police department immediately and arrest him for trespassing and endangering my husband. I don't need his toxic nature poisoning my sweet Carlos."

"Toxic?" Stacy said in an incredulous tone, then chuckled. "You are kidding, right?"

"I'm most certainly not!"

"Mrs. Ruiz, can I walk you to your car?" Colt asked, stepping out from behind the nurse's station and shooting a "shut the hell up" look over at Stacy.

"Like I have a choice," Consuela said as she made her way toward the hospital exit, showing no interest in hearing Colt's response to her question. Colt ran to catch up with Consuela and waited until they were outside of the hospital to freely talk.

"Mrs. Ruiz, I can't say that I know how you are feeling right now, but I do understand how scary something like this can be," Colt said, walking at a rather brisk pace to keep up with Consuela. "And it's moments like these that can sometimes bring even the most fractured families together."

Consuela spun around violently and had a madness in her eyes that terrified Colt. "Don't you DARE say anything about my family! Who says we are fractured?"

"I'm sorry, maybe I misspoke," Colt said, backtracking his comment but knowing full well he certainly hadn't misspoken. Speaking even a few moments with Consuela Ruiz made Colt realize how lucky he was. He'd have to thank Mark and Beth Humphrey the next time he spoke to them for being their wonderful selves.

"But Jacob…he's flown all the way here from Seattle with his son. He's left his restaurants and dropped everything to come back to Newport. I know you are only concerned for your husband right now, but do you think that maybe, just maybe, having Jacob here might help with Mr. Ruiz's recovery?"

This comment made Consuela Ruiz stop walking. She stood there motionless in the dark parking lot, silent. The jury was now deliberating, Colt thought, and he had just hoped that he presented a strong enough argument.

"You think that having Jacob around will help with Carlos' recovery?" Consuela asked quietly.

"I do," Colt replied.

"Very well. He can come in the morning. I'll be at church praying and will come over in the afternoon," Consuela said.

"That sounds like a good plan, Mrs. Ruiz. Thank you," Colt said.

"And Colt?"

"Yes, Mrs. Ruiz?"

Consuela turned and walked up to Colt until she was mere inches from his body. She was so close to Colt that he found himself taking a step back.

"Stay away from my son," Consuela said. She got in her car, not allowing Colt to ask what she meant by the command. The taillights of her car illuminated and the engine began to sputter out exhaust that blew in Colt's face. He got out of the way because he still had no idea if Consuela would run him over.

Consuela's words played over and over in Colt's head as he made his way back into the hospital.

What does that even mean? Colt wondered. He didn't think Consuela knew he was gay, but he did take Eli to Los Ruiz, so it might have been possible to put two and two together.

"What did she say?" Stacy asked when Colt rejoined her at the nurse's station, eager and nervous to hear his response.

"Jake can see his father in the morning. She'll come in the afternoon. Can you help me make sure those two don't get anywhere near each other again at the hospital?"

"You mean keep Mrs. Ruiz away from Jake, right? Because that lady is certifiably insane! How can she treat anyone, especially her son, like that?"

"I don't know," Colt said. "Can you do me a favor? Can you get me Helen Clayton's phone number?"

"Of course. We're still doing happy hour tomorrow, right? Because after that encounter, I could use a drink right now."

"I think we all could use one. And yes, happy hour tomorrow."

"And you're bringing Eli?"

"I am," Colt said. He thought about his boyfriend for a fleeting moment. And then all he could think about was Jacob Ruiz. How could someone so caring, warmhearted, and kind be from the same family as Consuela Ruiz? The two were night and day. Colt stood there and thought about Jake when they were growing up. He was always happy. He made Colt laugh and he wanted to be around Jake all the time. It hurt him so much when he and Jake had a falling out and weren't as close of friends as they had once been. It was a wound that hurt so much worse because Colt had feelings for Jake that had scared him as a teenager. He knew he was gay because of Jacob Ruiz. And now Colton Humphrey asked himself why he couldn't stop thinking about him, even when his boyfriend was mentioned.

CHAPTER 17 – OCTOBER 27, 2006

"Come on, please answer," Colt said with his cell phone pressed against his ear. After several rings, the other side finally answered.

"Colton? Honey, is everything okay?" Colt's mom, Beth Humphrey, asked through a restrained yawn. He had woken her up and had he not had a million other feelings going through his mind right now, he would have felt terrible.

"Mom? Is Dad there too?" Colt said. He could hear the shakiness in his voice. He was milliseconds from breaking down and crying.

"He is. Colton, please tell me everything is okay. You're scaring me," his mom said, sounding now entirely awake.

"No one's hurt and I'm okay…" Colt said, pausing.

"Okay, Colton, please tell me what's going on. You're scaring me. Your father is right here and he can hear you too."

"Hey, buddy. What's going on?" Colt's dad said through a quiet yawn.

"I'm just going to come out and say it. Mom…Dad…I'm gay," Colt said. Colt felt as though he had left a ticking time bomb at his parents' front door, run off, and now stood a safe distance away waiting to watch it explode in their faces. He had no idea how his parents were going to react, and the nerves in his body tricked him into thinking he was about to vomit all over the sidewalk.

Silence.

More silence.

"Hello? Mom? Dad? Are you still there?"

There was another moment of silence and then Colt heard his dad. "We're still here, Colton. Have you been drinking?"

"No, I mean yes, but this isn't like a drunk thing. I've been gay since like fifth or sixth grade. Well, I mean my whole life," Colt said.

"I'm sorry. I didn't mean to say it like that," his dad said.

"Colton, you know your father and I just want you to be happy," Colt's mom said, suspecting she was pushing his father's face farther from the phone in fear he may say something else unproductive. "I'm not going to lie. I imagine life may be a little harder for you being gay, especially if you plan on taking over your father's practice in Newport. Honey, this is a very conservative area. But we love you and will support you no matter what, okay?"

Colt slid down the wall of the building and began to cry uncontrollably. He couldn't remember the last time he had cried and felt himself begin to unravel in front of his parents. Had he known they were going to be this supportive, he may have come out sooner to them. But Beth Humphrey had a point. What would Colt do if he were to take over his father's practice? That had kind of been the entire plan all along, and now Colt was angry that his sexuality may have an influence on being able to go back to Newport.

"Your mother is right, son," Colt's dad said. "You are the best thing that has ever happened to us. And we are so Goddamned proud of everything you have been able to do in your life so far. And if you're gay, I bet you're going to knock that out of the ballpark too!"

"Mark!" Colt's mom screamed, and he heard a thud of what he imagined was a pillow being thrown at his dad's face. But his dad's comment was exactly what he needed to hear to help snap him out of his crying as he started to laugh.

"Your father is a great doctor, but he is a horrid motivational speaker," his mom said. "But he's right. We are so very proud of you, and I know the kind of person you are and your character. You are going to find a terrific man, and we are going to be so happy to finally be able to have two sons."

And just like that, Colt went from laughter back to crying. His parents were sending him on a roller coaster of emotions, which seemed only fitting given the entire circumstances of the night and how they had made Colt feel.

"Thank you…for everything. You really are the best parents," Colt said with absolute honesty. "I should probably go. I need to try and make something right."

"Be safe, honey. And Colton?" his mom said.

"Yeah?"

"If you need anything else, don't hesitate to call us. Okay?"

"Okay, Mom. I love you to the moon."

"And back," his parents said in unison, and the call ended.

Colt turned around and looked back in the direction of Dempsey's. He never imagined he would be able to start a relationship with a man. After the conversation he just had with his parents though, Colt knew what he had to do. He had to go back and make things right with Jake. He had to be honest with him. But all those hopes were crushed when he made it back to the doorway of Dempsey's only to find the bouncer who had kicked him and Jake out earlier.

"Oh come on, Charlie Chaplin," the bouncer said. "Once you're out, you're out for good!"

"I'm Jonas Salk!" Colt screamed. He made a promise to himself in that very moment that he would never for the rest of his life choose a costume that he found witty. Apparently, the only way to do Halloween was to go full skank.

"Oh wow! You think you're going to get in now?"

"No. Have you seen the people I was with? Pebbles and Bamm-Bamm?"

"Oh, that's what he was?" the bouncer said. "I thought he was an elderly Tarzan. Sorry, he came back and his friend met him outside right before you got here."

Colt groaned in frustration and stormed back down the street. He made his way back to Dewey's and looked inside the diner. They weren't there. He walked up the street and back into Blue Spark, where the night began, and there was no sign of them there either.

Colt opened his phone and scrolled through his contacts. As he looked at every person's name, he wondered if that contact would have Jake or Gigi's numbers. *BINGO,* he thought when he saw Stacy Morrell's name.

"HUMMMMMMMMMMPHREYYYYYYYYYYYY," a drunken Stacy said through the other line. "Are you coming to the house party? We are all trashed!" Stacy began to cackle in laughter, and Colt immediately regretted calling her.

"Stacy! Do you have Jake's phone number?"

"Yeah, why?"

"Just… Can you give me his number really quick? I need to call him."

"Sure, hold on. Let me text it to you," Stacy said sloppily and then hung up.

A few moments later, his phone buzzed and a phone number popped up in a text from Stacy. Colt memorized the number and then called it.

Ring.

Ring.

Ring.

Ring.

"Hello, you have reached 5-0-9-5-5-5-2-7-4-0. Please leave a message at the tone," the automated operator said.

"Jake, it's me. I'm so sorry about earlier. I don't know why I said that. The truth is: I'm gay. I always have been. I'm so sorry I didn't say that. I guess I was just afraid, but I'm not now. I don't regret that kiss at all and now I just want to see you again. Please call me back. Bye." Colt shut his phone and sat down on the curb. He wasn't sure if Jake would call him back, but less than two minutes later, his phone vibrated with a text message.

> **5095552740 10/27/06 11:26 p.m.**: Asshole…lose this number and never speak to me again

"SHIT!" Colt screamed as he shoved his phone back in his pocket. *Did he even listen to my message?* Colt was certain that his voicemail would be enough for Jake to call him back but clearly, he had underestimated how pissed he made Jake.

"Colton? Is that you?" a voice behind Colt said.

He spun around in hopes that he would be looking at either a red-headed or white-haired prehistoric child, but instead there stood Carmela, along with Sweeney and Harrison.

"Humphrey? What are you doing sitting on the street?" Harrison looked down at him in disgust. "God knows what you may be sitting in."

"Oh, hey, guys," Colt said quietly, his hopes obliterated by the sight of the three of them.

"Is everything okay?" Sweeney said, sitting down on the curb next to Colt.

"No, I screwed something up that could have possibly been great," Colt said. "You guys, I'm gay."

"I know," Carmela said matter-of-factly.

"What? How?" Colt said, shocked.

"Oh, it's a gift of mine," Carmela said. "Like Harry, for instance. He's gay too."

"WHAT!" Harrison screamed in horror.

"Oh, don't worry, sweetie. You won't realize it until you've probably been married for several years to Claire with two kids and are running for a Republican seat in the Senate and are found with your pants down in an airport bathroom."

Colt and Sweeney could not contain their laughter, while Harrison stood there, looking like he was about to piss himself. He didn't know Carmela too well, but after that last comment, Colt was beginning to think he may have to become better friends with her.

"I don't know what you're talking about," Harrison said defensively, as if he were repulsed at the idea of being gay.

"Of course you don't, honey. I already told you—you won't know for several years," Carmela said reassuringly. "Anyway, Colt, thank you for telling us, but that certainly doesn't change how we see you. If anything, it helps me see you a little more clearly now."

"Thanks," Colt said as Carmela wrapped an arm around his shoulders. "I kind of blew it with someone."

"Bamm-Bamm?" Sweeney asked.

"Yeah," Colt said. "I've known him my entire life and he was my high school crush. And I kind of screwed things up with him, and now I can't find him."

"Well, let's fix things," Sweeney said. "We will help you find him."

"Who's *we?* I'm going back to the hotel," Harrison said, storming off down the street.

"Thank you, guys," Colt said. "I'm really glad you came on this trip. And I owe you one!"

"Oh sweetie, you have no idea," Carmela said. "But not because of this. You owe us because you ditched us with that trust-fund baby."

"I'm so sorry," Colt said, realizing how awful it must have been for the two of them to spend the evening drinking with Harrison. The three began to make their way down the street, peeking into every restaurant and bar they passed. "So Carmela, that gaydar thing… Is that really true?"

"Nah, Harry pretty much stewed in anger the entire time about how you ran off with a nearly naked cave boy. If you read between the lines, there was a novel there," Carmela said.

"She's not exaggerating," Sweeney said. "The way he went on about Bamm-Bamm's and I quote 'toned brown thighs' was borderline obsessive. I'm pretty sure he can identify those legs in a police lineup."

"Jeez," Colt said, thinking about Harrison and how awkward it was going to be when he went back to the hotel room tonight. He couldn't imagine what was going through Harrison's head, and he certainly had no desire to find out.

The three of them continued walking up and down the streets, stopping every so often to look into a bar to see if Jake or Gigi was in there. After about an hour without any luck, Colt was starting to feel like Jake was less of a Bamm-Bamm and more of a Cinderella, disappearing into the night without any trace, except one very rude text message. Carmela and Sweeney didn't need to say what Colt was already thinking. He would not find or hear from Jake tonight. And with that, the three made their way back to the hotel.

CHAPTER 18 – JUNE 19, 2013

Colt opened the door from his apartment building and stepped onto the sidewalk of Seattle in the Ravenna neighborhood. He began to stretch next to the stoop of his building before his morning jog, catching the attention of a couple gay men who passed him.

"Hey, handsome," one of the guys said as he looked back at Colt, who smiled at the two. He knew that he was considered to be an attractive man, but the unwanted attention made Colt feel awkward. It had been almost seven years since he had come out to his parents and his close friends, but he had never got used to the attention from both sexes. He put in his earbuds and started playing his music before setting out to jog.

Jogging helped Colt clear his head. He often found that sometimes the time would make him think of things he hadn't thought of in a long time. He started to think about the two guys who had flirted with him and he wondered if he should have said or done something. He was horrible at all of this and he was starting to realize he needed to stop making work his excuse for not dating. Colt was about to enter his fourth and final year in the resident program at Virginia Mason and his father had already started making plans to transition the practice over to his son in a year. Everything was falling nicely into place for him. Everything except his love life, which was a dumpster fire.

"Sweetie, you know your father and I fully support you marrying a man, right?" His mother had told him on the phone not too long ago.

"I know, Mom. It's just, I'm busy."

"Colton, everyone is busy. That's the whole point of life," Beth Humphrey had said. "You just need to make it a priority. I hope you're not still hung up on Jacob."

"Mom. It's not that. I promise!" he said. This time, Colt was genuine in that response. "I moved on from him a long time ago."

And that was the truth. It was painful, but the last words he had ever heard from Jake Ruiz was through text. "Asshole…lose this number and never speak to me again." Then nothing. He never heard another word from Jake after that. In fact, he hadn't thought about Jake for a while, until he read an article about a rising Seattle chef who had opened his first restaurant, Viva la Vida Cocina. He made it as close as the entrance to Viva la Vida. The building's facade was a warm Mediterranean putty color with a red fabric awning. Colt looked through the window, and the moment he had caught a glimpse of Jake laughing, he had realized Jake was happy. There was no point in dredging up memories and reentering his life, not knowing if he would even be welcome. He walked away from the restaurant and did his best to not think about Jake, which became increasingly difficult, as Viva la Vida Cocina began to establish a cult-like following and was talked about by everyone Colt knew. On several occasions, he turned down meeting the other residents in the program after their work rotations, whenever they suggested getting drinks at the restaurant.

Colt stopped running when he got to Carmela's house. He had really solidified his friendship with her on Halloween night. He had also grown close to Sweeney, but after med school, she moved to Baltimore for her residency program at Johns Hopkins, and Colt continued to grow closer with Carmela.

"Hey, gorgeous!" Carmela shouted, stepping onto her porch and locking her front door. The two had made a routine of a morning jog whenever their rotations fell in sync and gave them the free time to do so. And given the hospital was short-staffed at the moment, their morning jogs had become more infrequent.

"Hey, beautiful," Colt said, smiling. "You look like you got some sleep!"

"Kind of," Carmela said. "I didn't get off until midnight and then I was so hungry I went to Dick's for a cheeseburger. What you're looking at is the product of about four hours of sleep and a cheeseburger. And a strawberry shake."

"It's a good look on you," Colt said reassuringly, even though Carmela didn't need it.

"Hey, so…um," Carmela paused. "Did you look at *The Stranger* this week?"

"No, but the way you say that makes me think that I should have. What's in the issue?" Colt asked, wondering what could be in the weekly newspaper that Carmela was asking about.

"Well, when I was reading it, I came across an article about Jake," Carmela said. Ever since she helped Colt try and find Jake on Halloween night, Colt had detailed his entire history with Jake so vividly, Carmela felt as though she had somehow known Jake personally. The funny part was that she had never even met him, aside from catching a glimpse of him on Halloween night as she walked past him.

"You know what? Don't tell me. Probably better I don't know whatever the article said," Colt said. By the sound of her voice and her demeanor, whatever it was couldn't have been good.

"Okay, I'm sorry," Carmela said, worried she had reopened a wound that had healed.

"No, don't be sorry. There's nothing to be sorry about," Colt said, putting his hand on Carmela's shoulder.

"Cool. So, I have to tell you about last night's shift. It was slow for most of the night and then…" Carmela continued telling the story about a man who had been hit by a car driving down the wrong side of the street, but as she got further into the story, Colt's mind began to wander as they ran. What could possibly be written about Jake that could merit the type of concern and hesitancy from Carmela? She never showed that kind of concern or caution when there were other articles about Jake opening his subsequent businesses. And she certainly didn't show that type of concern when multiple news outlets began running stories that Jacob Ruiz had received a James Beard Award for Viva la Vida. So what could it be? Colt knew there was only one thing that could cause Carmela to show this level of concern. Jake Ruiz was either getting married or he was dead.

"Okay," Colt said, interrupting Carmela, unaware of what she was talking about or what happened to that poor man hit by the car. "What was the article about?"

"Huh? Maybe you're right," Carmela said. "It doesn't matter."

Colt stared at Carmela and couldn't believe she would bring up a topic that touched a nerve and wouldn't follow through with sharing once Colt finally showed interest. He looked past her and there, at the end of the street, was a *Stranger* box. Colt went from a casual jog to practically a dead sprint, to ensure he could get to the box before Carmela realized what he was doing and talked him out of it. He opened the door and pulled out a copy. He flipped through the issue, scanning each page quickly. He could see Carmela standing to the side from the corner of his eye, silent—further indication whatever he was about to find out would not be good. He was nearly at the end when he flipped the page and there he was, staring back at Colt.

God, he's even hot in newsprint, Colt thought. But it was who was standing next to Jake that caught Colt's attention. He was nearly as beautiful as Jake and they were holding hands.

Renowned Seattle Chef Marries Business Partner

By Alexander Jackson

If you haven't heard of Chef Jacob Ruiz by now, you may be living under a rock. Ruiz came onto the Seattle food scene a little over four years ago like lightning in a bottle. And in that time, Ruiz has opened three buzzworthy food establishments, redefining the very food each of those restaurant's genre represents. And now, Ruiz is making an investment of another kind by saying "I do" to longtime business partner and co-owner, Paxton Cooper. The two wed on Saturday, June 1ˢᵗ in a private ceremony at Cooper's family ranch in Selah, Washington.

Before becoming a local celebrity chef, Ruiz grew up in eastern Washington in the small town of Newport. He found his love of food as he helped work in his family's Mexican restaurant in the town of just over 2,000. Ruiz later attended Gonzaga University, earning his degree in business before moving to Illinois to attend Kendall College, School of Culinary Arts. After finishing at

Kendall, Ruiz moved to Seattle and worked as sous chef to another Seattle renowned chef, Arthur Maxley, for a year before branching out and opening his first restaurant, Viva la Vida Cocina, with a local business partner, Cooper.

When asked why he made a risky investment during the recovery of the global recession with such a new chef, Cooper replied, "I saw so much potential in Jake. He is passionate about anything and everything he puts his mind to. I just knew that if he had the opportunity to put that passion into his own restaurant, he would leave a mark on the world that would never disappear." And Cooper was right. Viva opened to rave reviews and in less than a few months from opening his first restaurant, Ruiz and Cooper began work on their second restaurant, Beacon Hill Barbeque. This, of course, was followed by Blue Agave, and the upcoming Maple Point Bakery. If the previous openings of those restaurants are any indication, the fourth restaurant in the Ruiz Kitchens portfolio will be a smash hit when it opens later this year.

Cooper's love of food runs a parallel story to Ruiz's. Cooper grew up just on the outskirts of Yakima, Washington, on his parents farm in Selah. There, Cooper learned how to run a business at a very young age, helping his parents. Cooper later attended Central Washington University, earning his degree in business, before moving to Seattle and working his way through the ranks of the major building firm, Faye Construction, where he worked up until starting his business venture with Ruiz.

The two plan on remaining in Seattle, where they call home. Prior to their wedding, when asked about any new additions to Ruiz Kitchens, Jake said, "I think right now all my investments will be into my family." Ruiz later shared that he and Cooper are already considering starting a family of their own in the next couple years.

"Oh wow," Colt said quietly as he finished the article. It had been years since he had last seen Jake, but that article finally gave him something he had long needed: closure.

CHAPTER 19 – PRESENT DAY

"Do you think this is really a good idea?" Colt asked nervously.

"What? Inviting an old high school friend to happy hour with us? Of course it is," Stacy said. The two had been at Jersey's for less than an hour and Stacy was nearly finished with her second drink.

"No, I mean Jake coming to happy hour *and* Eli also coming to happy hour," Colt said. When Stacy had proposed the idea, Colt hadn't seen any problems with it, and now all he could see were problems. This would be the first time that Colt's sexuality would be a focus of attention with Jake in person, and that didn't seem like such a big deal. Except that it was. Jake Ruiz was his high school crush. Aside from that, Jake Ruiz was also the first boy he had ever kissed. And if he wasn't mistaken, Jake Ruiz was also the first boy whose heart he broke. The last time he had talked about his sexuality with Jake, it ended disastrously with that awful text message. And now, he was hoping for a better outcome in person so many years later. Unfortunately, the presence of Stacy and his over-the-top boyfriend made such a personal conversation all the more awkward.

"Oh relax, it's not like they are going to fight over you. What are you worried about?" Stacy asked.

"I guess I'm just starting to realize maybe I should have talked with Jake about how things were left with that text message before Eli shows up." Colt said.

"Colt, you haven't seen Jake in years. You don't owe him an explanation of anything. You went after him, remember? You tried to talk with him and he was the one to tell you to lose his number and he called you an asshole," Stacy said, recounting the story Colt had told her about the night the two shared a kiss.

"Yeah, I guess so," Colt said, still not confident of the decision to invite Eli and Jake to the same happy hour.

"Everything will be fine, but there's no turning back now. Look who just walked in," Stacy said, looking toward the door. Colt glanced over and saw Jake walk into the bar. Before his reappearance in Newport, it had been years since Colt had last seen Jake, but somehow he looked as youthful and beautiful as he always had. The light and happiness in his brown eyes had seemed to be less evident nowadays, but that made sense, Colt thought, given all the amount of stress and loss that Jake had experienced. He stood there in khaki shorts and a navy blue polo. Jake's caramel skin and toned calves were works of art, Colt thought. He couldn't pull his eyes away from Jake's legs. Colt had two thoughts in that moment: First, Jacob Ruiz was gorgeous. Colt bit his lower lip. Second, Colt realized how bad of an idea this was.

"Jake!" Stacy slid out of the booth, running over to squeeze him. Colt watched Stacy embrace Jake and felt a tinge of jealousy. She pulled him over to the booth where Colt was sitting. "I'm so glad you came. It's like a mini-reunion!"

"I guess it is. I just got off the phone with Gigi and she'll be here next week too," Jake said. The news of Gigi's imminent arrival didn't exactly thrill Colt. He got along with her and they had shared the same group of friends in school, but Colt had attributed the loss of his friendship with Jake partly to Gigi. The minute those two had started to be friends seemed to be the exact moment a wedge was formed between him and his friendship with Jake.

"Oh my God! When's the last time the three of us were together? I think it was Halloween night!" Stacy asked. Colt felt like he had just been punched in the stomach. Of all the memories that Stacy could have shared, she chose the worst. "Anyway, I'm glad we are all back together again. Hey, why don't you go catch up with Colt and I'll get us some drinks?"

There was so much Colt could have said when he and Jake found themselves alone. The problem, though, was that Colt felt like his mind was paralyzed. He had so much he needed to share but had no idea what to address first.

"It's kind of weird being at a bar in Newport," Jake said, breaking the awkward silence.

"Just wait. It gets even weirder when people see us here and try to practically get their physical taken in the middle of the bar," Colt said, thinking about the last time he was at Jersey's with Stacy. Mr. Martin, one of Newport's lifelong residents, dropped his pants to the floor to ask Colt about a mole on the inner part of his thigh, giving no thought of where he was or what it would look like to the rest of the customers in the bar, who thought Mr. Martin had had one too many drinks and was flashing Colt and Stacy. The comment made Jake laugh so hard he snorted a little, and Colt felt a jolt in his heart and the smallest flutter in his stomach. It was a cute sound that Colt hadn't heard in a very long time.

"Serious. It's why Stacy and I hide out in the back now," Colt said, reclining in the booth and resting his eyes on Jake's.

"Well, I hope they at least buy you a drink before they pull their pants down in the bar," Jake said.

"So many visuals with that, Ruiz," Colt said as he looked at Jake. Something about sitting across from Jake Ruiz made Colt feel like no time had passed since their last encounter.

Colt wondered how he had been so stupid to screw things up on Halloween night with Jake. It was those events that he felt had cursed the relationships that followed that night. First, there was Adam, who turned out to be a pot-smoking kleptomaniac. That relationship lasted a few weeks. Then there was Jason. Colt dated Jason for about a month before realizing he was a serial liar. There was a string of garbage dates that made Colt more cynical about the possibility of finding a long-term relationship with a man. After that, Colt decided to take a break from dating because he was having no such luck until Harrison Peak came back into his life. Several years following the events of that Halloween night, Harrison and Colt had reconnected and Harrison apologized for how he had treated Colt. He had done some self-reflection and realized he was gay. His girlfriend, Claire, had apparently done the same kind of soul-searching and realized she was a lesbian. It was something Carmela pointed out, as she had guessed that both Harrison and Claire were both gay on Halloween night in 2006.

Colt and Harrison continued dating and eventually became boyfriends. Harrison wanted to avoid any type of public displays of affection with Colt, which confused him, considering the two lived in Seattle, but he respected Harrison's wishes since he wasn't out to everyone yet. But that was what Colt had got wrong. He mistook Harrison's desire to not be affectionate because he wasn't out, when in fact he didn't want to be affectionate because Harrison was sleeping with half of the gay men on Capitol Hill behind Colt's back. Colt had learned that Harrison Peak had been by far the worst of all his exes. From that point on, he remained single and jaded until Stacy eventually introduced him to Eli.

"Sorry it took so long. I asked Art to make something sophisticated for our city friend here, and you would have thought I asked him the meaning of life. I gave up and he gave us three rum and Cokes. Cheers!" Stacy arrived back at the table with three drinks in hand and Colt realized his window of opportunity to talk with Jake was now gone.

"Do you guys remember homecoming night?" Stacy asked Colt and Jake before she took another sip of her rum and Coke.

"Do *you* remember homecoming night?" Jake asked, which in turn made Colt laugh into his drink.

"No, that's why I was asking. I don't remember it at all," Stacy said.

"Stacy, you were an absolute mess. We had to sneak you out the back of the gymnasium doors, and then we got locked out and had to leave early. Gigi drove you home," Jake said.

"Ah, I'm just messing with you," Stacy said.

"Oh, so you do remember that night?" Jake asked.

"God no. Colt told me though. I was a bit of a mess in high school. Thank GOD I've turned over a new leaf. Art! Can you bring another round of rum and Cokes to the table on my tab?" Stacy yelled to the bartender, who was speaking to two old men sitting over at the bar. Stacy continued a trip down memory lane, telling a couple more stories that practically made Jake's eyes bug out of his head at what a mess Stacy had been in high school.

"Colt, do you remember Bradley's party in the woods when we were sophomores?" Stacy stopped and then looked over at Jake, remembering the story of how Consuela had made him stand up and confess his sins in front of a Bible study group because of that night. "Oh God. Jake, I'm sorry. I completely forgot."

"Don't worry about it. My mom is, well…I'm sure she means well in her own head," Jake said slowly. "Unfortunately to everyone else, she's…"

"Too much?" Stacy said, interrupting Jake. She could see he was struggling to find words that wouldn't disrespect his mother but were still an honest description of the person she was.

"Exactly. Thank you Stacy," Jake said. Colt saw gratitude in Jake's face from Stacy's interjection.

"Well, that was hands down one of the funniest nights of my life. We were all playing strip poker when someone dared Bradley to pee on the electric fence to see if anything would happen. And of course, something happened and he said he almost shit himself. I don't think I've laughed harder in my life, until the sheriff pulled up. And there we all were, running through the woods after Bradley had peed on the electric fence," Stacy said. She began to laugh so hard that Colt noticed tears running down her cheeks.

"Who would have thought you two would end up together?" Jake's comment silenced Stacy, who just looked at him dumbfounded.

"Oh my God, we aren't together! Colt is dating Eli. And there he is now!" Stacy said.

Out of the corner of his eyes, Colt saw Stacy turn to face the entrance of Jersey's, but Colt's eyes were locked with Jake's.

"You're…gay?" Jake stammered.

"What? I told you. You knew this," Colt said defensively. How could Jake pretend to not remember the voicemail Colt had left him on Halloween night, followed by the text message Jake sent back telling him he was an asshole and to lose his number?

"Nope, you definitely didn't," Jake said. The anger in Jake's eyes made Colt realize Jake somehow actually believed this. He could also finally see that Jake was in fact the son of Consuela Ruiz, who had given him that same exact look of anger when she forbade him from going anywhere near Jake at the hospital.

"Hey there," Eli said when he arrived at the booth.

"Eli," Colt began. He had no idea where he was taking this though. *This is my childhood crush? This is the person I was once in love with?* Colt sat there and realized he had been quiet for far too long. "This is one of our oldest friends and classmates, Jake."

"Hi," Jake said in an octave or two deeper than Jake's regular voice. Colt looked over at Jake, surprised, and smiled. Clearly Jake was trying to make some sort of impression as well, which made Colt feel optimistic, but he had no idea why. Why did he want to feel optimistic with Jake when he was dating Eli?

"Nice to meet you. So, what are we talking about?" Eli asked. To Colt's surprise, Eli seemed to be very even-keeled at the moment, which relieved Colt.

"Oh, just some of my more scandalous stories," Stacy said as she laughed.

"And there's plenty of those, you crazy slut!" Eli screamed before high-fiving Stacy, catching the attention of Art over at the bar. Colt groaned, then worried that perhaps it was audible to the rest of the table. There was no saving Jake from Eli now. All Colt could do was wince at whatever would happen next.

"What about you Jake? Any scandalous or salacious stories?" Eli asked.

"No, not really," Jake said.

"What about Halloween night? You know when you and Co—AHHH!" Colt's leg shot up under the table and connected with Stacy's shin before she could finish that sentence and make an already tense situation even worse.

Colt watched as the remainder of Stacy's drink spilled into her lap. She grabbed a bunch of napkins and then squeezed past Jake out of the booth. She stood there, dripping rum and Coke.

"I'm sorry, Stacy! Here, let me help you with that," Colt said, grabbing her by the arm and making their way over to Art at the bar.

"Are you out of your mind?" Colt asked Stacy, pulling her away from the table. She looked furiously at Colt as she wiped her hands downward and beads of rum fell to the floor.

"WHAT?" Stacy practically screamed. She waved down the bar to Art for another round of drinks. "What are you talking about? You're the one who kicked me with what I can only assume are steel-toed boots!"

"Were you really about to bring up Halloween night to my boyfriend *and* my childhood crush?" Colt whispered furiously at Stacy as he pulled her into the hallway of Jersey's that led to the restrooms.

How can she be so daft to not realize what she was about to do? Colt thought.

"I…" Stacy finally realized what she'd done. "I'm sorry, Colt. But to be fair, nothing happened between you and Jake besides a kiss. And it's not like Eli's never going to learn about that."

Stacy was right and Colt couldn't be mad at her. Nothing happened. It was just a kiss and nothing else. Except that he always wanted it to be more than just a kiss. He could continue to stand here and argue with Stacy about this but Colt knew he had to get back to the table. Jake was sitting there with Eli in what Colt could only assume would be one of the most awkward and likely outlandish conversations Jake ever had.

"Anyway, can you believe him? He's pretending like he never heard the voicemail and that he never sent the text." Colt said.

"Well, I mean, weren't all of you really drunk that night? Maybe he doesn't remember," Stacy reasoned.

"But wouldn't he at least see the text when he sobered up? Wouldn't he hear the voicemails?" Colt asked.

"You know, though, he could have erased those messages when he was still drunk. Maybe he was too hurt and deleted them while he was angry and didn't remember the next morning," Stacy said.

"Yeah, I guess so. Well, what should I do now?" Colt asked.

"Nothing, don't even worry about it. Like I said, you don't owe Jake an explanation. But maybe we should get back there before the situation gets any more awkward between those two."

When Colt and Stacy arrived back at the table, however, Eli sat there alone and Jake was nowhere in sight.

"What happened to my drink?" Colt asked.

"Jake must have drunk it," Eli said, shrugging. "By the way, he had to leave."

"What? He practically just got here," Stacy said, sliding into the booth.

"I thought it was weird too. He's a bit sketchy if you ask me," Eli said. "Didn't you go to order more drinks, babe?"

Colt realized Eli had just set a new record for how quickly he could piss off Colt. He knew full well Jake didn't just leave, and if he had to guess, Eli said something to make a very awkward interaction worse.

Then again, Jake seemed really angry after finding out that Colt was gay. Maybe Jake left because of him.

Art walked over from the bar, delivering another round of drinks. Eli grabbed for one and began to sip.

"What were you guys talking about? Did he say anything?" Stacy asked.

"Oh, he just went on and on and on about how he was a chef in Seattle and ran a bunch of restaurants. Honestly, I couldn't get a word in with all the bragging," Eli said, taking another drink.

"That's odd. That doesn't sound like Jake at all," Stacy said.

Colt knew that wasn't Jake. Jake had never been the bragging kind the entire time he had known him, and Colt could see right through this. If there was anyone at this happy hour who you could not get a word in with, it was the one who was now peddling this story about Jake. Colt looked over at Eli. He had been dating him for several months, hoping to find redeeming qualities where his personality fell short. But the more he got to know Eli, Colt was beginning to see there weren't any redeeming qualities. In fact, Colt Humphrey was beginning to suspect that Eli was not going to be the exception to his roster of garbage boyfriends.

PART III

TODAY

CHAPTER 20

The following morning, after the disastrous happy hour, Jake woke to find that there was now a new houseguest at Helen's. Gigi had arrived in the middle of the night, a week earlier than expected.

"Please, do you really expect that I'd just sit in Seattle after Colt's bombshell? Clearly Newport is more interesting right now!" Gigi said over breakfast with Helen, Charlie, and Jake. Jake had called her right after he had left Jersey's to tell her that not only was Colt gay but that he was also dating the biggest jerk he had ever met.

"I feel bad for making you come out here," Jake said.

"Don't be," Helen and Gigi said in unison. The looked at each other and giggled. The way the two acted whenever they got together was more like an older and younger sister.

"I've got a free place to stay and all the time in the world... Well, actually it's more like four weeks."

"What do you mean?" Helen asked.

"I had so much PTO stored up and we just wrapped up the latest software release, so I'm taking a little sabbatical. Helen, aren't you so excited?"

"And you're staying here the entire time?" Helen asked nervously.

"Be careful what you wish for, Helen," Gigi said, taking a bite of plant-based bacon.

"You two are welcome to stay as long as you want. I just figured if you're taking that much time off, you'd want to go somewhere...international?" Helen said after a long pause. She knew her daughter well enough to know that after a week back in Newport, the novelty would quickly wear off and Gigi would be itching to go somewhere, anywhere else.

"Fair point. I'll play this by ear," Gigi said.

"I must warn you that tonight I'm having an art class on aging with dignity here at the house. You're welcome to stay, Gigi, if you'd like. But Jake, it may not be the place for Charlie."

"Oh, okay. Why's that?" Jake asked.

"Well, I'm doing a series of classes with some women from the community center and this class is on the female figure after menopause. We are doing portraits of each other…in the nude."

"Say no more," Jake said. He really didn't want to know any more details, especially where the class would be sitting since he was still staying with Helen.

"What's nude?" Charlie asked between a mouthful of vegan scrambled eggs. His plant-based bacon had remained on his plate, untouched.

"Naked, darling," Helen said, patting Charlie on the head and scooping another heap of scrambled faux-eggs onto his plate.

"Eww! That's disgusting," Charlie said.

"It's the human body, Charlie. There's nothing disgusting about it at all," Hellen said matter-of-factly.

"This coming from the woman who last year illustrated a book about a talking giraffe that wore red rain boots and had a starfish as a friend. Now she's painting old lady areolas," Gigi said.

"Gigi, seriously! It's okay. Charlie, why don't we go on an adventure tonight and grab some food?" Jake said. Charlie's eyes lit up in a way that basically said, "*As long as actual meat is on the menu, count me in!*"

"Yes!" Charlie said excitedly.

"The class should be over around seven, so I wouldn't arrive any earlier. Unless you want Charlie to appreciate art at an earlier age," Helen said.

"Oh God!" Gigi groaned, drooping her head into her hands at the table, mortified at Helen Clayton's total lack of awareness at just how inappropriate that comment was. "Can Aunt Gigi tag along on your dinner adventure?"

"I think Aunt Gigi is going to be spending some *much-needed quality time* with Helen tonight," Helen said, kissing Gigi on the head. Jake looked at Gigi and could see the faintest traces of regret already that she was beginning a four-week sabbatical under Helen Clayton's roof.

Jake looked at the time on the car's dashboard when he finally arrived to the hospital later that morning. He promised he would pick up Charlie, who stayed behind with Gigi and Helen, before Helen's nude art class. There was no way he was going to have Charlie deal with the trauma of being around Consuela followed by the trauma of seeing a bunch of naked old women. It was ten a.m. He had a few hours to spend with his dad before Consuela would show up. As he looked at the clock, he couldn't help but feel as if he had shared some sort of bizarre custody agreement with his mother over his father.

When he walked through the entrance, he was surprised that Stacy wasn't sitting at the nurse's station. Instead, another woman around his mother's age was sitting at the desk. Jake checked in and then made his way to his father's room.

"Hey, Pa," Jake said, taking a seat next to his father. The monitor next to the bed bounced with each of his father's heartbeats, showing that there was still life in his father, even though he sat there in his medically induced coma. As strange of a thought as it was, Jake couldn't help but think his dad somehow looked peaceful or happy. It was the most time he had ever taken off from the restaurant and his dad wasn't around his mother, so maybe he was.

Shoot, he probably thinks he's on vacation, Jake thought. The thought, as inappropriate as it was, made Jake begin to laugh.

"Why'd it have to take something like this to bring us all back together, Dad?" Jake asked. "You probably planned all this, didn't you? A grand scheme to get me and Mamá talking again, right? You forget just how stubborn she is though."

Jake walked to the foot of the bed and lifted his father's leg, repositioning it to help his father avoid getting any bedsores. He took his father's other leg and moved it as well before sitting back in the chair. Jake had no idea what to say to break the silence in the room. All he could think to talk about was the grievances he had with his parents, but he knew that was the last thing to do with someone who had suffered a major medical emergency and was now in a coma. Instead, he took his father's hand in his.

165

"I'm here, Pa," Jake said. He set his head down on the bed, and before he knew it, he had fallen asleep.

Jake was startled awake when he felt a hand on his shoulder. For a second, he thought it was his father.

Has he woken up to find me sitting here with him? Jake wondered as he shot up and looked at his father, who was still asleep. When Jake turned around, he saw Colt.

"Oh God!" Colt yelled and jumped back. The sudden upward bolt of Jake was so jarring, it had scared Colt as well. "I'm so sorry!"

"Are you trying to have another Ruiz patient in the ER?" Jake asked, panting.

"Sorry. The nurse said you were here," Colt said. "I just wanted to come and apologize."

"For what?" Jake asked, confused.

"About yesterday. I guess you were kind of blindsided," Colt said.

"Uh, yeah. You could say that," Jake said. "I guess I'm just surprised that if you've been out for this long, why didn't you tell me sooner?"

"Jake, we haven't seen each other in years. We went our own separate ways, and…I don't know. I guess I didn't think I needed to come out to you a second time."

"What do you mean?" Jake asked.

"Huh? The voicemail I left you on Halloween? And then that awful text you sent," Colt said. He figured this would jog Jake's memory.

"What are you talking about?" Jake asked.

"You really don't remember?" Colt asked in disbelief. Maybe Stacy was right. Perhaps Jake had been more drunk than he thought that night and ended up deleting the messages when he was angry and had no memory the next morning.

"No. Colt, I never sent a text, and I certainly didn't receive a voicemail from you," Jake said.

Colt looked into Jake's eyes for far longer than he should have. He had known Jake long enough to know that Jake genuinely had no idea what Colt was talking about. And as he sat there looking at him, Colt couldn't help but mentally fall down a rabbit hole of what-ifs. What if he had tried harder to find Jake? What if he had just told him he was gay after that kiss? What if that moment in time would have set him on a different course in life; one that involved Jake?

166

"Are you sure?" Colt asked, still reeling at the revelation that Jake never heard the voicemail.

"Colt, I would remember a voicemail from you. What did it say?" Jake asked.

Colt wasn't quite sure how to answer the question, or even if he wanted to. So much time had passed. Jake got married. He had a child. Colt was dating Eli, and although that relationship was quickly seeming like a dead end, he was still in a relationship. And Jake was a widower. Colt didn't think detailing how he had left a voicemail to him nearly two decades ago professing his love for Jake would be helpful to either of them. He also came to the realization that if Jake hadn't been the person he called, he had just left a drunken message professing his love to some random person. Some random person who just told him to lose the number possibly because it was the wrong number.

"I don't know if it matters now. But Jake, I went back there that night," Colt said quietly.

"Where?"

"To Dempsey's. After we kissed," Colt said. "The voicemail I left was me telling you that I liked you and I really was gay. *Am* gay. I was just afraid after we kissed, and I was going back to the bar to tell you everything, but the bouncer said you left. That's when I called you."

Jake sat there. He was about as motionless as his father who sat in the bed who was in a coma. Colt watched as Jake's eyes darted back and forth. He was probably processing every moment of that night, but with the newfound information that shined a different light on the entire evening.

"You were gay…this…entire…time?" Jake said slowly. His eyes were fixed on the floor. He appeared shocked. Not only had his entire world been rocked at the revelation his childhood crush was also gay, but now Jake was learning that Colt was going to tell him about this nearly two decades earlier. Much like Colt, Jake's mind also began running through a series of what-ifs, but for Jake, these were much different. What if Colt had succeeded in telling Jake about his feelings? What if this caused Jake to not meet his husband? Jake realized he would have never had the memories of his husband, and more importantly, Charlie would have never been born. Jake's mind remained fixed on this last point.

"You know what, Colt? It's water under the bridge," Jake said, and he meant it. The mere thought of a life without Charlie was unthinkable. "I've had a great life that may have otherwise not happened. And you seem to be happy with Eli."

That last point Jake did not mean. Eli was unbearable and most of Jake's questions now centered on how Colt could even be dating someone as loathsome as Eli in the first place.

"Yeah," Colt said a little too slowly. He tried catching himself, but it was too late. The look on Jake's face made it evident he could see Colt was not all that happy.

"What's the matter?" Jake asked.

"I don't know. Has dating men been this hard for you?" Colt asked.

"You're asking someone whose husband died almost two years ago and the only date they've been on since, resulted in them breaking down in tears and sobbing uncontrollably. So yes…dating has been this hard," Jake said. He laughed at his comment and realized it was the first time he had laughed at the thought of his last date. Usually all the other times resulted in him feeling a tidal wave of embarrassment.

"Are you serious?" Colt said, pulling up a chair and sitting next to Jake.

"It was awful. And to be honest, I haven't gone on a single date since. Unless you count meeting up with Gigi for margaritas," Jake said.

"Oh, that definitely counts," Colt said, grinning. This was the happy hour that Colt had kind of hoped for. Unfortunately, this happy hour was taking place in Jake's comatose father's hospital room, so there was nothing all that happy about it.

"So, Eli…" Jake paused, slightly regretting bringing up Eli's name, because this conversation seemed to be heading in a positive direction. He wanted to ask Colt what he was thinking, but knew better. Perhaps it would be better to start with something nice about Eli. If only Jake could think of a nice thing to say about Colt's creep of a boyfriend?

"I know, I know. He's a lot of personality. I've had no luck in the relationship department, and Eli… Well, he's kind of the 'best of the worst.' I don't really know how I feel."

He is a world class tool. Don't date him. You can do so much better. All of these thoughts popped in Jake's head, and he so desperately wanted to say them, but he knew it wasn't his place to criticize the boyfriend of someone he hadn't spoken to in years. At the same time, Jake was starting to look at Colt in a different light as another thought popped in his head. *You could date me.*

"Well, if you aren't happy, why are you staying with him?" Jake asked.

"I don't know. It's not like we see a lot of each other. And when we do, I need time to mentally regroup," Colt said. He looked at Jake, and they quietly laughed at the mutual understanding of why one would need time to recover from Eli's personality.

"I can understand. I needed my own time to 'mentally regroup' after that happy hour," Jake said.

"What do you mean?" Colt asked.

"Well, he was kind of interrogating me and then he made this comment about my parents' restaurant. That's when I knew it was time to leave."

"What did he say? Jake, I'm so sorry. All he told us was that you had to leave."

"I mean, he asked if the two of us had sex before. He was bad-mouthing Newport, and then he called my parents' restaurant something along the lines of a dump. I was going to wait for you and Stacy to return, but I couldn't sit there and hear anything else he had to say."

"Thanks for telling me, and again, I am so sorry," Colt said.

"No worries. It's really not that big of a deal. My parents do need to at least throw a fresh coat of paint on the outside of the restaurant," Jake said jokingly.

"It is a big deal, Jake. I don't want to be dating someone who is that much of a jerk to someone they've just met, or anyone for that matter," Colt said. Jake's eyes widened at the comment. He was probably worried he had caused this to happen, but all Jake did was let Colt see what was in front of his eyes the entire time. Eli wasn't the right person for Colt, and he never would be. The two had been absolute opposites in every possible way and no amount of time would help Colt find something that could possibly create a lasting relationship with Eli. Colt kept his gaze locked on Jake and realized the person for him might very well be the one right in front of his eyes.

CHAPTER 21

After Colt left the room, Jake sat there quietly.

Did Colt just tell me he was going to break up with Eli? Jake wondered. And if so, was he directly responsible for it? He wished he felt guilty about that being the case, but he kept thinking about his one and only conversation with Eli and realized he was doing Colt a favor. He looked over at his father, and Jake could have sworn that his dad's once peaceful expression had now shifted to a now judgmental look, even in his coma.

"What? Don't look at me like that," Jake said. He felt weird having an argument with his comatose father, but the expression on his dad's face was uncanny. "If that one conversation with Colt was what broke them up, then I'd say their relationship wasn't strong to begin with."

Silence.

"You'd understand if you met this guy," Jake continued. "He is horrid. A complete *pendejo.*"

Jake realized just how crazy he must have sounded having an argument with Carlos and quickly turned around to make sure no one had overheard. It was just him and his father, and he continued to sit there in silence until his phone vibrated. Jacob looked down and saw Consuela's name and phone number appear on the screen. Jake thought maybe she was calling to make sure he had left the hospital and the coast was clear.

"Hello?"

"Jacob. It's your mamá, Consuela."

"Mom. Caller ID. Besides, our phone numbers are literally one digit off," Jake said, reminding his mom that he had not changed his phone number since college and still had the number when he was once on their family's cell phone plan.

"Oh, right. I'd like to speak with you tomorrow morning and would like to come by the hospital when you're there," Consuela said. The news of this worried Jake.

"Is everything okay? Could we talk about it on the phone?" Jake asked. It would be so much easier if she would just say yes. That way, if an argument erupted, it would be much simpler to just hang up.

"Everything is fine, but it should be in person. I'm on my way to the hospital, but I'll see you tomorrow then," Consuela said and promptly hung up. Jake had to hand it to his mother for somehow being a master at being able to control any situation, even a phone call, and ensuring she had the last word. It was one of her more frustrating traits, as it benefitted no one except Consuela.

"Babe," Eli said, in a drawn out whine when Colt answered his fourth call.

"Hey," Colt said flatly. "I'm on shift right now, so I can't really talk."

"Why are you ignoring my calls?" Eli pouted and then made an overly dramatic huff.

"I'm not ignoring you. Like I told you, I'm on shift," Colt said through gritted teeth. He couldn't stop thinking about what Jake had told him. It was the last piece of information Colt needed to realize he was done with Eli. They had no future, but Colt didn't want to say this over the phone. "I'll be heading out in a few hours. Why don't I head to Spokane and we meet for dinner?"

"Somewhere nice?" Eli asked.

"Sure, I'll pick you up," Colt said. He knew he had no intention of taking Eli out to dinner. In his head he was already planning how to end things. Go to his house and let him know. There was no way he would break up with that ticking time bomb in public. He had no idea how Eli would react, but Colt imagined it would be loud and dramatic.

"Fine. Call me when you're on your way," Eli said, hanging up.

Colt sat there in his office, turning his phone in his hands, and then finally set it down. He flipped open his laptop and pulled up his Internet search browser and typed Jake's name. When the results appeared, he clicked on the images link and a few photos of Jake appeared. He clicked the first one, which was an image of Jake in his chef's jacket. The image was tied to an article of him opening his second restaurant in Seattle, Beacon Hill Barbecue. Jake looked so happy in the photo. He was beaming from ear to ear and looked so cute in his chef's jacket, Colt thought. This wasn't the first time he had searched Jake's name and this was by far the best photo; it really captured his personality. Jake had gone through so much loss that Colt wondered if he'd ever see this smile on Jake's face again. He shut his laptop when he began to wonder what he was doing.

The office phone began to ring and when Colt looked down at the display. It was a call from the nurse's station.

"Yes?" Colt said.

"You have a call from a woman. She says she is a patient, but wouldn't give me her name. She..." The nurse on the other line paused and was silent for so long that Colt looked down at the phone, thinking they had been disconnected.

"She what?" Colt asked.

"She said her uterus fell out of her vagina and she needs to speak to Dr. 'Hump House'," the nurse said hesitantly, clearly not wanting to finish the sentence.

"Thanks, transfer it over," Colt said. He had heard a lot of things as a doctor, but that one was new. This had to be a prank, Colt thought. The fact they had used the horrible nickname his childhood friends had given his home, Colt knew it had to be someone from his high school class. The nurse disconnected and the phone began to ring again.

"Hello? This is Dr. Humphrey."

"Doctor, doctor. Help me, I'm staring at my uterus. It's right here on the floor," the voice on the other line said in a dramatic tone.

Colt sat there momentarily and then realized there could only be one person who would pull a stunt like this on him. "Hey, Gigi."

"Hey there! I figured that would get me transferred to you quickly," Gigi said.

"You really are something. You know someone could be having a legitimate medical emergency right now and you are taking up the line."

"I'll be quick then. I'm going to the pizza place tonight with Jake and his son. You should come too!"

Colt thought about the offer. Having dinner with Jake and the possibility of rectifying the events of happy hour from the day before sounded like an opportunity that he couldn't turn down. But then there was the matter of Eli, who he had already made plans to break up with.

"So, I'd be crashing the dinner party?" Colt asked.

"Just show up," Gigi said. "Once you're there, come sit with us."

"You sure? Jake's probably seen enough of me between the hospital and happy hour, which I'm sure he's already told you about," Colt said.

"Trust me. Jake hasn't seen enough of you," Gigi said.

The way Gigi said that made Colt feel like there was something that Gigi knew that she didn't want to tell Colt.

"Fine. What time?" Colt asked.

"Hmmm…I think six should be fine. See you there!"

"Bye, Gigi."

Colt looked back down at his phone and knew what he needed to do. He opened his phone contacts and found Eli's phone number.

"Did you miss me already?" Eli asked when he answered Colt's call.

"Hey, so I can't go to Spokane tonight. Sorry, just some last-minute things came up," Colt said.

"You're kidding, right?" Eli was annoyed at this news.

"Sorry, but I do want to see you. In person. How about tomorrow?" Colt asked.

"In person? Uh-oh, you're not breaking up with me, are you?" Eli said, and then began to cackle in laughter. "Whatever, tomorrow's fine."

"Cool. I'll see you then," Colt said.

"Byeeeee," Eli said, somehow making a one-syllable word five.

Colt hung up and didn't even feel guilty about now feeling excited. Before Gigi had called, he was kind of dreading tonight, but now he was looking forward to it. Breaking up with Eli would have to wait one more day, because Colt had plans with Jake Ruiz tonight.

173

CHAPTER 22

The menu of Pend Oreille Pizza hadn't changed since the last time Jake had ate there nearly two decades ago. In fact, as he sat in the booth, he looked around and he could probably bet his entire restaurant company that nothing had changed during the last twenty years. Even the smell of the pizza parlor somehow reminded Jake of a time when he lived in Newport.

"Have you guys decided?" the server asked unenthusiastically.

"The usual?" Jake asked Charlie, who nodded eagerly and then made an excited grunt.

"Can we have a half cheese, half meat lover's pizza?" Jake asked.

"And make sure there's *real* meat on it, please!" Charlie added.

"Anything to drink?"

"SODA!" Charlie screamed.

"Two waters, please?" Jake shot a look at Charlie that made him sit back in his chair. The waiter walked away and Jake laughed. "Nice try, mister."

"One of these days, Dad. One of these days, I'll get you," Charlie said, holding up a scrunched index finger with one eye closed as if he were an old witch casting a curse.

Jake's phone rang and he looked down to see Gigi was calling him. He figured that she was already looking for any excuse to call someone and escape momentarily from Helen's nude art class.

"Hey, what's up?"

"Oh nothing. I just wanted to see if your appetizer arrived yet? I ordered it especially for you," Gigi said.

"What are you talking about?" Jake asked.

"It's six o'clock, right?"

"Yeah," Jake said. He heard the bell hanging on the front door of the pizza parlor ring. When he looked up, Colt was standing in the doorway. His eyes caught Jake's. Colt smiled and waved and began to make his way over to the table.

"Gigi, you didn't," Jake said quietly. His hand was wrapped around his mouth and he crouched slightly down so no one could hear.

"Oh, I guess it's there. Don't burn your tongue. I'm sure it's hot," Gigi said and promptly hung up.

"Colt!" Jake said, throwing his phone into the booth as if it had just caught fire in his hands. He had no idea what Gigi had told him, but Colt Humphrey was now standing there in front of him. His dirty blond hair was a little tussled, most likely because he had just left the hospital.

"Hey!" Colt said, smiling back at Jake. "Gigi invited me to your guys' dinner. Is that weird?"

"Not at all," Jake said. "I should warn you, however, Gigi isn't here. I think this may have been part of some grand plan that she was cooking up."

Colt's smile faded and he looked embarrassed to be standing at Jake's table. "Oh... You know, don't worry about it. I was actually thinking of just getting something to go."

"Colt, sit down. What are you going to do? Take your pizza home and then eat it?" Jake asked. Colt didn't move and Jake thought that maybe a formal invite would help the situation. "Colt, I'd really like it if you would join me and my son for dinner. As a thank you for everything you've done for my dad. Please, I insist."

Colt sat reluctantly without any rebuttal. He was next to Charlie, who smiled and waved before going back to drawing on the paper tablecloth with the can of crayons the waiter had brought over for him.

"Hi!" Charlie said.

"Colt, this is my son. I believe you only met him when he was sleeping. Charlie, this is Dr. Colt," Jake said.

"Hi, Dr. Colt,"

"Hi, Charlie," Colt said. He looked at Charlie, who kept smiling back at Colt. In the few moments that Colt had met Charlie, he had somehow reminded Colt of Jake, but he didn't look anything like him. He couldn't help but wonder if Jake had adopted Charlie, or perhaps if Jake and his husband had used a surrogate. "It's nice to meet you. You know, your dad and I have been friends ever since we were about your age."

"Dad was never this small," Charlie said. He started to color in what looked like a giraffe's neck on a hippo's body. "He's always been big and strong."

"Yeah, I suppose he has," Colt said, looking at Jake. This time, however, he didn't look away. Jake would have done anything just to know what Colt was thinking in that moment.

"Dr. Colt is helping my dad," Jake said.

"Is he going to die?" Charlie asked so matter-of-factly it was jarring.

"I promise I'll take good care of him. You see, Charlie, people get sick all the time and the hospital is there to help take care of them and try to make them feel better. And sometimes as doctors, we try our hardest but that isn't always enough. But I will try my hardest and try to help your daddy's father." It was as though Colt understood the dynamics of the Ruiz family when he opted to not refer to Jake's father as Grandpa.

"That would be good," Charlie said. "I lost my other daddy, so I know how sad I was, and I don't want Dad to feel that way."

"And that is very kind of you," Colt said. "You've got a big heart!"

The two sat there silently, smiling at each other. In any other given situation, the prolonged silence may have been awkward and uncomfortable, but Jake thought it felt natural.

"Well, I'm glad Gigi invited you to dinner with her." Jake said jokingly, breaking the silence and pulling the conversation back into lighthearted discussion.

"Yeah, me too. I'm so glad I get to catch up with her after all this time," Colt replied, and then the two chuckled.

"Is the pizza still okay here?" Jake asked.

"I mean, it's no Powers Pizza, but it's decent," Colt said. Just the mention of Jake's favorite pizza parlor that was about thirty minutes away in Sandpoint, Idaho, made Jake's mouth water. He felt like he came from a position of good authority to be able and declare Powers Pizza quite possibly the best pizza Jake had ever had, and he had tried pizza from some of the best restaurants in the country.

"As long as there aren't any jalapenos, any pizza is good," Colt said, beginning to laugh.

"I can't believe you remember that!" Jake said, laughing too. Jake's parents took Colt and Jake to Powers Pizza after one of their soccer games when they were in second grade, when Jake had played sports. Jake's father had ordered a meat lover's with raw jalapenos on it and the heat from the peppers had caused both Jake and Colt to cry within the first couple bites of eating their slices. This was followed by a second round of crying in the car ride home when Colt rubbed his eyes and the oil from the jalapenos scorched his eyeball and sent him into a fit of tears.

"How can I forget? I'm pretty sure your father permanently burned off my taste buds and a layer of my cornea from that incident. I can't ever look at a jalapeno now without feeling a tinge of heartburn. And PTSD," Colt said jokingly.

"Yeah, he did things like that a lot," Jake said. There was a time when his parents were enjoyable. They had loved to pull practical jokes, but over time they just became more conservative, stronger willed, and considerably less fun.

"So, you've known my dad a really long time?" Charlie asked Colt.

"Pretty much our entire lives. Well, at least the life we lived when we were still in the same city. Your dad and I have been friends since kindergarten," Colt said.

"Yeah, and then Colt here got too cool in fifth grade when your dad showed no ability to play sports," Jake said jokingly.

"Hey, that's not true," Colt said defensively. Something about his face made Jake think that Colt actually believed that.

"Are you kidding? As soon as sports came into the picture, you kind of stopped hanging out with me," Jake said, reminding Colt.

"No, as soon as Gigi came into the picture, you stopped hanging out with me," Colt said. If Jake wasn't mistaken, a hint of anger was behind Colt's defense.

"Well, agree to disagree," Jake said, taking a sip of his water. Did Colt really believe what he was saying? Jake looked at him, who looked like he had somehow been insulted.

"Anyway," Colt said, and Jake couldn't believe how with one word Colt channeled a passive-aggressive tone that he had only seen come from Gigi. "Your dad and I used to do a lot of fun things together. You remember Indiana Jones?"

"How could I forget?" Jake said, thinking back to when they were kids and would go cliff diving near Colt's house. "I nearly drowned. Don't you remember I nearly cracked my head open on the rocks?"

"Yeah, that sucked. But come on, we had fun over there up until that point, right?"

"What's Indiana Jones?" Charlie asked.

"Oh, it's basically just jumping off the rocks, pretending we were being chased by Nazis and looking for treasure."

"You guys were weird," Charlie said, taking a sip of his water before going back to coloring his girafopotamus.

"Yeah, I guess we kind of were," Colt said, laughing.

After that, there was hardly a moment of silence as the two caught up. Colt filled Jake in on all the major things that had happened following that Halloween night. Colt finished up medical school and then did his residency at Virginia Mason in Seattle, where he ended up becoming a full-time physician after the program.

"How did I not know you were in Seattle that entire time?" Jake asked.

"I don't know. The Newport gossip chain has failed us all." Colt smirked.

"Apparently! So, your dad's practice was what made you want to come back here?"

"Yes and no. My ex and I were actually about to buy a condo in Belltown." Colt stopped, realizing he had charted the conversation on a course he didn't want to go down. "That fell through."

Jake wasn't sure if Colt was talking about the condo or the relationship, but based on what Eli had shared, Jake assumed maybe Colt meant both. Colt said that after he and his ex-boyfriend broke up, he ending up leaving Seattle and working with Doctors Without Borders in Guatemala for two years, much to his father's dismay. After all, Mark Humphrey had already been planning his retirement. Colt eventually returned to Newport, which was a combination of taking over his father's practice and a desire to never return to Seattle.

"So, you'd never live in Seattle again?" Jake asked.

"I didn't want to back then. I kind of joined Doctors Without Borders largely to get away just because of the bad memories," Colt said. Staying in the same city where Harrison was didn't sound like a good idea to Colt after they had broken up. Jake had also started becoming a household name in Seattle, and Colt couldn't help but see his name all the time, creating more incentive for Colt to not want to return. "I have the practice here now, so it'd be difficult, but I don't have anything against Seattle now."

Hearing this gave a sense of relief to Jake, but he had no idea why. It wasn't like Colt was available to date in the first place, and it wasn't like Jake was mentally and emotionally available either.

"What about you? Fill me in on everything Jake Ruiz has been doing since…" Colt paused, and both knew the moment Colt was thinking of.

"Not much," Charlie said between mouthfuls of pizza. Colt and Jake laughed before Jake began to fill in the blanks for Colt. Although, he knew some of the details Jake had shared since the area newspapers would do periodic articles about Jake and his restaurants.

"So, Jacob Ruiz graduates college with a degree in business, decides to go to culinary school, becomes this famous chef, and then opens a ton of restaurants that all receive awards. Not to mention, he gets married and becomes a dad at the same time?" Colt said, recapping highlights of their conversation.

"Pretty much. I guess that's the abridged version. But I wouldn't say I'm *that* famous," Jake said, downplaying the compliment.

"No, no, you are. I saw your face in an in-flight magazine to Ontario, California, a couple years back. They were talking about your food," Colt said.

"Well, I didn't realize you knew about the in-flight magazine on Ontario-bound flights. That does appear to change things," Jake said, taking a bite of his pizza. He looked at Colt, who appeared to be thinking about something that brought a smile to his face. "What are you thinking about?"

"You remember that time in Mr. Graham's class when we had to dissect the pigs?" Colt said, trying to hold back laughter.

"Great conversation for dinner, Colt. How can I forget? It's one of the most humiliating moments from my childhood," Jake said,

179

remembering how he started to cry when Mr. Graham had told him that he had to use the scalpel to cut open the tiny pig. "I remember Ben Deavers called me Pig Lover the rest of the day after the incident."

"Pig Lover?" Charlie said with both eyebrows raised and a look of either disgust or concern on his face. His expression made Jake and Colt laugh.

"Yeah, and he didn't call you Pig Lover after that day either, after I told him I'd kick his ass," Colt said, taking a drink of his beer.

"Really? You did that?" Jake asked. He wasn't sure if this is what Gigi had intended when she tricked Colt into showing up at the restaurant, but Jake felt like the Grinch. It was as if he could feel his heart growing the longer he talked with Colt. And at the same time, he felt his heart begin to hurt ever so slightly. Here Jake was, beginning to feel the tiniest sliver of feelings toward another man, and once again it was emotionally unavailable Colton Humphrey. "I had no idea. Thanks."

"Of course," Colt said. He stared into Jake's brown eyes and couldn't look away. It was as if they were a black hole, pulling him into Jake. In the forty minutes he had been at the pizza parlor with Jake and his son, Colt had already felt far more with Jake than the three-and-a-half-month-long relationship with Eli.

"I forgot how nice this is," Jake said.

"What?" Colt asked.

The response made Jake wonder himself what exactly he had meant. Catching up? Having dinner with another man? There were a number of things that Jake was thinking about that made this dinner special, and he wasn't sure how to finish that comment now.

"Spending time with you," Jake said.

"I agree," Colt replied.

"Dr. Colt?" Charlie asked.

"Yeah, what is it?"

"Do you like my dad?"

All the air seemed to vanish from Jake's lungs, and his stomach felt like it exploded.

"Of course. He's an old friend," Colt said.

"Yeah, I know that. I mean, are you going to date my dad?" Charlie asked matter-of-factly.

"Okay, okay, okay. Let's just eat our pizza, all right?" Jake said to Charlie, who was trying to play matchmaker. Charlie huffed in frustration, and his mannerisms were so distinctly Jake's.

"He's just like you," Colt said and then laughed.

Five years ago, Jake and his husband had decided they wanted to start a family. And at the suggestion of his husband, they decided to go the surrogate route and use Paxton's DNA. Jake wasn't really sure why he wasn't upset that they hadn't initially used his, but he considered Charlie a blessing in more than one way. Not only did Jake and his husband get blessed with the sincerest, most kind, and sometimes overly honest boy they could ever hope for, but now Charlie was a living reminder of Paxton. Charlie was a literal piece of him left on Earth that Jake would forever have. His curly brown hair and dark olive skin always made Jake think he was a miniature version of Paxton, and whenever anyone would comment how Charlie resembled or was just like him, Jake always knew they must have only been speaking of personality.

"Hey, Charlie? You ever play air hockey?" Colt asked.

"No. What's that?"

"Only like the coolest game ever invented. You want to go learn?" Colt stood up and Charlie followed him over to the air hockey table at the other side of the restaurant. Jake watched as Colt showed Charlie the basic mechanics of air hockey, and he couldn't help but look at the two of them and how Colt seemed to get along well with Charlie. He disapproved of what his son had just done, but Jake was curious as to how Colt was going to answer the question that Charlie asked. Jake thought about something Helen had told him as he stared at Colt and Charlie on the other side of the restaurant now in an air hockey match. Maybe his heart really was close to mending all the brokenness he had felt after losing his husband.

CHAPTER 23

When Jake and Charlie walked through the entrance of the hospital the next morning, another nurse that wasn't Stacy sat at the nurse's station.

Apparently, Stacy does leave the hospital, Jake thought. He checked in with the nurse and then made his way to his father's room. And just as he expected, sitting at his father's bedside was his mother.

"Hola, Mamá," Jake said quietly when he walked into the room. Consuela turned around and looked at Jake and he could have sworn he had almost seen the faintest trace of a smile in her stern face.

"Hi, Mrs. Ruiz," Charlie said.

And just like that, the smile faded and Jake's mom looked as though someone had delivered the biggest insult to her.

"Hello," Consuela Ruiz said before turning back around to face her husband.

"Here," Jake said, pulling out a tablet and handing it to his son. "Why don't you sit here and watch something?"

"Cool," Charlie shouted.

"And it better be appropriate, *mijo,*" Jake said. Charlie was already swiping through movies and when Jake looked up at his mom, the smile was unmistakable. Jake froze with the realization that, for better or worse, he had sounded exactly like Consuela Ruiz just now.

Charlie grabbed the phone and plopped down on a chair against the wall on the other side of the hospital room. He threw on his headphones and became an instant zombie. Jake thought it was probably good he was wearing headphones, just in case anything dramatic happened here with his mother.

"How's Pa?" Jake said, joining his mother at his father's bedside.

182

"The same," Consuela said. Jake was surprised that she didn't bring up what Charlie had just called her and hoped that this might be a sign that today may not be as contentious as he thought it would. "You know your father. He's milking this stroke for all it's worth. He's probably fine and just using this time for a little R&R."

"Ma, I don't think that's what's going on," Jake said, unsure if his mother was being serious or just trying to make herself believe this. Either way, it wasn't lost on Jake that he had the exact same thought the day before. *Oh my god – I think like her*, Jake thought.

"Oh relax. I was just joking," his mom said.

"You said you wanted to speak to me about something?" Jake asked.

"I think we need to discuss the restaurant," Consuela said. "Your father is going to need some recovery time. If you're planning on staying in town for a while, we...*I* could use help at the restaurant."

Jake was floored. Was Consuela Ruiz asking for help? That was unheard of. Apparently, someone had prayed to Saint Jude—the patron saint of impossible causes. Jake had no idea how long he was going to stay in Newport when he had first arrived, but that answer was starting to look as if it would be a while.

"Of course I can help," Jake said, masking the reluctance he felt in saying yes to being around his mother more than he needed to. "How about I handle the restaurant and you take care of Dad?"

"What? Oh no, no, no, no, no," Consuela said vehemently. "Your father would not like that."

"Okay, well, I will take care of dad at your house then while you take care of the restaurant," Jake said.

"I don't think so. I'm taking care of your father," Consuela said.

"I'm confused. What exactly did you need help with then, if you do not want my help at the restaurant and you don't want my help with Dad?" Jake asked.

Consuela sat there, running her rosary beads through her fingers, and Jake could tell his mother was stressing out. She was beginning to realize she didn't have a plan for what Jake would do. She only knew she needed his help but wasn't willing to actually give up any responsibility.

"I guess it's settled then. I'll run the restaurant." Jake didn't want to waste any more time going back and forth, when he knew that this would be where their discussion would end. Consuela's jaw nearly dropped to the floor at the realization that while she was playing checkers with her son, he was playing chess.

"Running a business is complex," Consuela began. "I don't think you can handle it."

"You're kidding, right? Ma, I think you are forgetting that I run five restaurants in Seattle that not only have received multiple awards, but also survived Covid," Jake said.

Consuela looked at Jake incredulously, realizing she was wedged between a rock and a hard place.

"Okay, fine," Consuela said. "You can run the restaurant under one condition: Absolutely no changes to the menu or the restaurant."

"Deal," Jake said, realizing that would be a discussion for a different day. After all, as far as Jake knew, Consuela still had no knowledge of what Jake's dad did during his Seattle trip, when he offered thirty percent of the restaurant to Jake. And if she didn't know that, she certainly had no knowledge that not only did Jake take his father up on that offer, but he gave him more money to become an equal partner in Los Ruiz Restaurant and Karaoke Lounge, with a fifty percent stake in the family business. Jake had enough authority to make any changes he saw fit to increase the bottom line of the business, but he didn't need to share this information with his mother yet.

"Knock, knock."

Jake jerked around the second he heard Colt's voice. There he was standing in the doorway with his white doctor jacket and a stethoscope draped around his neck.

God, he looks cute, Jake thought.

"Hi, Colt," Charlie said, looking up from Jake's phone.

"Hey, dude, whatcha watching?" Colt said, kneeling and looking at the tablet.

"I don't know. Some random show so I can't hear Dad argue with Mrs. Ruiz," Charlie said matter-of-factly. As soon as Charlie finished talking, Consuela cleared her throat in a dramatic fashion, showing her disapproval at being called "Mrs. Ruiz."

"And how's that working?" Colt asked.

Charlie shrugged at the question and put the headphones back over his ears. "Whatever they're talking about, it's very loud and doesn't sound good."

Colt stood up and walked over to the bed, where Carlos was sleeping. "I can come back if you two need some time."

"No, it's fine," Jake said, a little embarrassed.

Colt walked over to the machines that his father was hooked up to and began making notes on the patient file he held.

"Your husband's vitals are looking really good," Colt said to Consuela. "Everything is looking promising."

"*Ay*, thank you, Jesus!" Consuela said, clapping her hands. "So when can he go home?"

"Well, I think we need to keep him here for at least another day or so. And we need to start talking about recovery and physical therapy," Colt said. "But we took him off the medicine that had him in the induced coma, so now we just need to wait for him to wake up on his own."

"How long will that be?" Jake asked.

"Depends on the patient," Colt said. "It could be a couple hours or more."

Just then, there was a knock at the door and a woman walked into the room, holding a clipboard. "You must be the Ruiz family," the woman said.

"Consuela, I'd like you to meet Dr. Mathison," Colt said. "Dr. Mathison is going to be taking care of Mr. Ruiz from here on out."

"What? No ,Colton, please. You've done such a good job so far," Consuela implored.

"I'm sorry, Mrs. Ruiz. It wouldn't be appropriate for me to continue his care, considering that I'm so…" Colt paused, thinking of the right words. "I'm a little too close to this patient."

"You're a little close to *every* patient," Consuela said. "You know every person in this town. Why is Carlos any different? Please…" Consuela was practically begging, and you could hear it in the shakiness of her voice. She wanted the very best care for her husband, and Jake didn't blame her. Jake had felt the same once before.

"How about this? Dr. Mathison will take over the case, but I'll work closely with her to ensure that we have many eyes on him," Colt proposed.

"Okay, that may be fine," Consuela said in defeat.

"Excellent. I'm just going to get Dr. Mathison up to speed on everything and we'll be back," Colt said.

"It was very nice to meet you, Mrs. Ruiz," Dr. Mathison said before leaving the room.

"I honestly don't know why he won't just help your father," Consuela said, still irritated.

"Mamá, you need to trust Colt...er...Dr. Humphrey," Jake said. Just saying it felt foreign as it came out of his mouth. Consuela shot him a look with a raised eyebrow.

Shit, Jake thought, realizing the slip-up had triggered Consuela like she was some sort of sleeper cell who had just heard her activation word. She was now suspicious.

"Second Timothy two, twenty two, Jacob Ruiz; stop lusting and pursue a life of love and peace," Consuela said, squeezing her rosary beads tightly before turning to look back at Jake's father.

Jake's mother was like some sort of Google for the Bible. He had no idea how someone who could never find their reading glasses and habitually forgot things could come up with a Bible verse in an instant for any given occasion as if she had photographic memory.

"I really hope you are right in everything you believe in, Mamá," Jake said. The words piqued Consuela's interest, and she turned back to face him. "Because I can't fathom the unimaginable heartbreak and remorse you may feel after you've pushed everyone that has cared for your out of your life."

Silence lingered in the room, and Consuela sat there frozen. Jake wondered if perhaps his mother listened to the words and was possibly thinking about them, but given how stubborn she was, he knew that was unlikely.

"Oh my God!" Jake said, startling Consuela.

"Jacob!" Consuela said, angry at his choice of words, but Jake ignored her running over to the bedside as he watched his father's fingers begin to twitch on his right hand.

186

"Dad? Can you hear us?" Jake said, a little too loudly.

"*Dios mio.* Carlos, *mi amor*," Consuela said, placing her hand on his arm. "I'm here, my love. Jacob is here too."

Jake looked at his mom, and it really was incredible how she could change her demeanor so quickly. If he knew his mother from how she just spoke, he would have thought that she was the sweetest woman rather than the unpleasant person she mostly was.

"Hey, Pa," Jake said. "I'm here. And so is Charlie. Charlie!"

Charlie looked up from the chair and walked over to his dad next to the hospital bed.

"Can you say hi?" Jake asked.

"Hi, Abuelo," Charlie said, and then made his way back to the chair with his tablet. Consuela shot a look at Jake that was smoldering.

"OH!" Charlie said once he got back to the chair, realizing the mistake he had made. His face looked like he had just broken something priceless and was caught. Jake shook his head and smiled, putting Charlie at ease. He threw his headphones back on and continued his movie on the tablet.

"So, he gets an 'Abuelo,' but I don't get an 'Abuela,'" Consuela said.

"Mamá, really? Not right now," Jake said, drawing his attention back to his father laying there with his eyes closed. Just then, the two of them saw Carlos's eyes begin to flutter and he appeared to be mumbling something.

"What, Dad?" Jake said, inching closer to his father.

"Bananas seat fur me," Carlos said a little more clearly. Consuela and Jake looked at Carlos, puzzled at what he was saying.

"Jacob, go get Colt and the other doctor," Consuela said.

Jake ran out into the hallway. *What the hell is Dad saying?* he thought. *He isn't making any sense.* He saw Colt and Dr. Mathison talking at the end of the hall and he ran toward them.

"Colt…Dr. Humphrey," Jake said, shaking his head after realizing his mistake. "He's awake and speaking nonsense."

"It's okay, let's go see," Colt said, walking back quickly with Jake and Dr. Mathison.

"Mr. Ruiz, I'm Dr. Mathison," she said once she arrived at Carlos's bedside. "You are at Newport Hospital. How are you feeling?"

Jake's dad just groaned. He looked as though he were looking for words to speak, and as he moved his lips, Jake could see how part of his mouth looked as though it were frozen while the rest of his facial muscles moved.

"He said something about bananas and fur," Jake said.

"It may just be a slight case of aphasia," Dr. Mathison said. "Words sometimes get mixed up as they're recovering.

"Mr. Ruiz, you suffered an ischemic stroke at your restaurant. You're very lucky you got here early. We were able to give you a thrombolytic drug that helped break up the blood clots. Your wife and son are here with you."

"Ja...ja..." Carlos began to say and slowly moved his head around, looking at the people around him. He finally found Jake's eyes and stared at his son. "Jacob...my Jacob."

"Hi, Dad," Jake said. He could feel his throat start to tighten and his eyes begin to burn as they welled up. It was taking every ounce of his willpower not to cry in front of everyone. "There's someone else here. Charlie?"

Charlie walked over to the bed and stared at Carlos. He didn't say anything but just held up his hand to wave at him and then smiled. Jake thanked God silently that Charlie didn't call Jake's father "Abuelo" one more time, because he didn't want his father's first moments back in consciousness to be one where he heard Consuela's irritation.

"*Mi amor,*" Consuela said, squeezing Carlos's hand. "You gave us a fright. *Ay,* don't do that again."

"Connie," Carlos said, struggling to say words. "Jacob, he owns..."

"Shh... Carlos, you need to rest," Consuela said, cutting off his father.

"Stop," Carlos said, looking at Consuela.

"Mrs. Ruiz, I think your husband is trying to say something," Dr. Mathison said.

"Connie," Carlos said again, though it was mostly slurred. "Jacob owns half the restaurant."

Consuela looked at him blankly, and Jake felt his heart begin to race. When he had agreed to invest in the restaurant and give his father the money, it had been under the stipulation that they wouldn't discuss this with his mother. And here was his dad, just seconds out of coming back to consciousness from a stroke, dropping the biggest bomb on Jake's mother. Jake knew he would be the one dealing with the fallout. But then Jake began to realize that maybe his father had heard their conversation earlier when Jake agreed to take over the business.

At least this will give me the leverage to run the restaurant as I see fit, Jake thought.

The room was silent. Consuela looked as if she had been personally insulted. She glanced over at Dr. Mathison, and in the most serious tone, asked, "Is this the aphasia talking?"

CHAPTER 24

After Consuela stormed out of the hospital room at the revelation that her husband had sold off half the restaurant to a son she had practically disowned, the room felt somehow a little less dramatic. Dr. Mathison and Colt talked more about Carlos's stroke to him and what the recovery may look like. Fortunately for him, Carlos had arrived at the hospital early enough that both doctors felt he would make a full recovery, but it would still require time and help from his family. Carlos looked around the room, likely looking for Consuela, but she was nowhere to be seen. Jake couldn't believe the audacity of his mother.

"I think we will want to keep your father here for a couple more nights," Dr. Mathison said. "I want to make sure you and your mother fully understand the therapy and treatment steps that are going to be critical for your father's recovery.

"I'll go see if I can find her," Jake said, making his way toward the door. He leaned over to Charlie, who was still focused on the movie he was watching. "Can you stay put here for a couple minutes?"

"Yeah." Charlie looked up for a moment and then went straight back to the tablet.

Jake didn't have to walk very far to see his mom sitting on a bench outside the hospital with her arms folded in her lap. She sat straight up; her posture looked as stiff as the bench itself.

"Can I sit?" Jake approached his mother and waited for her response.

"Not like I have a choice now. Right, *boss*?" Consuela said. Jake felt as if he were about to have a conversation with a moody teenager rather than his middle-aged mother. Jake could already sense that this conversation was going to be anything but pleasant.

190

"Really, Mom? Is this what you're going to do, right after Dad wakes up?" Jake asked, sitting next to his mother on the bench. She didn't even look at him. She just stared straight ahead into the distance. When Jake leaned forward to block her view, Consuela jerked and shifted her entire body in the other direction, like a petulant child.

"Wow, you really are the most stubborn person I have ever known," Jake said. He stood, realizing anything he would say wouldn't get through to his mother when she was in that kind of mood. "And Mother? I wouldn't get upset that Charlie doesn't call you Abuela. If you expect to be called Abuela, you need to start acting like a mother before you expect to be seen as a grandmother."

Jake stormed back through the sliding doors of the hospital, determined to not turn around. But something told him his last comment probably was like a gut punch to his mom and he had a feeling she was now watching him walk away, slack-jawed.

"Is everything okay?" Colt asked, stopping Jake as he made his way down the hallway.

"Do you ever just wish you were adopted and your real biological parents are about to show up any day now?" Jake asked.

"I'm sorry. How about we have Dr. Mathison go talk to your mother about the physical therapy?" Colt said. "Maybe that might distract her from the other news about the restaurant."

"That's probably a good idea," Jake said. "I'm really sorry you had to witness that."

"Hey, I'm sorry you had to go through that," Colt said. He placed his hand on Jake's shoulder, and the gesture almost made Jake forget why he was angry. Colt pulled his hand away, and Jake wished it was still there.

"Thanks."

"This may not be the best moment but are you doing anything tomorrow night?" Colt asked. Colt seemed to shift nervously as he asked the question.

"I don't think so. Why?" Jake asked.

"I…um…" Colt paused.

"Just say it," Jake said.

"I was hoping I could take you to dinner." Colt said. He spoke so quickly it was as if his brain was forcing him to speak before he could change his mind.

"Like a date?"

"Well, yeah. It would be a date. But we don't have to call it that if that makes it…"

"No! I'd like that. But what about Eli?" Jake's heart raced, and he felt it beating in his stomach as well.

"I'm meeting him tonight – to end things with him," Colt said.

"Oh, I'm sorry," Jake lied. Hearing the news that Colt was ending things with Eli thrilled Jake. The guy was awful.

"I'm not. It wasn't going anywhere," Colt said. He looked at Jake and wanted to tell him the truth: that he felt more connected to Jake and his son last night than the entire time he had been with Harrison and the few months he had been with Eli. But Colt was smart and knew sharing that much information before they'd gone on a date would make him seem like a certified weirdo.

"Well then, a dinner date with you sounds great," Jake said. "I'll talk with Helen and see if she can watch Charlie tomorrow night."

"You're pretty close with Gigi's mom, huh?" Colt asked.

"Yeah, she's pretty much the mom I wish I had. The other one… Well, she hasn't been like a mother in—"

"Jake," Colt said.

"—years. And she clearly doesn't really care about me and Charlie. My dad is really my only family."

"Jake," Colt said quietly, tugging Jake's arm. Jake turned around and saw his mother standing directly behind him. She looked blankly at Jake and then pushed past him.

"Shit," Jake said. "How much of that did she hear?"

"A lot," Cold replied.

CHAPTER 25

Jake knew better than to follow Consuela after his slip of the tongue. Trying to speak with her right now would only escalate things, and since she was back in his father's hospital room, that was the last thing he wanted to do. But now Jake was left standing in the hall of the hospital, unsure of what to do.

"Should you go talk to her?" Colt asked.

"You're kidding, right? You know my mom. Do you think bringing that up would be a good idea right now?"

"That's a fair point," Colt said.

"Can you do me a favor? Can you tell Charlie to stay in the room until I get back? I'm going to give it a few minutes."

"Of course," Colt said.

Jake walked out the doors of the hospital and sat on the bench at the entrance. His chin fell into the palm of his hand as he sat there, thinking about everything he had said that Consuela just heard. How could he feel sorry for speaking something that was the truth? Jake hated that he felt guilty, especially when in all these years, Consuela seemed to lack the genetic programming to be the kind of mother he had needed. He felt his phone buzz in his pocket and when he looked at the caller ID, he felt a second wave of guilt.

"Evelyn, how are you?" Jake said. He couldn't have asked for a better mother-in-law than Evelyn Cooper. Jake had always considered himself lucky when he had first met Paxton. He wasn't only beautiful but also was one of the kindest and most sincere people Jake had ever met. And when Jake finally met Paxton's parents, Peyton and Evelyn Cooper, it was clear they had a significant influence on the man Paxton had become. They were wonderful people and Jake still spoke with both on a regular basis; Evelyn a little more frequently. Jake wasn't the only one who felt a major crater in their heart since Paxton's death.

"I'm doing just fine, sweetie. I wanted to check in on you. I called Forchette and they said you took time off for a family emergency. Is everything okay?"

"Oh, I'm so sorry. Charlie and I are both fine, but my father had a stroke and he's in the hospital, so I came back to Newport," Jake said.

"Are you doing okay?" Evelyn was silent for a moment before asking the question. She had known Jake for years and had become quite familiar with the complicated and strained family dynamics that was Jake's family.

"Well, my mother just overheard me basically saying what an awful person she was and that I only consider my dad family. And when I arrived, she tried to forbid me from seeing my dad altogether," Jake said.

"Oh goodness. I'm so sorry, Jacob," Evelyn said.

"It's okay. It's been kind of a nice trip, all things considered. My dad actually just woke up and the doctors said he should make a full recovery," Jake said. "Gigi is here with me too."

"Tell her I say hello. She is such a character." Evelyn thought Gigi was a riot the first time they had met. Paxton's parents had come to Seattle to spend the weekend with him and Jake, and Gigi had somehow tagged along to dinner with them. The night culminated with Peyton and Evelyn at a drag show, where Gigi and Evelyn took shots of Fireball whisky.

"That she is," Jake said.

"Well, you sound good. I panicked when they told me that, but it sounds like you are in good spirits, and I'm glad your dad is doing better."

"Thanks. Evelyn, there's one more thing." Speaking with Evelyn and not telling her about his planned date with Colt tomorrow evening made Jake feel like he was somehow cheating on his dead husband. He thought about not saying anything for a second. After all, who knew where this might even go, but then he remembered he had told her about the last date he had gone on and she had been supportive. Later, she shared in Jake's tears and laughter as he recounted the breakdown he had on the date. She and Paxton's dad were always there for them, and he knew sharing the news of a date would be met with support. "I…I'm going on a date tomorrow night."

Evelyn was quiet for a moment. "Jacob, I'm happy for you. And I think this will be good for you."

"It's just… How do I know if I'm ready?"

"Well, I don't know if anyone can answer that for you but you. It's going to be different for everyone. One of my girlfriends met her second husband at her first husband's funeral. She didn't want to be lonely. And then I have friends who have never married after, saying they couldn't get lucky twice. What does your heart tell you?"

Jake thought about the question. He wanted to take away all the thinking about it and just go with his gut instinct. And right now, his gut told him to go after this. Someone like Colt was a rare find and Jake knew it. "I think my heart wants me to do this, but I think it's also nervous."

"Starting anything new is always a little nerve-wracking, but you deserve to be happy, and I know Paxton would want that also. I hope it goes well!"

"Thank you," Jake said. Evelyn was so positive, just as Jake had expected she would be. He thought for a moment about telling her of the other big news—the news that might take him and her only grandchild across the country to New York but then realized what an awful idea that would be, especially considering the position wasn't even his.

"I should probably get back to my dad," Jake said.

"Absolutely. Take care, dear. Oh, and kiddo?"

"Yeah?" Jake replied.

"I think you can get lucky twice. Give my little lovebug a big hug and kiss from his grandma. I love you!"

"I will. Speak with you later. Love you too," Jake said.

Jake ended the call and took a deep breath before reentering the hospital. Evelyn ended up being exactly the distraction he needed. It was as if the universe had known exactly what he needed and delivered. The moment the sliding doors opened, Consuela stood on the other side. Jake wished the universe would be able to deliver a second time and give him the words he needed to fix what he had said about his mom.

"Mom, I'm sorry." She may have said plenty of hurtful things to him in the past, but Jake had always tried his hardest to not turn into his parents. He tried living a more positive life.

"Psalm ten one. *Why Lord, do you stand afar? Why do you hide yourself in times of trouble?* I'm sorry that you feel I haven't been a mother to you, *mijo*. You may not think it, but I'm trying. I am trying, Jacob. And even if you think I haven't been the mother you've needed, it doesn't mean I haven't stopped loving you, which has been hard to do."

Jake had done the most important part, which was apologize. Any normal mother who had heard the hurtful words their only child had said about them may have taken a different approach than Consuela, who chose to respond through Scripture.

"It's times like this that I look around and can't help but feel alone. I feel the Lord testing me with your father's experience, and I constantly feel the Lord testing me when it comes to you. Jacob, my prayer for you is that you have a son that you are proud of and you have a great relationship with. Heartbreak comes in many forms, but I think the most painful is the heartbreak that comes from the profound disappointment in your children."

Consuela placed her hand on Jake's shoulder for a moment and then turned to head back toward his father's room. The words left Jake speechless. He couldn't believe the nerve she had to say these words and make it seem like she was coming from a place of love. He had no idea why he even tried with Consuela.

Chapter 26

When Jake and Charlie arrived at Helen's, Jake wasted no time filling in both her and Gigi on everything that had happened between him and Consuela, but more so what had happened between him and Colt. In less than twenty-four hours, Jake would be going on a date he had dreamed of since he was a teen and had always figured would never be a possibility. He had no idea what to expect from the date with Colt tomorrow night, and the thought of something more long-term coming out of this prospect seemed miniscule. After all, Jake's life was in Seattle and possibly New York City soon. Colt's entire life was in Newport.

After the New York opportunity came to mind, Jake couldn't stop thinking about it. He knew that without something significant happening, if things continued as they were, two of his restaurants' doors would be shuttered by the end of the year. His youngest restaurant, Forchette, had not gained the traffic he had with his other restaurants, and once Covid hit, it was a death blow to Forchette. Had it not been for Viva la Vida and Beacon Hill Barbeque, Forchette would have never survived past 2020. If Jake were to land a celebrity chef position on *Wake Up With Us*, he knew that would likely secure the future of Ruiz Kitchens. He also knew how hard it was going to be with his entire support group being in Washington. Jake didn't know a soul in New York.

Charlie had been asleep for a couple hours as Helen, Gigi, and Jake continued to talk into the night. Jake realized he wasn't going to sleep anytime soon when Helen came back into the living room with three glasses and a bottle of vodka.

"Helen, no!" Jake and Gigi said in unison.

"Oh, please. I didn't raise you to be a wet towel, Gigi. Besides, it's only nine p.m. in Hawaii!"

"Well, my hangover is going to be in Pacific Standard Time tomorrow, Helen," Gigi said, but still held her hand out to take the glass with a lime on the rim that Helen offered.

"Okay, Jacob, so this plan of yours…tell me again. You're going to go on a date with Colton and then what?"

"What do you mean?" Jake asked.

"Well, it's not like you can move back to Newport. Your entire livelihood is back in Seattle. Besides, it's not like this town is going to be hosting a Pride parade anytime soon."

"She has a point," Helen said. "I'm surprised Colt even stuck around."

"Well, let me just get through the date tomorrow night and take it from there. I think we are getting way ahead of ourselves. Anyway, I should probably call it a night. I'm stopping by the restaurant tomorrow to see what kind of situation I just got myself into. Good night," Jake said, setting the untouched drink back on the coffee table. He gave Helen a kiss on the cheek and made his way to the guest bedroom that he now shared with Charlie since Gigi had arrived. Charlie was fast asleep in the bed, snoring loudly. He loved his son, but he sounded like a freight train and Jake could hardly sleep with Charlie's monstrously loud snoring. He was incredibly grateful for Helen allowing them to stay with her, but Jake couldn't help but long for his own space once again.

Jake fell asleep thinking about his date with Colt tomorrow night. He wondered what Colt had planned. But to be honest, Jake couldn't care less what they did. The only thing that mattered was that Jake was going on a date with Colton Humphrey tomorrow night.

The next morning, Jake woke up with his nerves feeling as if it were the first day of school or he was starting a new job. He couldn't wait for his date with Colt tonight and he knew the day was going to go excruciatingly slow. Helen and Gigi decided to take Charlie miniature golfing in Spokane and have a day of fun, while Jake made his way to Los Ruiz Restaurant and Karaoke Lounge. Jake had to figure out what was going on with the restaurant so he could run it properly, which meant another conversation with Consuela, who agreed to meet him at the restaurant.

When he entered the restaurant, Jake felt like he had never left. Everything looked exactly the same since the last time he was there. He couldn't quite recall when that had been, but knew it had to have been more than a decade ago. Unfortunately for Jake, the traffic of the restaurant coupled with neglect and disrepair made the restaurant look awful. As much as he despised him, Jake couldn't help but think Eli was somewhat right in his assessment of Los Ruiz. The brand-new restaurant booths he and Gigi had helped his father unload during Halloween in college now had duct tape stretched across cracks that ran across the fabric's surface like spiderwebs. Grease had caked the lighting throughout the restaurant. The paint on the walls had faded and, in many areas, had begun to peel away from the walls. And the front windows of the restaurant were plastered with flyers and ads for other businesses around town. Jake looked and saw several flyers for events that had occurred six or eight months prior. He was sad to see a place his parents had once took so much pride in now fall to neglect.

"Mom, what happened here?" Jake asked in absolute shock.

"What do you mean, boss?" Consuela asked. She had apparently decided to keep up with at least a bit of the attitude from the day before. She walked to the back of the restaurant, blind to what Jake saw. To the side of the office door, he couldn't believe that an old metal stool he would sit on and take his breaks on when he worked there as a teenager was still there. In fact, he was certain the chair was in the same exact spot it stood when he was a teenager, which was saying a lot considering it wasn't bolted to the ground.

"The restaurant, Mom. It's…filthy," Jake said.

"Oh, it's not that bad. Nothing a good mopping can't fix," Consuela said, stepping into the office. She flicked on the light and made her way to the desk and began to rummage through one of the drawers.

"A good mopping? Mom, this place should be shut down and pressure washed with bleach," Jake said in disbelief.

"*Ay mijo*, why do you always have to be so dramatic. Here we are," Consuela said, holding up a shoebox.

"What is that?" Jake asked.

"These are all the receipts and invoices. Your father keeps the monthlies in here and then at the end of the month, we pay them and then they get filed away into the trash," Consuela said, pointing to a rusty old wire basket next to the desk.

"You're kidding," Jake said, even though he knew she wasn't.

"And this is our employee time log. This is where all the employees enter their time for when they work," she said, holding up a black college-ruled spiral notebook. "Everyone is paid minimum wage, and your father sends the final tallies to our payroll accountant in Spokane, who processes payroll for us on the tenth and the twenty-fifth of every month. Her name is Margaret, and her contact information is on the little note taped to the computer monitor. The food supplier's phone number is the other note, and we have a standing order that doesn't change."

Jake listened to all this and felt like he was about to have a stroke himself. When he was a teenager, he admired how entrepreneurial his parents had been in starting and running their own business. They made it look so easy, as if they knew what they were doing. But after running his own restaurant group and becoming quite knowledgeable on how to run it successfully, hearing how his parents were actually running the business made Jake want to scream. A child's lemonade stand was more fiscally responsible than Consuela's "sticky note" method of business operations.

Jake was embarrassed that his mother stood there showing him everything and still somehow seemed to have a look of pride.

It is a miracle they have survived this long, Jake thought.

"Mother…" Jake said slowly as he thought about every word he was about to say. The last thing he needed was her to blow up. "If you and Dad have a standing order that doesn't change, what was your food waste for last month?"

"Food waste? *Mijo*, we don't waste food. We cook it," his mother said, not understanding the question.

"No. Mom, how much money did you lose in spoiled food that wasn't cooked?"

"Oh, not much. Probably just a couple hundred dollars' worth."

"But you don't know for sure? What about your P&L? What was your bottom line for last month?"

"Last month? We actually lost some money," Consuela said.

"How much?"

"I think your father said about three thousand. It's okay though. This is the slow time of the year. It'll pick up again."

"When's the last time you had a positive net profit?" Jake asked.

"Jacob, I don't know. I think in December...or November," Consuela said. "Times have been a little tough, and after Covid, business never really bounced back."

Jake covered his face and took a deep breath in the palms of his hands. He knew his parents had been having trouble. It was the reason his dad had come to see him in Seattle just a few years ago, but now he could see why. He knew his dad had been much more organized. This looked like he had given up. They both had.

"Okay. I don't want this to become a fight at all, so let me take care of all of this. Do you need me to go back to the hospital and help with Dad?"

"No, they are running some more tests but said he actually might be getting discharged today. Isn't that wonderful, *mijo*? That's Jesus right there! Colton is letting us borrow a wheelchair that he had."

Jake knew full well Colton didn't just have a wheelchair lying around and likely was letting his parents either borrow it from the hospital or he was footing the bill. Apparently, Jake wasn't the only one who could see the truly dire financial challenges his parents were going through.

"Okay. Mom? What about medical? Please tell me you and Dad are covered. If not, we could lose this restaurant with his medical bills."

"Oh, we're fine. I already spoke with our provider and we set up a payment plan. Isn't that funny, *mijo?* It's like we're financing a coma. I hope your father enjoyed it." Jake tried his best not to roll his eyes and the news that his mother had at least set up a payment plan provided some sense of relief. "Anyway, do you think you have everything you need?"

"Yes, I believe I do," Jake said. "Go back to the hospital and take care of Dad."

Consuela lingered in the office before she was about to leave. This time, it seemed like she was looking for an excuse to stay at the restaurant.

"Well, here are the keys to the restaurant. Glen's been looking over things for the last couple days and can help answer any questions as well."

"Glen's still...alive?" Jake asked, thinking about Los Ruiz' oldest employee, who must have been at least in his seventies when Jake was a teenager. He was shocked to hear Glen wasn't only alive, but still working at the restaurant.

"Don't be rude," Consuela said. "He's not that... Okay, he's pretty old, but he's a big help. Anyway, call me if you need anything. *Adios, mijo!*"

The second his mother disappeared, Jake yanked out his phone and scrolled through his contacts until he found the accountant for his restaurant group. "Jessica?"

"Hi, Jake," Jessica said. "I heard what happened to your father. Is he okay?"

"Yes, everything is okay," Jake said. "Listen, I need your help. Do you think you can get on a flight to Spokane as soon as possible? I need your help with my parents' restaurant that I technically own a fifty-percent stake in. Don't worry, the company will pay for everything."

"Okay, what's the matter?"

"Well my mother just showed me a shoebox of receipts, which is their accounting system, and a black notebook that is their time clock. I'm worried that if there are financial issues with this restaurant, it's putting the entire restaurant group at risk. It might be what puts the final nail in the coffin for Forchette."

"Say no more. I'll look at flights and I can try and get there tomorrow. Does that sound good?"

"Thank you so much! Call me if you need anything from me to book the trip."

"What's the nearest hotel to you?"

"Umm..." Jake paused, not really wanting to answer this question. "There's actually only one in town. It's the Moose Nugget Motel."

"Okay, that has got to be a joke, right?" Jessica asked.

"I'm afraid not. But maybe you should just stay in Spokane and drive up," Jake said.

"Hey, if the...*Moose Nugget* is my only option, I think a hotel in Spokane is probably a good idea. I'll see you soon."

Jake sat back in the squeaky desk chair that was covered in practically an entire roll of duct tape and looked up at the ceiling. The yellowish fluorescent lights in the office flickered above and he closed his eyes.

"What have I got myself into?" Jake said aloud.

"Well, if it isn't Mr. City Slicker himself." Glen, the elderly cook, stood in the doorway of the office.

He doesn't look a day over two hundred years old, Jake thought.

"Hey, Glen. It's good to see you," Jake said, reaching out and shaking Glen's bony hand.

"You mean to say, 'Glen—I'll be damned. You're still alive?'" Glen said, chuckling. The years of smoking practically a pack of cigarettes a day made Glen's voice sound like a gravel truck.

"I'll be honest. When my mom said you were still working here, I was surprised. What are you, pushing a hundred now?"

Jake and Glen stared at each other for a moment in dead silence and then both started to laugh. Glen bent over and placed his hands on his knees and his laughing turned into wheezing. He sounded like an old squeak toy as his lungs continued to rattle.

"There's the smart-ass I knew," Glen said. "I was mighty sorry to hear when your husband died. When my Sheila passed, I didn't know what to do with myself. You know—I had to start doing my own grocery shopping? And that stuff's expensive. Did you know an artichoke is almost four Goddamned dollars? Four dollars! You know what you could buy back in my day with four dollars?"

"You mean to tell me there was currency during the Dark Ages?" The two laughed, but Jake thought about what Glen had said. He extended condolences to Jake. Glen had no idea that this small gesture meant so much. It made Jake feel that Glen saw his marriage to Paxton as valid and the heartbreak from the loss just as legitimate. It was a gesture much larger than anything Consuela had ever given to Jake, which was nothing. "But thank you, Glen. You don't know how much that means to me."

"So, what do you have going on here?" Glen asked.

"I have an accountant coming here to take a look at the books and help get the place organized," Jake said.

"Ah, I see your mom showed you the shoebox."

"You know about that?"

"Know about it? Of course I do. Hell, I have to 'clock in' and 'clock out' in her spiral notebook," Glen said, holding up his fingers and making air quotes. "You know, I never went to college, but even I know that this place is a mess."

"Well, I'm here now and I'm going to be making some changes," Jake said.

"Thank God. Maybe now I won't be worried if I'm being underpaid."

"Hey, Glen?" Jake asked.

"Yeah? What is it?"

"Do my parents ever talk about me?" Jake asked. He wasn't sure why he had asked the question, but curiosity got to him. He could see his mother shunning the topic of Jake and the very mention of his name by anyone else probably got a quick change of topic.

"Your mom not so much," Glen began. "But something tells me you already knew that, but your dad... Well, your dad talks about you almost every single day."

"Really?" Jake wasn't surprised to hear that his mother rarely discussed her son, but he was surprised to hear his father still talked about him on a daily basis.

"Oh sure. He's always showing me news articles or Yelp reviews on dishes at your restaurant in Seattle and asking me to help him 'add it to the menu.'" Glen held up his fingers in air quotes once again, talking about Jake's father. "Every time he saw what you were doing, he'd say, 'If my Jacob can do it, it must be out of this world.'"

"Okay, Glen, no need to embellish the past on account of me," Jake said in disbelief.

"Well, that's the God's honest truth, Jake," Glen said. "He made me work with him almost an entire day in the kitchen to recreate a pambazo dish he ate when he visited one of your restaurants. Your dad has never stopped talking about you. Your mom...well, she's always been as stubborn as a mule."

He shouldn't have laughed at the comparison, but the second Jake heard Glen's description of his mother, he realized there was no better comparison that could have been used.

"That's good to hear. Thanks, Glen. Hey, once we get the books in shape, we're going to have to focus on getting this restaurant back in order. And by the looks of it, this place is probably going to have to shut its doors temporarily while we do that." Jake saw a flash of nervousness on Glen's face with the thought of no paycheck. "And when that happens, I'd like to pay your full wages during that time, including a bonus for dealing with my mother for as long as you have."

"Ah, hazard pay," Glen said with a chuckle. "Well, thanks, city slicker. I have no doubt things are going to be on the up and up now that you're here."

Now that you're here... The words stuck in Jake's head as Glen left the office. Without realizing it, Jake had somehow gone from a quick trip to see and help his father to practically becoming a permanent resident of Newport once again. This was less frightening when the thought of Colt and their upcoming date came to mind. And then there was the opportunity in New York that Jake knew would become an issue at some point, but for now he pushed that out of his thoughts. For now, all he wanted to think about was the date with Colt.

CHAPTER 27

Jake had hoped to get ready for his date with Colt in peace, but those plans were thrown out the window when he arrived at Helen's house to find that she, Gigi, and Charlie had returned from Spokane earlier than he had expected. All three of them stood in the doorway of the bathroom watching Jake comb his hair and get ready, as if he were a high schooler all over again and this was his first date. As much as he acted slightly put out by Gigi's over-the-top antics and Helen channeling her more motherly instincts, Jake loved it. This type of interaction was something he never had with his own mother but was so common with his friends and their parents. Gigi had no idea the impact of something so trivial as standing in the doorway to watch him get ready had on Jake and she never would.

"Where are you two going?" Helen asked.

"You know, I'm not really sure," Jake said. All he knew was that Colt had called him at the restaurant when he was sifting through the shoebox to let him know he would pick him up at Helen's house.

"You don't think he's a murderer now, do you?" Gigi said.

"Jeez, you need to stop listening to so many serial killer podcasts. Not everyone is a murderer, Gigi."

"Hey, I've seen that house of his. There's plenty of places to stash a body. Besides, hot men in their thirties who are *still* single are very suspect. Do you know how many dates I've gone on in Seattle where if I went home with them, I would have ended up becoming a skin flute?"

"Skin flute? I don't think that's what you are meaning to say," Jake said.

"Oh? What's that?" Gigi asked.

"A penis, dear. It's a penis," Helen said before taking a sip of wine. Gigi scrunched her face as if she had taken a giant bite of a lemon.

"Penis!" Charlie said through giggles as he looked up at Helen. "Penis, penis, penis!"

"HELEN!" Jake yelled, causing Helen to lurch backward and nearly spill the entire contents of her wineglass.

"I'm so sorry. It's been so long since I've needed to use a filter," she said.

"Anyway," Gigi said, clapping her hands for every syllable of the word. "Do you need the pocketknife I carry around in my purse, just in case?"

"Oh sweetie," Helen said. "If this date goes well, that isn't the kind of protection he will need."

"ALL RIGHT, ALL RIGHT! All three of you out of here. NOW!" Jake said. He waved his hands and pushed the three of them out of the bathroom but then latched on to Gigi's arms and pulled her backward.

"Please try and have Helen keep it G-rated. I don't need Charlie talking like a sailor by the time we get back to Seattle," Jake whispered into her ear.

"Deal," Gigi whispered back and gave him an overly dramatic wink.

Before Jake could double-check to make sure Helen wasn't teaching Charlie how to throw knives at this point, the doorbell rang. Gigi's eyes lit up in excitement, and Jake, who still had his hand gripping her arm, squeezed it tightly.

"OW!" Gigi yelped. "If Helen's right about where this date is going, don't squeeze it that tightly. Colt won't call you for a second date."

"I really hate you, you know?" Jake said, letting go of her arm.

"Aw. And I hate you too," Gigi said. She gave Jake a big kiss on the cheek and then he moved past her and made his way to the door.

"I didn't know you were still doing those art classes." Jake walked into the living room to find Helen already in full conversation mode with Colt.

"Oh yes. Perhaps you can come and be a model for my class one day," Helen replied.

"Colt!" Jake said quickly. He tried cutting Helen off before she could finish what she was saying, but it was too late. It had already been said and a visual was already in Jake's head. He had no desire to do nude paintings with a bunch of old women, but a class where Colt was the model? Jake was ready to go on Amazon and buy his own set of acrylics and a canvas.

"Ruiz!" Colt said. He stepped forward and hugged Jake, wrapping his arms around him. The way Colt had said his name felt very bro-ish, but the way he hugged and squeezed him tightly was unlike any hug Jake had ever received from Colton Humphrey. "You look great."

"Thanks! I used soap," Jake said. The second it came out of his mouth, Jake had a *what the hell did you just say* moment in his head.

"It must be some good soap," Colt chuckled. He placed his hand around Jake's waist and walked with him to the door. "I'll have him back by curfew, Ms. Clayton."

"Please, it's Helen. Ms. Clayton is my daughter," Helen said.

"Goodbye, Colt. Bring him back in one piece," Gigi said. She waved at Colt and Jake, as they made their way out the door.

"Oh, hold on one second," Jake said. He left Colt on the porch of the house and ran back in to give Charlie a hug goodbye.

"Are you going to be okay tonight?" Jake asked. He felt the mounting anxiety of leaving Charlie to go on a date begin to surface and part of him hoped Charlie would ask him to stay.

"Don't come back until I have a second daddy!" Charlie said in Jake's ear in a hushed whisper. When he pulled away, he giggled.

"What?" Jake said. He practically choked.

"She told me to say it," Charlie said. He pointed to Helen, who raised an eyebrow and gave Jake a knowing smile as she took another sip of wine.

"So, where are we going?" Jake asked once he was in Colt's car.

"I thought you were planning the night?" Colt asked, looking over at Jake. The moment Jake heard this, he almost had a panic attack. "Relax, I'm just kidding."

"Oh jeez…Well, you got me," Jake said.

"I was thinking sushi, if you're up for it."

"They have a sushi restaurant in Newport?"

"No, but they have one in Spokane. I figured we could spend the drive time talking. Is that cool?"

"Sounds great," Jake said. He looked at Colt, who seemed so comfortable with being himself now. It was unlike the Colton Humphrey on Halloween night all those years ago. "Okay, so I'm just going to ask this really quick, and I promise not to bring him up ever again, but you did break up with Eli, right?"

"Oh yeah. I talked with him on the phone yesterday," Colt reassured Jake. "I told him it wasn't really going anywhere anyway and he took it well."

"He did?" Jake asked with a noticeable tone of shock in his voice.

"Actually, no. It was pretty bad, but it's over."

"Well, that's good." Jake felt his shoulders shrug upward and he settled back into the passenger seat as if that one question was the one thing that had him on edge.

He wasn't sure if he had steered the conversation in this direction, but Jake and Colt somehow spent a large part of the drive to Spokane talking about Jake's parents and their complicated relationship. Jake would have much rather talked about anything else, but one story led to another and then another, until they found themselves seated at the sushi restaurant in downtown Spokane.

"So, your parents really have only seen your son once?" Colt asked.

"Yeah, at my cousin's wedding a few years back. I tried to not make it awkward, but my entire extended family knows about my family drama, so it was like they were all watching us, waiting for us to create a scene."

"Well? Did it happen?"

"No, thank God."

Colt sat there, looking down at his glass of beer the server had brought to the table. He ran his finger around the bottom of the glass where beads of water had already started to pool at its base. "I'm really sorry."

"About what?"

"About…that night." Colt didn't need to clarify what night he was talking about. Jake knew he was talking about Halloween.

"You know, I should be the one apologizing," Jake said. He was hoping they could somehow forget about Halloween, but they had finally reached the topic he had been dreading during this entire conversation. The elephant in the room.

"Why should you be sorry?"

"Because you looked out for me. You saw there was an issue at the bar and you came to help. And then you kissed me to make my ex feel awful. I can't really think of a lot of people who would have done that. I guess I should have thanked you, but I was an idiot and kind of ruined our friendship."

"What? No, you didn't ruin it at all. Hey, I should've tried harder, but after the text message I guess I just kind of gave up," Colt said.

"I still don't know who you called and received a text from. I promise it wasn't me. If I got that message, I would've come back to you immediately." Jake hated thinking that Colt believed he had said those hurtful things all those years ago.

"Hey, it's all in that past now," Colt reassured him. "All we have is the future now, right?"

Colt reached across the table, and before Jake was able to process what was happening, he felt Colt's hand slide into his. The gesture by Colt had the effect of a defibrillator pumping a million volts of electricity into his chest.

"This is nice," Jake said. He looked at Colt and knew he couldn't hide the enormous smile on his face.

"It is," Colt said. "To second chances and new beginnings."

The two held up their glasses of beer and tapped them together. Jake had no idea where this was going, but he knew he would enjoy every single second of it. He never imagined he would find himself back on dates again after getting married to Paxton, but if he was going to have to do this, he couldn't think of anyone better than Colt.

As they drove back to Newport, Colt's hand didn't leave Jake's. He worried it might be a little dangerous to drive with just one hand, but Colt seemed to have the hang of it, and Jake didn't want to let go. Colt ran his thumb around the edges of Jake's thumbnail in a circular motion in the subtlest way; Jake wished he wouldn't stop.

The drive back to Newport was the fastest it had ever been, and before Jake knew it, he was staring at the door to Helen's house. He could see Gigi and Helen run up to the window and then hide inconspicuously, but both were probably drunk, so they weren't too successful.

"So, can we do this again?" Colt asked.

"Yes! Absolutely," Jake said. Colt laughed and pulled his hand out of Jake's. Jake felt Colt's hand run up his arm and then rest just above his shoulder blade. "Sorry, should I have played harder to get?"

"No, not at all," Colt said. He leaned over and then his lips pressed against Jake's. It was different than their one and only other kiss. There were no restraints. No false pretenses. Both knew what they were doing, and if Colt had any say in it, this was just the beginning. Colt pulled away and looked at Jake, who appeared to be feeling the same things Colt had felt.

"That was…perfect," Jake said. He looked at Colt and knew he wanted to take this slow but another part of him felt very differently.

"It really was. Jake?"

"Yes?" Jake replied.

"This was, hands down, probably one of the best nights of my life," Colt said. He leaned forward to kiss Jake one more time. He took a deep breath as he pulled away. Colt found the scent of Jake intoxicating. He looked at him one last time before Jake got out of the car.

"Good night, Colton Humphrey."

"Good night, Ruiz," Colt replied. He watched as Jake made his way to the front door of Helen's house. He could have never imagined the two shared the same thought. Neither wanted the night to end, and both saw the possibility of this lasting forever.

CHAPTER 28

One week had passed after Jake's first date with Colt. In the span of those seven days, Jake had somehow managed to spend three of them with Colt. And in that time, Jake felt himself slowly feeling further connected to the town he had once vowed to never set foot in again. Between the time he was spending with Colt, the countless issues that continued to be uncovered at the restaurant, the incredible support system he had found in Helen on nights she wasn't teaching nude painting classes, and his father, Jake was finding it harder to make his way back to Seattle.

Carlos had been sent home from the hospital and Consuela had focused all her efforts in helping Jake's father recover. This turned out to be exactly the distraction that Consuela needed. She had not been into the restaurant since the handoff to Jake, which was a good thing. Jake knew if his mother came in and saw the amount of changes he had made to their business ordering and management systems, she would have a blowup of "Consuela Ruiz" proportions. When his accountant had arrived after his call with her, the severity of how poorly his parents had been operating the business had been confirmed.

"Okay, Jacob. I'm really worried. Are we absolutely positive this restaurant isn't a drug front?" Jake's accountant, Jessica, asked. His head felt like a never-ending migraine after he did his best to sort through the receipts, invoices, and his parents' "payroll" system.

"If I didn't know my parents, I would think it probably was. Besides, I'm sure drug fronts have better bookkeeping systems."

Whenever Jake would uncover another colossal business liability, he couldn't help but fear that Los Ruiz would be the Achilles heel to Ruiz Kitchens. Somehow, this restaurant would be the thing that topples

Jake's entire house of cards. This in turn caused Jake to operate in "damage control" mode for the last several days at Los Ruiz. And after spending the better part of ten hours at the restaurant, Jake was on his way back to Helen's to get ready for his fourth date with Colt. However, tonight's date felt different for Jake. Something about being at Colt's house made this seem like a much more significant night.

Jake felt a sense of nostalgia as he pulled into the port cochere that extended over the rounded driveway of Colt's house. Colt's family had bought up about five properties before building their massive house on Sacheen Lake. During the summer, Colt would have friends over to go jet skiing, tubing, or just hang out. And now, Colton Humphrey's homestead was back in Jake's sight. He couldn't help but feel like he was visiting the ghosts of his past as he looked at the house.

Before he got to the entrance, Colt opened the door. Jake had thought Colt couldn't get any cuter than when he saw him in his doctor's jacket, but there stood Colt with an old Newport Grizzlies T-shirt on that his pectoral muscles filled in nicely. He had a pair of navy shorts that ended above the knee, revealing the fuzzy blond leg hairs on his toned legs. It was a look that made Jake get momentarily sidetracked.

"Why hello, Mr. Ruiz," Colt said, leaning forward to kiss Jake on the lips. Jake felt like he had started to melt the moment Colt's lips touched his. Colt pulled away from Jake, but his hands remained around his waist. "Did you find the house okay?"

"Hmm?" Jake replied, realizing he was doing something that Colt had called him out on so many years ago. He was staring. "Oh yeah. It hasn't moved at all, so it made it easy."

Although the exterior of the house had not changed significantly, now that Jake followed Colt into the kitchen, he could tell that the entire house had been renovated. The timbered look of the house with dark oak flooring had now been refinished with white walls and a whitewashed shiplap that extended to the peaks of the vaulted ceiling of the house.

"Oh wow! The house looks so different," Jake said.

"Yeah, I liked the idea of living in my childhood home, but I wanted something that still felt like my own. Everything's pretty much been redone," Colt said.

"Well, I'm just glad you got rid of your mom's couches," Jake said.

"You remember my parents' furniture? That was so long ago." Colt laughed.

"Colt, I think you are underestimating how much of an impression your mom's velour floral-printed sofa made on people," Jake said in his most serious voice. "The image of that sofa still haunts my dreams."

"Mine too. Mine too. You know, you were always my mom's favorite," Colt said.

"What? Really? Well, don't tell Helen, but Beth Humphrey was one of my favorite moms." Jake began to think about Colt's mom. She and Gigi's mom had actually become really good friends when they had all entered high school, and the two of them seemed to contend for the title of "cool mom." Meanwhile, Jake's mom was the undisputed heavyweight champion of the mom everyone avoided and was terrified of.

"My mom's amazing. My parents have been really supportive of me when others haven't," Colt said proudly. He opened the double fridge in the kitchen and grabbed a bottle of beer and handed it to Jake. "Care for a – what do you call it again? An 'eyepuh'?"

"Funny," Jake said, taking the bottle of beer. He thought about what Colt had said and it dawned on Jake for the first time that maybe Colton Humphrey's life wasn't as perfect as he always imagined it seemed.

"So, I don't know if this is too casual for a date dinner, but I figured we could barbeque. Does that sound good?"

"I'm not picky at all, and that sounds delicious. Can I help?" Jake asked.

The two made their way out to the deck that overlooked Sacheen Lake and Colt found himself thinking about Eli. Eli had been one of the pickiest, most selective eaters Colt had ever met, with an elitist mentality. If the restaurant wasn't fancy enough, Eli wanted no part in it. He also had expected people to serve him and never laid a finger in the kitchen during the preparation or the cleaning. To hear Jake say he wasn't picky and his offer to help were things Colt had always hoped to find.

"You like thighs?"

"Do I!" Jake said excitedly, looking down at Colt's legs and realizing about a second too late Colt was talking about the chicken on the barbeque grill.

"Whoa there. Did you just get out of prison?" Colt winked at Jake as he felt he cheeks turn red.

"Sorry," Jake said quietly.

"Don't be. Hey, can I show you something?" Colt said. He took Jake by the hand walked down the steps of the balcony. Colt brought him to the edge of the water where a singular tree stood. There, in the center of the tree, was a familiar carving.

JR + CH

"Where are the other trees?" Jake asked, looking at the only one left.

"A rainstorm washed them off the bank a few years back," Colt said. He pointed to the edge of the bank, where a giant cement retaining wall now stood. "I had to hire an engineering company to make sure nothing happened to this one."

"You saved this tree?" Jake asked. He couldn't believe that, after all this time, Colt had somehow managed to save a relic that proved just how long the relationship between Colt and Jake had been.

"I hope you don't think I'm a weirdo, but I had to save it," Colt said.

"When we did this, did you know that you were gay?"

"I didn't really have any type of attraction to anyone. I just did it for our friendship." Colt looked like he regretted what he had said and hoped Jake wouldn't get upset. "I'm sorry. What about you?"

"No...I get it. We were really young and I felt the same way. Though, a few years after that was a very different story."

"Listen, Jake, I know that you've moved on from Newport a long time ago. You built this really amazing life, and you have this remarkable son. But...you see...well, there was a part of you that always stayed here." Colt ran his hands across Jake's initials and looked at him.

Jake took a step closer to Colt until their chests were pressed against each other. He ran his hands up to Colt's shoulders, pulling Colt closer to him until they kissed once again. How could he explain to Colt the pain he felt whenever he came back to this town? Colt's experience with Newport had been entirely different. After all, he was still here. He had an amazing relationship with his parents. How do you explain to someone who has never been emotionally broken and isolated from their family what it feels like to return? Jake didn't want to believe that he had left any part of himself in Newport.

"Colt, I'm a big believer that things happen for a reason," Jake said. "You know, when I left Newport for good, I never thought I'd come back. My parents told me not to. They said they didn't want anything to do with me."

"Jake…" Colt started, but before he even realized what he had done, Jake held up his finger and Colt stopped talking. The mere action horrified Jake as the only other person he had ever seen hold up a finger with such force and command that it silenced anyone just so happened to be the person he prayed every night he would not turn into.

"After Halloween night, I charted a course for a really terrific life that ultimately led to a terrific son that I'm a dad to. And after Paxton's death, I didn't think I would ever want to date again. But I'm starting to realize that I may feel differently about that now."

Jake looked into Colt's eyes, which appeared to slightly well up. The sight was almost as shocking to Jake as the kiss from Colt on Halloween. He had never seen Colt cry.

"So, what do we do now?" Colt asked, wiping his face.

"I think…" Jake began. Truthfully, he had no idea what they were going to do now. He felt like he could finally date again after his husband's death but was now also dealing with his father's stroke. There was also that matter of a potential chef position with *Wake Up With Us* that could take him and Charlie to New York. Part of him said to go for it. This was his first love, his childhood best friend. This was the thing that movies were made of. Another part of him was telling Jake to be cautious. He had to think about Charlie as well and couldn't move too fast. And then there was another part of Jake, the more animalistic side of him, that wanted to rip Colt's clothes off and do everything he had ever imagined with Colton Humphrey.

"I think I would be an idiot to let you pass by me a second time," Jake said. He leaned forward and his lips met Colt's as they stood next to their tree.

It was Colt who eventually pulled away and took Jake's hand, leading him back to the house. Once they were inside, Colt placed a hand on Jake's lower back and his other behind Jake's neck and slowly lowered him backward onto the couch. He shifted on top of Jake with one leg to Jake's side and the other between both of Jake's legs. They fit together and it made sense. Colt leaned forward and began to kiss Jake softly. Jake was right, Colt thought to himself. Jake had such a beautiful life, and although it ended in tragedy, it had given him so much. Colt realized that his wish that Halloween night ended differently was essentially wishing away some of the best parts of Jake's life. He knew that wasn't fair to Jake.

"I don't want to lose you a second time," Colt said. He placed one hand on Jake's lower back. His other hand was free to explore as it slid up Jake's arm. Colt brushed his upper lip across Jake's bottom lip before kissing him again.

"You won't," Jake said. There was a lot of things that Jake would need to figure out. But he realized that Colton Humphrey was worth it.

"I could do this all night," Colt said breathlessly as he continued to kiss Jake. "But, maybe we should eat."

"Yeah," Jake said halfheartedly. He had no interest in the chicken thighs on the barbeque grill. There was an entirely different set of thighs he wanted his mouth on. "So, how'd you get all this food ready so quickly?"

"I left the hospital a few minutes early," Colt said unconvincingly. In fact, Colt had actually left nearly three hours early in order to get all of this ready.

"Oh okay. I was going to say that if you were able to cook all of this by yourself, you could have a career as my sous chef if you ever decide to make a career change," Jake said, playfully bumping his hip into Colt's as they stood next to each other by the grill.

"Deal," Colt said. He pulled the chicken off the grill and brought it over to the table, where the rest of the food was.

Colt served the plates as the two settled into the chairs on the balcony. Jake took a bite of the chicken. It was a little overcooked and their time at the tree by the water bank and inside the house was probably to blame, but overall, it tasted great. "So your parents—how did you tell them?"

217

"Um, I actually told them on Halloween night," Colt said between bites.

"Really?"

"Yeah. I kind of told them right before I went after you. But don't worry. I didn't tell them anything that happened that night, because you weren't out yet," Colt said reassuringly. "But I did eventually tell my mom about my unhealthy crush I had for you back in junior high and high school."

"I'm glad they are so accepting," Jake said.

"Me too. I kind of wish they weren't so – involved. Mom's been trying to play matchmaker for me anytime she runs into anyone who's gay and single. She's been pestering me for years to get married, but I'm a hundred percent certain it's just because she wants grandkids."

Jake thought about what Colt said. Hearing how Beth Humphrey embraced her son was a good sign for Jake. It was the same type of relationship Paxton had with his mother, Evelyn. Jake realized how wrong he had been about Colt.

"So, you want kids?" Jake asked curiously.

"Oh, of course. I love kids," Colt said. He took another drink of his beer and held his bottle up until Jake grabbed his and tapped the two of them together. "Cheers."

"Cheers."

"So, what about you? Have you ever thought of having more kids?" Colt asked.

Jake had now reached the point in the process of dating where the future was discussed. It was the thought about these conversations that Jake feared the most whenever he contemplated having to put himself back out there once again. Something about that part in dating felt so formal, as if you were being interviewed for a job or you were on some sort of game show. Say the right things and you get to move to the next round. Say the wrong answer and you find yourself plummeting down a chute after a lever is pulled.

"Yeah," Jake said slowly. He realized it was hard to answer this question without thinking of Paxton. After all, he was the one he had always imagined raising a family with, and Jake began to wonder if it was going to be like this…comparing everything to or thinking of Paxton.

"We had always planned on having more children. But then the unexpected happens and your life changes."

"I'm sorry," Colt said.

"No need to be. Sorry for being a damper to the conversation."

"You aren't. Jake, listen. I know you've been married. I know you've experienced loss and trauma…and so has Charlie," Colt said. "I guess I just want you to know that when I tell you I'm invested in wherever this is going, I understand there's a lot that comes with that."

"Thanks. Honestly…" Jake began. He thought about telling Colt about New York right there and then. They were talking about the future, and that seemed like the opportune time to bring it up. But then Jake realized he was putting the cart before the horse. The job offer was no guarantee, so why ruin such a nice moment? "This is all new for me again, but I'm really glad it's with you."

"Me too. You know, when I've dated in the past, I never really found the right man I wanted to settle down with. But things change…" Colt said and then smiled at Jake.

"And you think you found that person now?" Jake asked. The way he said it made Jake realize Colt was of the same mindset. This was much more than a fourth date. How could they pretend there already wasn't a history that the two could immediately build off of?

"Pretty sure," Colt said confidently.

"Phew!" Jake said dramatically. "I was going to say that if you were about to say no, we may need to have a different conversation."

"What about you?" Colt asked. The question could have had many different meanings, but Jake was no idiot and knew exactly what Colt was asking.

"I always figured I would know when I was ready to date and get into something serious again. And honestly, I had no idea when that might happen. But I know now. I mean, our tree is still here. That's gotta be a sign, right?"

"*Our tree…* I like it," Colt said. "I kind of always thought of it as the 'Ghost-of-the-Boyfriend-That-Never-Was-Tree.' 'Our Tree' has a better ring to it."

The two continued to talk about everything from the time they were both in Newport to the time where they parted ways. Jake thought everything about the night felt right. It didn't just feel like he was catching up with a friend. He had a deeper connection with Colt. It was something that Jake had prayed there was more than just one of after losing Paxton. And it turned out, there was. This entire night was proof of that. Colt stood and grabbed both of their plates and took them into the kitchen. Now that dinner was over, Jake had no idea what Colt had planned. Dinner was the only thing that Jake knew was definitely on the agenda. He was now in unknown territory.

"So…" Colt said slowly, returning back from the kitchen. Whatever he was about to say, he was nervous. "I was thinking of maybe hot-tubbing under the stars?"

"I didn't bring any shorts," Jake said.

"Neither did I," Colt said, grabbing Jake's hand and pulling him across the balcony to the hot tub. "If my memory serves me correctly, this isn't the first time we've gone skinny-dipping, Ruiz."

And just like that, Colt began to pull off his Grizzlies T-shirt, revealing his toned physique. *Damn, you can practically grate cheese on those abs*, Jake thought. Jake was thankful Colt was a doctor, because he was certain what he was witnessing was about to give him a full-fledged aneurysm and send him straight to the ER.

Colt unfastened the belt on his navy shorts, and Jake realized he needed to start taking clothes off, too, and it wasn't just to keep up with Colt. No, it was so he wouldn't have a heatstroke from watching him undress. Colt threw his shorts to the ground, revealing his muscular legs and calves that were covered in the same blond hair that covered his chest. His tight black boxer briefs left very little to the imagination. In fact, there was no need to imagine anything. The boxers made a very detailed outline of what awaited underneath. Colt tucked his thumbs under the elastic waistband of his boxers and before Jake could even mentally prepare or at least hold on to the wall of the house to brace himself, the boxers fell to the ground.

Jake knew he had been staring for far too long, but as much as he tried, he could not pull his eyes from anywhere other than the area that Colt had revealed. Jake bit hard on his lip, praying there wasn't drool coming out of the corners as he stared at Colt's entire torso.

"So…um… Are you joining me, Ruiz?" Colt asked. Jake began to worry that maybe things were moving a little too fast, but it was too late. A completely naked Colt Humphrey now stood in front of him and what else could he do? Look at Colt and let him know he changed his mind? *No way in hell*, Jake thought.

"Yeah!" Jake said, tearing off his clothes much faster than Colt's slow reveal. He disrobed in what felt like ten milliseconds. He didn't have as toned of a body as Colt did, but Jake thought he had a nice body. He had more of a swimmer's build, while Colt had a more defined physique.

"Wow," Colt said, taking in the sight of Jake, who was now naked. "You are…the most beautiful man."

Colt wasn't kidding. At least, there was no tone of humor in his voice and his face was dead serious. As a teen, Jake had ruined countless socks and underwear thinking and imagining an encounter like this with Colt. And it finally was coming to fruition, albeit almost two decades later.

"Come on." Colt grabbed Jake's hand and pulled him over to the hot tub. Crickets chirped in the distance and other than that, it was silent. It was such a change from living in Seattle for so long. Even the night sky looked different without all the lights of the buildings swallowing up the beauty of the stars.

"I forgot how peaceful it can be out here," Jake said. The glassy, still surface of Sacheen Lake reflected the trees that lined the bank of the water as the sun began to sink behind them. Jake felt his body begin to shiver. He couldn't tell if it was because of nervousness or the cooling summer night air. "It's a little colder than I expected."

"Don't worry. It'll be warm in just a minute," Colt said reassuringly.

"You're not going to pee in it or something?" Jake asked, wincing with regret as soon as the words left his mouth. He wondered what the hell was wrong with him. "I'm so sorry. I don't know what's wrong with me."

"Nothing's wrong with you, Ruiz. You're funny. And don't worry—I won't pee in the hot tub," Colt said, lifting the cover off and pressing a button to start up the jets.

"I like it when you call me Ruiz," Jake said. Colt was the only one who called him that.

"I do too." Colt stepped up the stairs next to the hot tub, bringing his lower half right to Jake's eye level. Jake felt the urge to reach out and grab his butt, but showed restraint. After all, by the looks of where the night was headed, there was going to be a lot more than just some ass-grabbing.

Jake followed Colt into the hot tub, and the moment his foot touched the surface, the rest of his body seemed to sink right in. Colt was right. The water felt amazing. Steam rose off the surface of the hot tub and Colt inched his way closer, until Jake could feel Colt's thigh pressed against his. He lifted his left arm and wrapped it around Jake's shoulder, pulling him closer.

Colt was silent and when Jake turned to look at him, he had his head pointed toward the night sky. His eyes were closed and he was smiling. Jake didn't need to ask what he was thinking about. It was obvious the same thing was on Colt's mind. *After all of these years, this is actually happening.*

"I could get used to this," Colt said, staring into Jake's eyes.

"Me too," Jake said, running his hand up Colt's chest to his pecs and resting it there. Even through the hot-tub jetted water, Jake could feel Colt's heart racing, which was surprising, given his calm demeanor. "I love your body. I always have."

"Jake, I love yours even more, now that I've seen all of it," Colt said, playfully squeezing Jake's thigh. "I always thought this would happen. I mean, I kind of hoped it would happen on homecoming night."

"You did?" Jake asked, surprised.

"I mean, yeah. I had this whole plan that you'd stay here that night and I could finally tell you how I felt," Colt admitted. "But then, you know...I melted the siding of the house. Even the accidental spooning couldn't snap me out of the fear I had of how my parents would react."

Jake sat there and couldn't believe what he was hearing. Was he being told that if Colt had listened to his warning and moved the fire back a few extra feet that Jake would have possibly lost his virginity to Colt? That he and Colt would have realized just how much they both felt about each other? That homecoming night could have drastically changed the entire course of Jake's life, preventing him from meeting Paxton and ultimately having Charlie? That bonfire was Jake's butterfly effect. It was quite possibly the only thing that assured he would end up having the life that led him to Paxton and Charlie. Fate didn't just work in mysterious ways. No, it worked in even the most minute of details.

"I had no idea," was all that Jake could say. He sat there, continuing to think about the bonfire and homecoming night.

"Well, we're here now." Colt lifted his hand out of the water and ran it along Jake's cheek. "Is it weird?"

"Is what weird?" Jake asked.

"Being back here?"

"It's different," Jake said. "After being gone for so long, it doesn't quite feel like the city I grew up in. Almost like some sort of ghost of the city I grew up in."

Colt sat there quietly, realizing he had charted the conversation into heavy territory, creating a somber mood in the hot tub. "Do you remember when you came out to me and I said I knew because you stared a lot?"

"Do we really need to bring this up right now?" He wasn't sure where Colt was going with the question but the last thing Jake wanted to be reminded of right now was Halloween night.

"Jake, the reason I knew you stared a lot was because I was looking at you as well. There were plenty of times I had no idea what was going on in class because of you. Your looks are…very distracting. I mean, I'm lucky I graduated from high school."

"Colt, you were third in our class and had like a 3.9 GPA."

"Yeah, but it was definitely touch-and-go there for a minute. Especially on the days you wore shorts!" They both laughed, thinking about their shared past. "So, what are things you like to do in your free time now?"

Jake thought about the question. He wanted to laugh and tell Colt he was cute for thinking that a single father to a five year old and business owner had free time. This was a secret better kept from individuals without kids so it wouldn't scare them off. And the last thing he wanted to do was scare off Colt. "Umm…We go kayaking on Lake Washington when it's warm and have started to go hiking quite a bit. What about you?"

"Well, I happen to love kayaking too. I also like to hike. I'm usually on trails when I'm not working. To be honest, tonight is kind of a one-off. I don't cook that often. Mostly because it's just me and also because the only thing I seem to do decently is grill. I eat out probably more than I should, and since the dining options are a bit scarce, I'm somewhat of a regular at Los Ruiz."

"So, what you're saying is that you're just interested in me because I can cook?" Jake asked playfully.

"No, I'm interested in dating you because you can cook *and* so much more," Colt said.

Jake looked at Colt. "You said you want to date me?"

"I mean, yeah," Colt answered. "I figured that's where this was heading. That's where we are headed, right?"

"If you're asking me if I want Colton Humphrey to be my boyfriend, the answer to that question is an unequivocal yes." Jake said. "It's just… How are we going to make this work? I've got my restaurants back in Seattle, and you've got a practice here in Newport."

"Ruiz, let's not talk about that tonight," Colt said. "But I can assure you of this. I'll make this work no matter what. If I have to get on a plane and fly over to Seattle to see you every week, that's what I'll do."

And here Jake was presented with another opportunity to share with Colt about the opportunity in New York. And just like last time, Jake decided to push past the moment. He leaned over and kissed Colt. He felt Colt run his fingers through Jake's hair and rest on his neck.

"Do you…want to go inside?" Colt asked Jake between kisses.

"Yes," Jake said breathlessly. He followed Colt into the house and straight into the bedroom.

CHAPTER 29

The reflection of the sun from the lake flooded into the room, and Jake pulled the covers over his head to hide from it the next morning. He felt the fabric of the comforter run across his naked body and rolled over, causing Colt to wake just enough to be aware of Jake's movement. Colt pulled Jake's body into his, and Jake felt Colt's chest push into his shoulder blades and the rest of Colt's naked body now enmeshed with Jake's. Jake knew he needed to find his phone and text Gigi to tell her he'd be coming back to Helen's in a little while, but for now Jake fell back asleep in Colt's arms.

When he woke up again, Jake found he was now alone in the bedroom. At the foot of the bed, there was a folded T-shirt and a pair of boxer shorts. They were Colt's clothes, but considering Jake's clothes were nowhere in sight, he threw on the shirt and boxers and made his way to the living room. When he opened the French doors leading from the bedroom, the warm smell of sausage and eggs overpowered his senses. Colt stood in the kitchen in his underwear and a tank top, cooking.

"Good morning," Jake said shyly, making his way into the kitchen.

"Hey!" Colt pulled his attention from the stove and looked at Jake. He walked over to him and put his hands on Jake's hips, pulling him closer and kissed him. "How'd you sleep?"

"There wasn't much sleep involved with last night..." Jake said, winking at Colt and then sitting on one of the bar stools that faced into the kitchen.

"Right..." Colt said. He laughed and made his way back to the stove. "Last night, by the way, that was...incredible. Best night of my life. Hands down."

"Yeah, it was a really good night. I mean, I'm a little sore, but it was definitely worth it," Jake said.

"You are," Colt turned to look at Jake from the stove with a devilish grin on his face, "surprisingly really flexible."

"I do yoga. I was actually thinking of cancelling my membership," Jake said.

"Don't do that. Definitely don't do that," Colt said, holding up a spatula and waving it as he continued to cook breakfast. "You look really cute in my clothes, by the way."

"That's what they were there for, right? Sorry, I didn't see my clothes anywhere."

"Totally. I set those out for you. I think there's a trail of your clothes somewhere near the slider. Oh…your phone was blowing up earlier too. You may want to check it."

Jake went over to the living room to find where his phone had landed in the rush to strip to go skinny-dipping. He finally found his clothes near the legs of a chair by the windows overlooking the lake. After unlocking his phone, he saw a missed call from Gigi and two text messages.

> **Gigi 6:13 a.m.:** Just tell me… 🍆+🍑= 🏃 ??

> **Gigi 6:46 a.m.:** Jacob Ruiz…I will never forgive you if you don't send some sort of details. Are we going to have to borrow your dad's wheelchair to come pick you up?

Jake looked down at his phone and rolled his eyes. Should he tell her anything? He looked down at Gigi's messages and typed:

> **Jake 7:28 a.m.:** Last night was amazing. I'll tell you more later, but let's just say it definitely was worth all the wait. Talk soon 😏

Jake made his way back to Colt in the kitchen. Now that the dream that was last night was over and they were back in the reality of this morning, he knew he had to tell Colt about New York. It was as if the universe was also aware of Jake's plan, because at that very moment, his phone rang. When he looked at the caller ID, his marketing manager, Marcia Schrader's name was displayed on the phone. He pressed decline and before he set the phone down, it began to ring again. Marcia was not okay with being sent straight to voicemail.

"You can grab that if you need to," Colt said from the kitchen.

"It's cool," Jake said, pushing decline again. "Hey, Colt? Can we talk about something?"

"Sure," Colt said hesitantly. "But you have me a little worried."

"Well, it's just…" Jake said, but then the phone rang again. *Dammit, Marcia—take a hint and just leave a message*, Jake thought.

"Jake, just answer it. I'm not going anywhere," Colt said.

"Okay," Jake said. The problem was, Jake didn't know if he could say the same. He pressed answer on his cell phone. "Hey, Marcia."

"Okay, I'm just going to brush past the fact that you sent me to voicemail three times."

"Marcia, I'm a little busy," Jake said, looking over at Colt, who just smiled.

"Well, you're certainly not too busy to answer my call when I have news that *Wake Up With Us* wants to fly you out to New York to appear on their Monday show."

"Monday? Like, this Monday?"

"Like this Monday! Jake, this is incredible news! This is going to be a massive injection of life into Ruiz Kitchens!"

"That's really great," Jake said, but after his night with Colt, Jake was starting to second-guess if this was something he even wanted to do.

"I'll take care of everything and will send over all the details to you later today. Oh, they've offered to fly Charlie out there as well, so you two can explore the city and you know, maybe look at places to live."

"He'll like that. Thanks, Marcia. Send me the details and I'll look everything over."

"Of course! I'll talk with you later," Marcia said before hanging up.

Jake set his phone down just as Colt handed him his plate. He figured Colt probably wasn't one to ask who was on the phone and be nosy, but Jake knew this was the time to tell him about New York.

"That was my marketing manager for the restaurants," Jake said.

"Marketing manager…that's when you know you've made it, Ruiz. When you have your own marketing manager," Colt said. He brought another plate of food over and sat down next to Jake on the stools at the kitchen island. "Breakfast is served."

"Thanks! Hey, Colt, I need to tell you something," Jake said.

"Uh-oh. That doesn't sound good," Colt said. "What's up?"

"Well, my marketing manager got me this opportunity to be a guest chef on *Wake Up With Us* this Monday," Jake said.

"*Wake Up With Us?* Oh my God, Ruiz! That's HUGE! I love Cookie Cochran," Colt said. It was cute watching him geek out over the co-host of the morning show.

"The thing is, it's not just a guest chef appearance. It's kind of like an interview."

"For what?" Colt said, but Jake had an idea that Colt already knew what for.

"To be their permanent chef for the program."

"Oh." Every indication of happiness and joy that had been evident on Colt's face seemed to wipe away. "So, what does that mean? That you'd have to move to New York?"

"If I get the job, yeah. I'm still not really sure about it though. Marcia, my marketing manager, is insisting it will help the restaurant group recover."

"What do you mean *recover?*"

"Well, when Covid hit, it kind of destroyed my company. We were able to survive because I have a really fantastic team and we had a lot in the bank, but Covid took its toll." Jake would have been embarrassed to share this information with anyone else, but not Colt.

"How bad are your restaurants?"

"Bad. We may have to close two of them, but Marcia thinks this might bring new publicity to the restaurants and save them."

Colt sat there silently, processing everything that Jake had shared. He woke this morning with a feeling of optimism. Laying in his arms, their bodies entwined with each other, was the man he had always thought was the one who got away. Jake was the one Colt had compared new boyfriends to. Over time, that barometer disappeared, which left Colt with boyfriends that were atrocious, like Eli. When Jake showed back up in his life and eventually in his arms, Colt had thought it was maybe too good to be true. And what Jake was now telling him was that Colt was right. This had been too good to be true. Colt knew there was only one thing he could do. He couldn't ask Jake to stay and have him potentially lose all his restaurants and resent Colt in the future for having him make that decision.

"You should do it." It took every bit of him to try and hide the hesitation and sadness, but Colt knew Jake could see right through him.

"What? You know that might mean I move to Manhattan," Jake said.

"Jake, I think you need to do this," Colt said. "I don't want to be the one who stood in your way. Besides, I've always wanted to see New York. I could come out there and visit."

"You'd do that?"

"Of course," Colt said. He was wondering what he was doing. Was he really so willing to send someone away that took years to get over the last time? "We can make this work."

"I think we can too," Jake said.

They sat there both thinking the same thing. *This will never work.* But instead, they falsely reassured each other while also trying to assure themselves that starting a brand-new cross-country relationship may work.

"I better get ready for work," Colt said. He stood up and kissed Jake on the cheek. Jake looked down at the breakfast Colt had made for the two of them. Colt's breakfast was left nearly untouched.

"I better get going too. Can we talk after you're off?" Jake asked.

"Yeah. I'm probably going to work a little bit late tonight, though, so I can call you after I'm off."

"Cool," Jake said. With the exception of an awkward kiss after Jake had gathered his things and made his way out the door, the rest of the time Jake was at Colt's was largely spent in silence. Jake knew Colt was upset, but maybe giving him time to process everything was best, Jake thought. As he drove away and Colt's house disappeared behind him, Jake couldn't help but think he was going to lose Colt Humphrey a second time.

CHAPTER 30

To say that Gigi took the news of Jake possibly moving to New York worse than Colt would have been an understatement. Jake was relieved there weren't any objects she could throw within reach when he told her after returning from Colt's.

"When were you planning on dropping this bombshell?" Gigi asked.

"This just kind of came up, and it's not even a guaranteed thing, okay?" Jake tried reasoning with her, but he knew that was going to be about as effective as reasoning with Consuela while Gigi was this angry.

"Is New York where all the superheroes are?" Charlie asked eagerly.

"Yes, Charlie. And the Son of Sam and the Long Island serial killer!" Gigi snapped back.

"Gigi, for God's sake!" Jake interrupted before Gigi could name off any other serial killers that would give his child nightmares about New York City.

"There's also rats the size of horses in the subway, Charlie," Gigi said and stretched her arms outward, emphasizing just how large she thought the rats were. This caused Charlie to gasp and whimper as he ran off to the bedroom.

"Why do you have to do that? He's going to be terrified of a city he's never even been to now!" Jake said. He loved Gigi, but she could sometimes be selfish and ignorant.

"I just don't really think you are thinking this all the way through. You seriously think that moving to New York and having your restaurants go on 'cruise control' will work? It's not a well-thought-out plan, Jake."

"Gigi, those restaurants do just fine without me breathing down my nose on them. In fact, they usually do better when I'm not there!" Part of that was true. Although the restaurants were now financially unsecure due to the massive hit they had taken during the Covid pandemic, each of Jake's businesses had a very capable manager and team. He knew that living in New York would require hiring some more people to handle some of the overall operational pieces, but he also knew this was none of Gigi's business.

"Well, what about Colt? Obviously, he is pissed about this too!" Gigi said.

"What are you talking about? Colt's fine!" Jake had told her how Colt had reacted to the news earlier of New York, but he had made no indication that he was upset about Jake's opportunity.

"Oh Jacob. Sweet, sweet, Jacob," Gigi said, patting Jake on the cheek. The gesture infuriated Jake; it was as if Gigi was talking to a child who didn't know any better. "If you think that man is fine after he just reconnected with his childhood crush, only to find out said crush may be moving across country after going on MULTIPLE dates with him, then you are very, very mistaken."

Gigi grabbed her keys and left the house. Jake knew she was angry. After all, she had offered to watch Charlie earlier, and second, where was she even planning to go? But the words Gigi said stuck in Jake's head long after she had left. He wanted to make this work with Colt but he also knew he needed to do something to help save his businesses. He wished there was someone who could make the decision for him, but there wasn't. He knew he was taking a gamble with these decisions, and Jake just hoped he had his chips on the right number.

CHAPTER 31

It was just before noon when Jake arrived at the hospital with Charlie in tow for his dad's physical therapy session. He hadn't planned on coming to this appointment, but his mother was told having a second person involved would be helpful. So, unfortunately, Jake was now walking right back into a potential conversation with his mom. Stacy was back at the nurse's station and as he passed her, she waved at him and then pointed to a rainbow lapel pin that was fastened to the pocket of her nurse's scrubs. He had to admit that it was nice to see Stacy was trying.

"Like the pin, Stacy," Jake said.

"Thanks!" she said proudly.

"Do you know where my dad's physical therapy is?" Jake asked.

"Oh, he's down at the end of the hall on the right," Stacy said.

"Hey, Charlie? Why don't you go down there and wait for me?" Jake handed him his tablet. "You can watch something, but only if it's appropriate, *comprende?*"

"*Comprende,*" Charlie said disappointedly. He grabbed the tablet and ran down the hallway.

"He's a good kid," Stacy said.

"The best. Hey, Stacy?"

"Yeah?"

"Is Colt here? I kind of wanted to talk with him."

"Oh, he actually left not long after he got here. Dr. Mathison is filling in his rounds. He said he wasn't feeling well."

"Oh, okay." Jake couldn't pretend Colt's departure was because of anything other than their conversation that morning. "Thanks, Stacy."

As he walked down the hospital corridor, Jake thought about how he had probably screwed things up once again. At this rate, and based on their history, it would be another two decades before Jake had another chance to make it right with Colt. He pulled out his phone and scrolled to Colt's name. Jake's finger hovered over the contact as he contemplated sending Colt a text message. If Colt really was upset though, Jake realized he needed to give him more time.

When he walked into the room where his father's appointment was, Jake saw Charlie standing next to his dad's wheelchair and his mom sitting next to Charlie. Jake was about to say something, but stopped as he eavesdropped on the conversation.

"And this is our house," Charlie said, showing a picture of their Phinney Ridge home to Jake's mom and dad from the tablet.

"It's nice," Jake's dad said quietly as he stared at Charlie.

"It's a bit extravagant for me," Consuela said dryly. The thought that a 1,200-square-foot house was a "bit extravagant" for Consuela made Jake roll his eyes. Nothing was ever good enough for Consuela unless she was part of the decision-making process.

"Oh! Here is a picture of me and my dads at Point Defiance Zoo," Charlie said. He giggled. "The peacock kept chasing Daddy Pax on the sidewalk." Charlie stared at the phone for a while before showing the picture to Jake's mom and dad. Jake bit his lip out of fear that the next words that would come out of Consuela's mouth would disparage Paxton right in front of Charlie.

"Aw, that looks like it was a fun day," Consuela said. She was quiet for a moment and then asked, "Do you miss your daddy?"

"Yeah," Charlie said, swiping through the photos. "He was really funny and made my Daddy Jake laugh all the time. See?" Charlie turned the phone and showed a picture of the three of them in front of a bakery in Ballard. Paxton had a cinnamon roll in his hand that he shoved into Jake's face right as they were about to take a picture.

"Oh my!" Consuela said, chuckling at the photo. "Your…Daddy Jacob has always had trouble keeping clean when it comes to sweets."

"That's just like me," Charlie said. "I'm a little sugar monster. I get that from both of my dads."

"I know your Daddy Jacob is a really great person. I didn't know your…Daddy Pax, but it sounds like you had two really good dads," Consuela said.

Jake turned for a moment to look around and see if he was on some sort of new hidden camera show. Was he in the right room, or did he fall into some sort of other dimension? With everything that happened between him and Colt the night before, and now this, Jake was beginning to believe that perhaps he was in a coma or all of these events were some sort of fever dream brought on by stress. There was no way this was his mom.

"Hey, Dad…Mom," Jake said quietly, tapping the door before making his way into the room.

"It was good talking with you," Charlie said and started making his way back to the chair on the other side of the room.

"Hold up, buddy. You can stay here if you'd like," Jake said, praying he wouldn't regret the decision.

"*Mijo*," Carlos said quietly and held up a hand to greet Jake.

"Hey, Pa," Jake said. "Try to take it easy."

"He's right, *amor*," Jake's mom said. "You're going to overexert yourself."

Carlos groaned and looked out the window. This was further proof for Jake that Consuela must have been body snatched and replaced with a lookalike. At no point in Jake's entire memory did he recall a time where Consuela admitted someone else was right, even when it came to matters this trivial.

"*Mijito*, can you help me with the paperwork at the nurse's station?" Consuela asked Jake as she made her way to the door.

Great, what does she have up her sleeve? Jake wondered.

"Sure," Jake said, following her. Out in the hallway, Consuela inched closer to Jake so that she could talk quietly.

"Your father's blood pressure is incredibly high. They are putting him on medication, but they said it would be best to create a stress-free environment for him. That means no fighting, *comprende?*"

"Yeah, of course," Jake said. There was about a million other things he could say as a follow-up. For starters, he could have said that most of the fights the two of them went through were results of his mom starting them, but he kept quiet. He knew better than to say anything that would provoke his mother's otherwise pleasant demeanor.

"*Gracias, mijo*," Consuela said, patting her son's cheek. "You look nice. There's a…glow about you."

Jake had to bite his tongue.

If only she knew what had caused the glow, he thought.

"Thanks, Mom. So, how have the other physical therapy appointments been?"

"They've been good. Your father – he's a fighter. He'll be back to his old self in no time. How's the restaurant?" his mom asked.

Jake wondered if he should tell his mom the truth, but he knew that if he did, there was no telling the type of response his mother would have. Instead, he decided to be vaguely honest. "There's a lot of work that needs to be done, Mom."

"*Ay*, it isn't that bad, *mijo*. We can't all be profitable restaurants like yours," Consuela said.

"Ma, that is literally the only goal EVERY restaurant has," Jake said. He thought Consuela was baiting him into an argument, but he couldn't quite tell. Either way, he was determined not to fall into the bear trap. "Anyway, I am heading out of town, but I'll be back in a few days."

"Who's going to take care of the restaurant?"

"Well, Glen's there. And I actually have one of my restaurant managers flying in to help with a couple things. The restaurant will be in good hands," Jake reassured his mom.

"Fine, if you say so," Consuela said. "Where are you going?"

"New York. I'm actually going to be on *Wake Up With Us* as their guest chef for the Monday show."

"*Wake Up With Us*? Like the *Wake Up With Us* that is on TV every morning and has Cookie Cochran?" As far as he could remember, Jake's mom had never sounded as excited as she did right now.

"That's the one," Jake said.

"That's huge, *mijo*! You need to tell your father. He'll love to hear that," Consuela urged him.

"You think?"

"*Ay*, your father is proud of you when you sneeze. Can you imagine how excited he'll be to hear this? He'll be so proud. You know, your father always wanted to make a name for himself. 'I'm going to do something big. Just you wait and see, Connie.' He'd always tell me that. When he opened Los Ruiz, he felt like he finally made it. That is, until he had you. That's when he felt like he made it. And every success you've had, your father feels like he's part of it. *Wake Up With Us…* Can you imagine? Your father will be so thrilled to hear!"

And just like that, Jake felt like he had been pushed further into the New York opportunity and further away from whatever had begun with Colt.

CHAPTER 32

Colt had been conveniently busy at the hospital and on shifts in the days leading up to Sunday, when Jake and Charlie had to get on their flight from Spokane to New York. Jake had talked with him on the phone, and it was unmistakable that Colt's demeanor had shifted since hearing the news of Jake possibly moving to New York. Of course, he had said all the right things to Jake. *Have a safe flight. Just have fun and don't overthink things. If you get the opportunity, we can try to make this work. You're worth it.* But it was the uncertainty in Colt's voice that made Jake nervous. *Try?* You would have thought that the years and years of history and feelings the two shared would have produced a more assuring response, but all Jake received was a *try.*

Maybe I'm expecting too much, Jake thought. What had he been expecting? Colt to drop everything for him and move to New York? That the two would marry in a Central Park wedding and go to Broadway shows every weekend? Jake understood the distance that Colt was placing between the two of them. He just wished Colt didn't feel the need to do that.

Helen drove to the airport to see Jake and Charlie off, and Gigi had begrudgingly come along. After checking their bags in with the airline, the group shared last hugs. When Jake went to hug Gigi, it was like hugging a pole, as she kept her arms down at her sides. Charlie wrapped his arms around Gigi's waist, but again there was no hug in return.

"Call us when you get there, okay?" Helen said, squeezing Jake and Charlie one last time. "I hope you two have fun!"

"I hope it's awful," Gigi said drolly. "I heard the garbage men are on strike and all the heat in the city right now is making the entire city smell like piss and cabbage."

"I'm going to miss you too, Gigi." Jake tried giving Gigi one last hug, to no avail, and decided to make his way to the security gate.

"Is it true that there are alligators that will swim up through the toilets when I'm going potty?" Charlie asked as the two made their way to the line waiting to get through security. "Aunt Gigi said thousands of alligators are in the sewers and pipes because people flushed them down. She said they are going to bite my butt."

"Your Aunt Gigi is unhinged, Charlie," Jake said. He swore that if Charlie didn't take a shit during this entire trip, he would sue Gigi.

"RUIZ!" The sound of his last name being screaming in the echoing chamber of the airport startled Jake. For a split second, he expected the drug dogs to tackle him at any moment, but when he turned around, he saw Colt bolting down the airport corridor toward Jake. Jake's heart began to race. He felt like this was a scene ripped right out of the end of a romantic comedy. Colt continued sprinting toward the security gate, which was no small feat, considering he was wearing skinny jeans. Jake pulled Charlie out of the security line and made their way to Colt.

"Colt?" Jake looked at him as he stood there panting. He put a hand on each knee and hunched over as he caught his breath.

"Are you okay?" Charlie asked. He looked up at Jake with an expression of worry on his face.

"I'm…fine," Colt said between panted breaths before standing back up. "I…was…an…asshole."

"Uh oh," Charlie said, looking at Colt who had his hands on his waist and was still trying to catch his breath.

"Sorry! I…was…an idiot."

"What are you talking about?" Jake looked at Colt. He couldn't tell if the pained look on Colt's face was because Jake was about to get on a plane or if he was about to pass out from the marathon sprint through Spokane International Airport.

"I was pushing you away. I don't want to do that," Colt said. He placed his hands in Jake's. "I'm sorry. I should have been more supportive of this opportunity for you. It sounds fantastic."

"Colt, you are absolutely fine, but thank you." Jake squeezed Colt's hands.

"I should have told you to have a safe trip and I can't wait to see you when you return," Colt said. He leaned forward and kissed Jake before pulling back and letting go of Jake's hands.

"Oh! I also found this, Charlie. My dad brought this back from a medical conference when I was a kid and gave it to me. I thought you might like it for your trip." Charlie reached into a plastic bag Colt handed him, finding a baseball cap with an embroidered apple, with the words that read "Lil apple in the Big Apple."

"Thank you!" Charlie put the hat on and hugged Colt.

"Dad thought it was a bit ironic." Washington was known for its apples, so Colt could appreciate how next level his dad was. Mark Humphrey had always come through with his dad jokes.

"That's really kind of you. Thank you. I'll call you when we land," Jake said. He kissed Colt one more time and then took Charlie by the hand and made their way back to the line that went through security. He looked one last time before he rounded a wall and waved at Colt. He felt an ache in his chest and recognized the familiar pain of losing something. And although Jake wasn't losing Colt, he couldn't help but think the chances of a cross-country relationship succeeding seemed very slim.

"Dad?" The plane was somewhere over the Midwest by the time Charlie got bored with the movie he'd been watching. He turned off the tablet and removed his headphones before he tugged on Jake's sleeves.

"Yeah, buddy? What's up?"

"Can we talk for a minute?" Charlie asked. Jake couldn't handle when Charlie sounded grown up. Part of him found it adorable and the other part found it terrifying that Charlie was growing up so fast.

"Always. What's on your mind?" Jake asked.

"You know I miss Daddy Pax," Charlie began. "But I just thought I'd tell you that Colt is really cool."

"He is pretty cool, isn't he? Why do you say this though?"

"Just in case you want to marry him," Charlie said.

Jake chuckled and patted his son on the back. The mere thought of marrying Colt gave Jake a sense of elation, but how could he tell his son that the idea of marriage after only a week of dating was, well, a little premature?

"That means a lot, Charlie. You know I've always been honest with you and I always will, so I will tell you that I do like Colt. He's the first man I've liked since Daddy passed away. And I'm glad you like him too. We will just have to see where this goes."

"So, you aren't marrying him?" Charlie asked.

"Well, I don't know. It's really way too early to talk about that, okay?"

"Okay," Charlie said gloomily and looked out the window.

"Why do you sound sad?" Jake asked.

"I just want two dads again," Charlie said with an honesty that broke Jake's heart. Jake would have given anything to make Charlie feel better, but he knew what Charlie wanted right now, Jake could not give.

"You might again someday," Jake said. "It's just not going to be today. I really like Colt, and he likes me too."

"Okay, so how can we speed things up?"

"You can't speed these things up, Charlie. It will happen if it's supposed to happen in its own time, okay?"

"Fine," Charlie said and turned to look out the window.

The rest of the flight to LaGuardia Airport was fairly quiet after the conversation between Jake and Charlie. After finishing his movie, Charlie fell asleep, and it wasn't until they got into the car service that picked them up from the airport that Jake realized Charlie was upset with him. He was silent for the entire trip to the hotel, which was unheard of for a five-year-old, especially Charlie. After they checked into the hotel, Charlie walked into the room in silence and threw himself onto one of the beds.

"Are you okay?" Jake asked his son.

"I'm fine," Charlie said flatly. Jake knew to let Charlie deescalate on his own. If he tried to press the issue, Jake knew he risked Charlie having an epic meltdown. So when his phone began to ring, Jake gladly stepped away from his son, who was still acting like he had somehow been personally scorned. When Jake looked at the screen, he saw that it was a video call from Colt.

"Hey!" Jake said when he answered the phone.

"So how was the flight?" Colt asked. He wore his medical jacket and was on shift at the hospital.

"It was much faster than I thought. And when we got here, there was a car service waiting for us. They had the sign that read *Ruiz* and all."

"Well, that makes it official then," Colt said with an obvious sound of disappointment in his voice.

"Makes what official?" Jake asked.

"You're big time now, Ruiz. A celebrity. I hope you remember us small people!" Colt said jokingly. Although he sounded excited and happy for him, Jake wondered how many times Colt had to rehearse this to sound supportive of the opportunity.

"Shut up!" Jake laughed and rolled his eyes.

"Is that Colt?" Charlie shot up on the bed with more energy than Jake had seen from him in the last several hours.

"It is. Do you want to say hi?" Jake asked and turned the phone around so Charlie could see him.

"Hi, Colt! I still have your hat on, see?" Charlie pointed to the top of his head.

"Looks good on you, buddy! Hey, when you get back, maybe I can get a rematch with you at that air hockey game," Colt said.

"It's a deal," Charlie said. He looked like he was about to wander off and go check out the hotel room, but at the last moment, Charlie turned back around to look at Colt. "Oh, my dad likes you and wants to marry you."

Jake dropped the phone, which was still aimed at Charlie, and Jake was terrified to turn the phone back around to see Colt, who just seemed amused when Jake finally found the nerve to flip it around.

"Charlie! What was that about?" Jake asked.

"Relax! I'm just speeding things up," Charlie said and walked off toward the bathroom.

CHAPTER 33

"So…" Colt said slowly before laughing somewhat nervously. Jake wanted to crawl under the hotel bed and stay there. He loved his son, but sometimes Charlie could be a real asshole, Jake thought.

Jake held up his hand, looking down at the ground. "I pretty much want to die right now, just so you know. He asked about us and was asking questions about marriage. I told him that isn't something that just happens and takes time. I'm so sorry."

"Hey, don't worry about it," Colt reassured him. "At least I can say it's a safe bet that Charlie likes me then, right?"

"Oh, for sure."

"Okay, I'm getting up early and I'm watching the East Coast viewing of *Wake Up With Us* so I can see my boyfriend's big break!"

Hearing Colt refer to Jake as his boyfriend seemed to cause a temporary paralysis in Jake. They had talked about it the other day, but hearing Colt say it now in conversation made it seem so much more official. When Paxton had died and Jake had been getting ready for his first date after his husband's death, Jake thought about what would happen and how he would feel when he was finally referred to as someone's boyfriend again. The thought had terrified him, and he should have taken that as a clue he wasn't ready for dating, but the emotional breakdown he had later that night on the date confirmed that. But when Colt said it, Jake heard the words and they seemed to fit. They made sense. Jake and Colt made sense.

"Uh-oh, I think I lost you. You're frozen," Colt said. Jake could see Colt moving around, trying to get better reception.

"No, I'm here," Jake said.

"Oh, you froze up for a second."

"Sorry. I just like hearing you call me your boyfriend. It's a nice feeling." Jake knew there was no way he could hide the smile on his face. *I have a boyfriend again.*

"What time do you have to be at the studio?" Colt asked.

"I'm not even going to be on until the nine-o'clock hour, but they have a driver picking me up at five a.m., so we'll need to get up at four. I'm just having Charlie sleep in sweats so I can throw some shoes on him and head out the door."

"Oh damn. Jake, I'm sorry. Are you going to be okay with him and the show?"

"Yeah. They have a children's center there at the studio, and they have a day pass for Charlie to go there. I'll be up to my neck in pambazo tomorrow morning." After his conversation with Glen and hearing how his dad had been trying to recreate one of Jake's most popular dishes from Viva la Vida, Jake had decided to make pambazo for the cooking segment. The dish, a Mexican sandwich filled with potato and chorizo, was fairly simple. The version that Jake made also included cilantro, diced peppers, and onions on the inside, and then the entire sandwich was drenched in guajillo pepper sauce. He often referred to it as a Mexican sloppy joe, and it had been one of Jake's favorite meals growing up.

"Well, you probably need to get some rest, so I won't keep you. You're going to do great tomorrow," Colt reassured him. "Call me after the show."

"I will. Talk with you later."

"Oooooohhhhh," Charlie said loudly from his bed, making kissing sounds when Jake got off the phone. Jake grabbed one of the larger pillows from his bed and threw it at his son, knocking him backward into the bed. Charlie laughed, grabbed the pillow, and heaved it back at Jake.

Later that evening, Jake and Charlie ventured out into the city and had dinner at Shake Shack before going back to the hotel and getting ready for bed early. He didn't want to think too much about the show, because Jake knew that if he did, his nerves would get the better of him if he processed the millions of viewers who would see him tomorrow morning. Instead, Jake thought about Colt calling him his boyfriend, and that was enough for Jake to fall asleep without even giving *Wake Up With Us* another thought.

Jake had been having a dream that quickly turned into a nightmare when the wake-up service called his room. He had returned to Spokane and Colt had been standing there with a string quartet. He was down on one knee, ready to propose, when Jake realized he had accidentally left Charlie in New York City. When he turned around to run back to the plane, there was a massive three-story Consuela Ruiz, who laughed and began to throw kitchen knives at him as if she were the final boss in a video game. Jake bolted upright in his bed and instinctively dodged a dream knife one last time before realizing none of it was real.

After getting ready and slipping shoes onto Charlie, Jake arrived at the curb just as the driver taking him to *Wake Up With Us* pulled up. The show had been a staple on network TV for as long as Jake remembered. He would wake up as a kid with his mom watching the show, so for Jake to appear on the show and possibly become a part of it really made him feel a huge sense of pride. He had never dreamed of being an actor or anyone famous. He just wanted to be happy, and that was what cooking provided for him.

"Mr. Ruiz, I'm Patty," a woman whispered when Jake walked in the security entrance to the studio. She looked at Charlie, who was still fast asleep, and smiled. This kid could sleep through a nuclear explosion, Jake thought as he shifted Charlie to his arm that wasn't numb.

"It's nice to meet you, Patty."

"Follow me," Patty said. She passed the security guard station and through a set of double doors that led to a long white corridor. "The children's center has a nap room with little beds that Charlie can sleep in. We had someone get there early since the center doesn't open officially until seven a.m. There is a team prepping your food as well, per your instructions."

"Thanks," Jake said. He couldn't help but feel a bit dishonest that he was appearing on the show as a guest chef and there was a group of people already working on the food he would present as his own. But then he realized that was what a restaurant was like. His teams prepared the recipes he had created that he'd taught them to make, and the thought of this helped Jake feel less like a fraud.

After getting Charlie situated at the child care center and having his makeup done, Jake was ushered onto the soundstage, where *Wake Up With Us* was filmed. He saw the anchor desk that Cookie Cochran and Jim Forrester sat at every morning to talk with the millions of viewers that watched the show. Jake looked at the desk and couldn't help but think about his mother. She would go nuts right now if she could see where he was and what he was looking at.

Jake made his way over to the kitchen set and met the two girls who had been helping to prepare his cooking segment. Cami and Mona were interns for the show and tasked with helping get various segments underway. Jake was nervous at first that interns with no cooking experience had been given this assignment, but he found Cami and Mona were quite skilled and enjoyable to work with in the kitchen. For the show's segment, Jake was cooking five different pambazos, each at different phases of the cooking process. This was to be able to show the audience what the process looked like from start to finish. Cami and Mona helped get the first four phases completed, while Jake prepared the only iteration of the pambazos that would be tasted by Cookie Cochran during the segment.

As he finished touching up the entire presentation, Jake began to wonder what it might be like if this was his life. Could he be happy if he moved to New York and worked in a kitchen with three false walls? Would Charlie be happy in a new city and so far away from Paxton's family, Gigi, and Helen? Question after question popped up in Jake's head, most of them surrounding Colt. He knew he could be successful in New York with this opportunity, but there was one question that Jake fixated on: Was he willing to risk everything and possibly lose Colt again?

CHAPTER 34

"Things are getting hot and spicy in the kitchen when we return with award-winning chef, Jake Ruiz. He's looking pretty *caliente!*" Cookie Cochran said, before the cameras cut to commercial break. Part of the schtick that was Cookie Cochran was her uncanny ability to somehow make anything sound somewhat inappropriate. She had once been covering a hurricane down on the Gulf when she said on live TV that the hurricane was blowing so hard she was in disbelief the stop sign was still erect. The clip had gone viral on the Internet and earned *Wake Up With Us* a dedicated fan base, who tuned in to see what she would say next. In the age of scandals across multiple networks, Jake was shocked that nothing had come up regarding Cookie Cochran. She was the cross between a serious journalist and an Internet personality, which came as no surprise since her mother had been a Pulitzer Prize journalist and her father had been the bassist for a rock band in the seventies. It was for all these reasons that Jake was flabbergasted that *Wake Up With Us* was one of his mother's favorite shows and Cookie Cochran was one of her favorite TV hosts.

"Well, what do we have here!" Cookie Cochran said as the production assistants wrapped an apron around her waist and a stylist touched up her makeup.

"I'm cooking my own take on pambazo. I hope you don't mind, but it can get a bit messy," Jake said. Cookie eyed the prepared dish, and he couldn't tell if she looked disgusted or delighted.

I should have played it safer with a stupid enchilada, Jake thought as he tried to figure out what Cookie was thinking.

"That's what this apron is for, honey!" Cookie said.

"My mom's a big fan of yours. She was sad when you first replaced Hope Covington, but she adores you," Jake said. He realized as soon as he finished talking what an idiotic comment it had been to bring up the person Cookie had replaced, but it was too late now.

"We all miss Hope, but it sounds like your mom has a good judge of character."

Not in the slightest, Jake thought.

"And we're back in five…four…three…"

Jake felt a sudden thrust in his stomach, as if Cookie Cochran had lobbed a punch right into his appendix. The sudden jolt was enough to make him want to double over and throw up on Cookie's heels. Instead, he gripped the counter so tightly his knuckles turned white until the feeling subsided.

"And we're back with Seattle's award-winning chef, Jacob Ruiz." Cookie looked ahead at the camera, and when his name left Cookie's mouth, Jake felt the palms of his hands get sweaty.

I can't do this, Jake thought. He wanted to run off the set and never come back, but he couldn't. He knew if he did, his restaurants would be doomed and Cookie's erect stop sign video would no longer be the most watched clip from *Wake Up With Us*. It would be Jake running off set in a fit of panic. "He's the brains behind some of Seattle's hottest restaurants and hidden gems, including Viva la Vida Cocina. So, Chef Ruiz, what do you have in store for us today?"

It was as if he was having an out-of-body experience. He wanted to talk and yet, his body stood there paralyzed in silence. He thought about how excited his mother had sounded and knew his father was going to be watching this as soon as it aired on the West Coast, but it still wasn't enough for Jake to snap out of it. Instead, it was Colt's words of encouragement and the knowledge he was watching the East Coast airing that broke Jake's TV paralysis.

"Sorry about that, Cookie. Just taking this all in," Jake said, laughing, going off what was written for him on the teleprompter. Cookie laughed nervously, as if she was saying in her chuckles, "*What in God's name are you doing, kid?*"

"Just like I'm taking in all these TO DIE FOR smells. You need to tell me what I'm smelling!" Cookie said dramatically, pulling it back to the script on the teleprompter.

Don't screw this up; we're on live TV. This was the message spelled out in Cookie's eyes, which looked like they were about to explode right out of their sockets.

"Well, I've made pambazo for you today. This was one of my favorite dishes growing up and is one of the most popular dishes back at my restaurant, Viva la Vida. Pambazo is a bread that we coat with a red guajillo sauce and then fry. Most of the time, it's filled with potatoes or chorizo, but I like to add a little more to it."

"This kind of sounds like a sloppy joe, Chef Ruiz." Cookie walked down the table alongside Jake as he showed her the pambazo at different phases.

"That's what I always say! And the best part is that kids love this too," Jake said. He knew the segment had pretty much started as a complete and utter train wreck, but Jake had found his groove with Cookie the more they talked until he pretty much forgot they were being watched by millions of viewers. Jake had found that talking with Cookie was quite easy, as she reminded Jake in some small way of Gigi. Jake walked her through the entire process of preparing the pambazo, which was quite simple, but the end result was nothing short of pure, fried, guajillo-soaked bliss.

The sound that came out of Cookie's mouth after taking a bite of the finished pambazo should only have been heard in her bedroom, not national television. Jake instinctively laughed while he watched Cookie lean down and take another bite. And another.

"Pretty good?" Jake asked, breaking the on-air silence.

"Pretty good? Chef Ruiz, I would move to Seattle for these pambazos! Shoot, I'd let you adopt me just so I can request these for EVERY meal! Tell us about what inspired you to cook." Cookie bent over and took another bite.

Of all the questions she could ask, she had to choose this one, Jake thought. Sure, he had loved cooking, but there was no way he could answer this without speaking about the two people he didn't really want to talk about on national television.

"Well, I grew up in the restaurant business," Jake said. He knew he would need to move through this next part of the interview surreptitiously, as if he were navigating a mine field to avoid having Cookie Cochran ask too many questions. "I guess you could say the love of cooking runs in the family."

"You apparently have had some great teachers," Cookie said through another bite of the pambazo. "Chef Ruiz, this has been an absolute delight! Coming up next – a water-skiing squirrel spotted on Lake Michigan? We'll be right back after this commercial break."

"AND WE'RE CLEAR!" The camera crew shouted across the studio. The assistants and the makeup artists came running up to Cookie to help her out of the apron before the next commercial break. They were like tiny worker bees and she was the queen.

"You scared me, Chef Ruiz," Cookie said as her assistants untied the apron. "Started off a bit rough, but you really pulled through. I like you! And this food? Well, let's just say I'm probably going to be a hundred pounds heavier if you start full-time! I'll put in a good word for you."

"Thanks!"

"Hopefully we'll see you again soon!" Cookie waved as the assistants pulled her away from the pambazo and the kitchen set and back to the anchor desk.

Jake couldn't believe that was it. Had he really been flown across country for a little less than a five-minute cooking segment? The producers came up to him and thanked him for coming out to be a part of the show and led him off the stage and back into the hallway. He couldn't tell if Cookie had been polite, because this was starting to feel like they were trying to get him out of the studio. Had he really been that bad, he wondered.

Jake went to the daycare center to collect Charlie and prayed that the segment hadn't aired in the daycare for his son to watch him fail miserably. He was so thankful he had not talked to his son about what he was doing, because he couldn't imagine the expectation Charlie would have had after hearing his father was going to be on national TV, only to see him freeze and appear for a fleeting second. Jake had just experienced his fifteen minutes of fame, except it was more like four minutes and thirty-six seconds.

"Ruiz! You were amazing!" the encouraging voice of Colt said on the other side of the phone when Jake answered it on the way back to the hotel. "You were also very, very cute!"

"Colt, I completely screwed it up," Jake said. He appreciated Colt's enthusiasm, but it seemed like borderline pity. "I can't imagine anyone seeing that segment and thinking I was amazing."

"You are being too hard on yourself. Listen, you had a split second at the beginning where you froze. So what? The rest of the segment made up for it. I'm so, so proud of you!"

"Thanks, I love you."

Silence. On both ends. Had those words just come out of Jake's mouth? He looked down at Charlie, whose mouth was agape as he stood there in stunned shock on 7th Avenue.

"Holy shit," Charlie said quietly, but not quietly enough for Jake not to hear.

"CHARLIE!"

"What? You just said you love him," Charlie said, and Jake couldn't even be mad at him. After all, he heard the same thing in his head as soon as he had said it. Jake thought maybe he could tell Colt he suffered from a medical condition called verbal diarrhea and then just pretend it never happened.

Meanwhile, a stunned silence still hung over the other side of the phone. Maybe there was a bad connection, but when Jake pulled the phone from his ear, he was disappointed when he saw five solid bars.

Well, so much for this, Jake thought. *I've scared him off.*

"I…" Colt said and then paused. "I love you too, Jake."

"You don't have to say—"

"Yeah, I know. And I'm not. I really do. I love you," Colt said reassuringly. "I know this may be way too early to say this, but maybe in our case, it isn't."

Jake was in one of the largest cities in the world and had just finished doing a cooking segment, if that was what you would call it, on a show watched by millions. And all he wanted was to be back in Newport. It was a sentiment he never believed he would have again in his life. As he stood feet away from Times Square, all he wanted was to be back in his hometown. "I wish I was back there right now."

"Me too. But you'll be back tomorrow. I *can't wait* to see you."

"Same, I'll talk with you later," Jake said.

Charlie had a giant grin on his face. It was the same grin Charlie had whenever Jake cursed at home and had to put a quarter in his piggy bank; a deal that nearly bankrupted and then quickly reformed Jake's choice of words whenever he was around Charlie.

"You like him! You love him," Charlie said, but drew out "love" for about five seconds while he wiggled his entire body in the most five-year-old manner possible. He may as well have been teasing a friend on the playground about a crush they had.

"I do," Jake said, processing the realization. He couldn't believe that a slip of the tongue had caused the most wonderful thing to unfold.

"Cool! Can we go into M&M's World?" The gravity of what was said between Jake and Colt was clearly lost on Charlie, who already had moved on and was eyeing the massive, two-story chocolate store. A large LCD screen showing chocolate candies practically hypnotized Charlie, who started pulling Jake's arm.

"Oh no, I'm not putting sugar in you this early in the day," Jake said.

"Take me in there and I'll forget about you cussing," Charlie said with a devilish grin.

"I didn't say anything. You were the one that said *shit*," Jake said.

"Aha, see? Now you have to take me there!" Charlie giggled. Jake gave up. His son was either going to grow up to be a lawyer or a con artist, Jake thought. And by the time they had left the chocolate store, Jake had somehow managed to spend enough money to walk out with two shopping bags. Charlie had already begun to dig into them before they had barely reached the sidewalk.

Jake's phone buzzed, and their otherwise pleasant day was interrupted when Jake saw Consuela's name flash across the screen of his phone.

"Jacob. It's your mamá, Consuela."

"Mom, remember? Caller ID…"

"*Mijo, your* father found you on the Internet and we watched your appearance already. I thought you were doing a cooking segment?"

"That was the segment, Mom."

"*Ay*, they gave more time to that squirrel on the water skis."

Show me the last time you were on a nationally broadcast show was what Jake wanted to say. Instead, he gritted his teeth and said, "Did you need something, Mom?"

"Well, your father loved the segment. Said you did fantastic," Consuela said.

"I'm glad one of you thought it was good," Jake said dryly.

"*Ay mijo*, it was good. I already told you that," Consuela said, but she hadn't. Jake could never tell if his mom truly believed what she said or if she had become an expert at gaslighting others. "Anyway, when are you coming back to Newport?"

"We fly back tomorrow evening."

"Would you and Charlie like to come over for lunch on Wednesday?"

Jake knew what Gigi would tell him to say. No, this was a trap. He could practically hear Gigi tell him not to go or he would end up waking in a tub of ice with jumper cables clamped to his body at some "pray the gay away" conversion facility.

"Sure," Jake said slowly. Gigi had warned Jake to never trust his mother on countless occasions, so Jake knew she was going to throw a fit when she heard Jake had accepted the invite.

"Bueno! You need me to send you the address?"

"Did you guys move?" Jake asked.

"No, we're in the same house."

"Mom, I think I can remember the address of the house I grew up in," Jake said with irritation. He knew it was his mom's passive-aggressive way of pointing out how infrequently he had seen his parents. No matter how hard he tried, every conversation with his mom ended up with several eye rolls and muffled sighs or groans. She was good at what she did, Jake thought.

"Okay, okay. Well, have a safe flight back, *mijo*. Love you."

"Thanks, Mom. See you Wednesday."

Apparently, this was a good day for Consuela. Either that, or she was up to something and Jake had just agreed to meet them in a non-public setting. He now wished he had agreed to meet them somewhere in town, but he didn't want to have this conversation hang over the rest of his and Charlie's time in New York. The two spent the rest of the day doing all of the tourist things that New York City was known for. They went to the Vessel at Hudson Yards and then went to Central Park later in the day. Jake had plans to take Charlie to a Broadway show, but after about an hour in Central Park, Charlie began to complain and say that all there was to do in New York was walk and that he wanted to go back to the hotel. Jake recognized he was on the precipice of a five-year-old meltdown. Charlie barely made it to the bed before he dropped onto it and fell asleep.

The next day, Jake and Charlie went to the Empire State Building before taking a taxi back to the airport. Neither had any desire to stay in New York any longer. Jake felt fairly confident that his appearance on *Wake Up With Us* was hardly his big break. There was no way he would get the offer to be a regular on the show, and he knew that. Charlie had no desire to stay in New York any longer because he said he was tired of walking and the city smelled funny.

As the plane flew back to Washington, Jake contemplated his and Charlie's future. He knew he needed to get back to Seattle. He could always hire additional operations staff to manage the restaurant if he were to stay in Newport, but he also knew his company was not in a position to be able to add additional staff. The writing was on the wall, and sooner than later, Jake and Charlie would need to return to Seattle. He just hoped he could somehow manage a long-distance relationship with Colt at the same time.

CHAPTER 35

When Jake and Charlie walked back through the security gates of Spokane International Airport, there was one person standing there waiting for them. Colt stood at the bottom of the escalator in a dark navy suit with a navy shirt and mustard yellow tie. And in his hands was a handwritten sign that read: *I really do.* Jake smiled at Colt, who flipped the sign over and it read: *I love you.* He had obviously put some thought into the first time they were going to see each other since he left for New York, and Jake wished he had at least done the same. Instead, he was covered in crushed cheese crackers Charlie had spilled on his sweats and hoodie. He felt like how someone would feel after a six-hour flight and he worried the airplane smell would be enough to have Colt write a new sign that read: *Sorry, I changed my mind.*

"Hey, handsome," Colt said, hurrying to grab Jake's bag and kiss him at the same time. The result of which was the two of their heads hitting each other.

"Ow!" Jake said, pressing his hand against his head.

"Jeez, I'm sorry! I guess I'm just excited to see you," Colt said, laughing as he held his head too.

"It's okay. You look amazing, by the way. I probably smell like a dumpster," Jake said. He looked down at Charlie, who just scrunched his nose and nodded in agreement. Leave it to Charlie to be brutally honest when you least needed him to be.

"You don't, and I wouldn't even care if you did," Colt said. "I've been wanting to kiss you since our phone call. And to also say this in person: I love you."

"I love you too," Jake said.

"I love you too, but can we please get some food?" Charlie asked both of them. He nudged his way through Colt and Jake and continued to proceed to the baggage claim area.

"Is he okay?" Colt asked.

"Well, let's just say New York wasn't really his cup of tea. His idea of New York was that it was going to be some kind of amusement park where alligators in the toilet bit your ass. I think he is over all of it."

"Do you think he'll like it if you end up getting up the job?" Colt asked, while the two trailed behind Charlie toward baggage claim.

"I guess we'll have to see if I get it," Jake said. He didn't want to tell Colt that he didn't have high hopes in getting the job because he didn't want to get Colt's hopes up. Jake also thought saying something like that made him seem like he lacked self-confidence. But after he spoke, Jake could see the trepidation in Colt's face and knew he needed to give him more. "But even if I do, I'm going to make the decision that's right for me and Charlie. I want him to be happy too."

After stopping for an early dinner at Colt's favorite Italian restaurant in Spokane, the three of them drove back to Newport. Half the drive was filled with Charlie talking about the things he liked about New York and the things he didn't like. It came to no surprise to Jake that most of the things that Charlie listed were things he didn't like and Jake began to wonder if perhaps Charlie was intentionally trying to find things to complain about regarding New York City. Everything started to make sense why Charlie had made such a fuss while they were there. Charlie had no desire to move to New York City, and Jake felt like an idiot that after all the complaining Charlie did, it hadn't even registered until Charlie talked about how a donut he had in New York just "wasn't as soft as the ones in Washington" and that the pigeons in Central Park seemed "to be very rude compared to the nice birds in Washington." Jake and Colt kept eyeing each other as Charlie talked and tried their hardest not to erupt in laughter at him as he moved on from the pigeons and was now describing in great detail all of the "nasty smells" that New York had to offer.

"I take it you weren't a fan of New York then, Charlie?" Colt asked.

"Oh, don't get me wrong," Charlie said in the most matter-of-fact tone he could muster. "It was a perfectly lovely city, but it certainly isn't a Newport!"

"Perfectly lovely? Who are you? The Queen of England? I'm pretty sure you are the first and definitely the last to say that New York City doesn't hold a candle to Newport, Washington. Kid, you are crazy," Jake said through fits of laughter at Charlie's ridiculous comments.

When they had passed the "Welcome to Pend Orielle County" sign, Jake's phone rang. He saw Marcia Schrader's name scrawled across the screen. If there was any name that could pull him out of this lighthearted moment and back into the possible decision of a lifetime, it was Marcia's.

"That's my marketing manager," Jake said, looking at Colt.

"Are you going to answer it?" Colt asked quietly.

Jake grabbed his phone and turned it over and over in his hands. What news would be on the other end? Jake had hoped he would at least be able to enjoy a few days with Colt before hearing anything about the *Wake Up With Us* opportunity, but it appeared that this was not going to be the case. He saw Marcia's name disappear and, in its place, the phone displayed "One Missed Call." He sat there silently as Colt continued to drive toward Newport, fully expecting Marcia to blow up his phone a second and possibly third, fourth and fifth time in true Marcia fashion. The two didn't say a word. Charlie didn't say a word. If Jake were to guess, they were probably just as nervous as he was. His phone chirped again. This time, indicating there was a new voicemail from Marcia. The fact that she left a voicemail when Marcia usually sent text messages if she couldn't get a hold of Jake was enough to cause his heart to race.

"She left a voicemail," Jake said cautiously.

"Play it! Put it on speaker," Charlie called out from the back of the car.

Jake unlocked his phone and then went to his voicemails. He had a feeling that whatever was on this message was going to change his life.

"Jacob, Jacob, Jacob. Call me back as soon as you get this message! I have amazing news to share with you. You've got an offer! Call me." The excitement in Marcia's voicemail was prominent.

Oh my God—I got the job, Jake thought. *How is this even possible?*

"Do you need to call her?"

"Maybe," Jake said hesitantly. When he looked at Colt, disappointment could not be hidden in his expression. He looked down at his phone, and before he had a chance to second-guess himself, he called Marcia back.

"Are you sitting down?" That was how Marcia answered the phone.

"I am. I'm heading back to Newport, but I'm not driving. So, I got the offer?"

"What? For the show? Sorry, I think they are going with their first choice…some YouTube chef sensation. No, you got a different offer," Marcia said.

"What is it?"

"Ridgeline Hotel Collection reached out with an offer to buy Ruiz Kitchens," Marcia said excitedly. "They already have The Crab Quarter and want to create a massive restaurant group and feel that RK is the fastest way to build a diverse portfolio."

"I don't know." This wasn't the offer Jake had expected to hear, and he had never given any thought to selling off the restaurants he and Paxton had built together as a team. In some ways, the restaurants felt almost as much of a child as Charlie, but Jake knew in a matter of months two or more of those would likely need to close.

"Jake, they've been putting together an offer for the last couple months and when they saw you on *Wake Up With Us*, they reached out. Jake, this is the lifeblood that RK needs."

"What's the offer?" Jake asked. He saw Colt swallow hard and bite his lip. Jake realized it probably wasn't the best thing to say after seeing Colt's reaction.

"They're offering to purchase the entire group of restaurants, and they're offering you five million."

"Dollars?"

"They want an answer, though, by the end of this week. Jake, this will save the group. It will save jobs," Marcia implored. "Please consider this."

"I will. Can you email more of the details, so I can look it over?"

"Of course. I'll give you a call tomorrow."

The sound of the gravel under the car leading up to Colt's house muffled the silence that filled the car. Jake sat there thinking about the offer that was now in his hands. The idea of selling his restaurants was never anything he had considered. But the offer of five million dollars was something he couldn't ignore. It would be more than enough for him and Charlie's future.

"So, I guess congratulations are in order," Colt said in a rather unconvincing enthusiastic tone, once the car came to a stop.

"Oh, I didn't get the New York job," Jake began. He told Colt about the other offer that Marcia shared, leaving out the details of the amount offered.

"How do you feel about that? I'm sorry it wasn't the offer for New York." Colt reached over and placed his hand on Jake's knee.

"I'm not. To be honest, when I was there I realized something."

"What's that?"

"I want to see what happens with us, and New York just isn't a realistic option for that to happen."

"So, we're staying in Washington?" Charlie asked from the backseat.

"Yeah, buddy." Jake knew that much at least was true. They would not be moving to New York, but the decision with the restaurants had to be made.

Later that evening, the three of them sat in the living room and watched a truly awful movie about a ninja cat that Charlie had picked. The movie was horrid, but the moment was something Jake didn't want to end. Colt's arms were wrapped around him tightly and Jake rested his head on Colt's shoulder. He didn't want to let go of Colt. Ever again. The possibility of moving across the country was what Jake needed in order to finally see it.

"So, I kind of accepted an invite from my mom to go to their house for lunch tomorrow," Jake said quietly to Colt. Charlie was too focused on the movie to hear what Jake had said.

"That sounds..." Colt paused, unsure of how to finish that sentence.

"Horrifying? Yeah, I know. I was going to see if you wanted to go, so I could introduce them to my boyfriend." Jake felt Colt's chest tense at the offer. He hadn't really been entirely serious with the invitation.

After all, he didn't want to have to put anyone through the ordeal of spending unnecessary time around Consuela if they didn't have to.

"Relax. I'm just kidding," Jake assured Colt.

"Oh, thank God. Your mother is kind of the most terrifying person I've ever met. But it at least sounds like she is maybe rounding a corner, right? I mean, that offer might be like an olive branch."

"I think she's just not wanting to stress my dad out. Or maybe she is actually trying. I mean, she seemed somewhat pleasant on the phone at least."

"Well, I'll cross my fingers her kindness lasts through tomorrow at least. You know, I don't have to take you over to Helen's tonight. Maybe you two can spend the night here?" Colt said. He pointed over at Charlie, who was in the middle of a gaping yawn. "The little guy can sleep upstairs in my old room."

"I think I'd like that," Jake said.

When it finally came time for bed, Jake walked Charlie up to the bedroom that had once belonged to Colt. Jake looked around the room and was shocked to see it somehow still felt like Colt's room. The room was still painted a dark navy blue and the bed that used to belong to Colt was in the same exact spot.

"You know, I used to sleep in this room when I was kid and had sleepovers here," Jake said, thinking back to his childhood when him and Colt were almost inseparable. He opened the suitcase from the airport and pulled out a pair of pajamas for Charlie.

"Colt is really cool," Charlie said. "I like him."

"I know, buddy. Go ahead and get your pajamas on and then brush your teeth. We've got a long day ahead of us tomorrow," Jake said, thinking about the lunch at his parents' house. Just the thought made his nerves seize up in his body.

"Night, Dad," Charlie said, taking his pajamas and toothbrush to the bathroom connected to Colt's bedroom.

"Good night, buddy," Jake said, making his way downstairs.

"How does your room look exactly the same?" Jake asked.

"Easy," Colt replied. "My mom begged me not to change it. Also, that room is so dark that after I found out I would have to put a primer over the blue before actually painting a new color, I realized listening to Mom would be easier."

Colt grabbed a large throw blanket and wrapped it around him and Jake when he sat down next to him on the couch. "So, can I be honest with you?"

"You can, but that question makes me nervous."

"I just want to say how relieved I am that you're staying in Washington. We could have made New York work, but at least Seattle is so much closer."

"I'm glad we're staying too," Jake said. The two cozied up on the sofa and Colt began to flip through several streaming services trying to find a movie before settling on *The Goonies.*

"You remember when you used to say I reminded you of Chunk?" Colt asked Jake.

"No! You clearly hit your head at the airport harder than you thought because I would have never called you Chunk," Jake said defensively.

"The last time we watched this when we were kids, you said that I reminded you of Chunk," Colt replied.

"No, I said that you reminded me of Chunk because you make me laugh," Jake said, at least mildly confident he had said the second part. "Besides, I said that in, like, third grade. You certainly didn't look like Chunk, though, and you definitely don't now!"

"Thank you for that reassurance," Colt said, wrapping his arms around Jake as the two slid downward into the sofa.

Laying in Colt's arms was the most comfortable thing to Jake. He knew that if everything went how he hoped it would go, this was going to be the start of something really fantastic. They hadn't even reached the part where the kids found the secret entrance underneath the fireplace before Jake realized he wasn't interested in watching a movie right now.

"We can watch this later," Jake said. He turned to look at Colt and their lips touched, parting as they kissed passionately.

"What do you have in mind?" Colt asked.

"Let's go to bed," Jake said. He threw the blanket off them and pulled Colt upward as the two made their way to Colt's bedroom for the night.

CHAPTER 36

"Jacob. It's your mamá, Consuela Ruiz," Jake's mother said through the phone the next morning. He slid away from Colt and reached down and slipped on his boxers, quietly making his way into the bathroom that was connected to the main bedroom.

"Oh my God, ma—"

"Yeah, yeah. I know… *caller ID*. Sorry, *mijo*. Your mamá's memory isn't like it used to be. I'm getting old," Consuela said, trying to make Jake feel sorry for her. But Jake knew better. Stubborn people somehow seemed to outlast everyone. "Anyway, what time are you coming over?"

"Aw jeez, Mom. It's like six a.m. How are you even awake?" Jake rubbed his eyes. All he wanted to do was get back into bed with Colt.

"I have to get your father to physical therapy. I feel like I'm a carpool mom again and your dad is going to school," Consuela said, chuckling.

"I thought we agreed noon. Does that still work?"

"No, no, no. I can't get lunch done by that time and get your father back from the doctor."

"Well, why don't I come over at noon and I can help cook? Does that work?"

"I cook a special way, *mijo*."

"Ma, I know *exactly* how you cook," Jake said. Both of his parents were fantastic at cooking, but anytime Consuela Ruiz cooked, it tasted a little bit different. This was because the *Consuela Ruiz Method* of cooking never used any type of measuring device. Consuela would measure ingredients and add ingredients by the smell of the food.

"Fine, come over. And you are bringing over little Carlos, aren't you?"

"His name is Charlie."

261

"Oh, Charles is just the gringos' version of Carlos," Consuela said matter-of-factly.

"He goes by Charlie, Mom. I'll see you at noon," Jake said.

"Okay, fine. I'll see you then, *cariño.*"

Jake felt like he had a hangover from a two-minute conversation with his mother as he propped his head in both his hands.

Do I really want to do this? This seems like a bad idea.

The thought of spending lunch with two people who had essentially shunned him from their lives for the better part of a decade was beginning to settle in for Jake. Consuela may have had one pleasant, redeeming moment of character at the hospital, but his mother's personality was so volatile that Jake couldn't be sure the Consuela he saw in the hospital talking to Charlie about his other dad would be the same Consuela he was about to have lunch with. He hoped for everyone's sake it would be, because the last thing Jake wanted was to cause any undue stress in front of his father during his recovery. He tiptoed into the bedroom and slipped back into the bed.

"You calling your other boyfriend?" Colt asked as he rolled to his side and wrapped his arms around Jake.

"My mom," Jake said.

"Whoa, mood killer," Colt said as he laughed. His hands ran down Jake's chest until they met the waistband of his boxers. "And you're wearing underwear now? Damn, this is not going to be my day."

"Here," Jake said, reaching down and yanking his boxers off. "But I have to warn you: you have exactly thirty minutes before we have a five-year-old awake on the other side of that door pounding on it and yelling for breakfast."

"Well, I will try to be as efficient and thorough as possible," Colt said, rolling on top of Jake before he disappeared underneath the covers.

After taking a shower together, Colt and Jake crept out into the living room about forty minutes later. The two looked around and were relieved to notice Charlie was still asleep upstairs. Colt went into the kitchen and pulled out two bowls, filled them with cereal, and handed one to Jake.

"You're probably the only man in his thirties still eating Cinnamon Toasties." Jake chuckled, shoveling a spoonful into his mouth.

"What can I say? I'm a creature of habit," Colt said. "So...with everything that's going on at the restaurant, it looks like you'll be here for a while. I guess I was just wondering how we should address our relationship around others."

"What do you mean?"

"Like, can we tell people we are dating?"

"Oh!" Jake said. "I mean, yeah. Do you want to tell people?"

"Jake, of course I want to tell people. I feel like the luckiest guy in the world," Colt said with a huge smile on his face.

"Please, that's how I feel," Jake said. "I guess if that's the case, and you're comfortable with it, let's tell people. But maybe we should start with our families first."

"Deal!" Colt said, kissing Jake before he pulled away.

"Good morning," Charlie said, joining Jake and Colt at the table. "What are you guys eating?"

"Cinnamon Toasties. You want some?" Colt asked.

"Sure!" Charlie said with excitement. "I never get to eat this kind of food at home."

"Hey, Charlie, can we talk with you?" Jake said.

"Yeah, Dad?"

"Well, it's about Colt and me," Jake said nervously. He didn't know why he was so nervous. He knew Charlie would be ecstatic to hear Jake was officially dating Colt. But something about this conversation was like he was opening a new chapter in his life. "You know that I really like Colt and he likes me too."

"No – you love him," Charlie said. He once again wiggled his entire body as he spoke.

"Yes, I love him. And well, we decided we want to see where things go and would like to date each other."

"YES!" Charlie squeezed his fist and shot it up in the air in triumph. "Does that mean you guys are getting married?"

"Well, no," Jake said. "I think that is something we would talk about further in the future, right?"

Jake had no idea how to answer that question and was worried that what he said may have been too much, but when he looked to Colt for validation, Colt was nodding and smiling.

"Absolutely," Colt said.

"So, does that mean we aren't going back to Seattle?" Charlie asked.

"Well, I need to make a decision on the restaurant offer, but I think we will probably stay here through the summer and then we will have to figure things out," Jake answered.

"What about my toys?" Charlie asked.

"We can get those. Does that sound good?"

"Sure! So, are we going to stay here or at Grandma Helen's? Is that going to be my room upstairs?"

Jake looked at Colt. Charlie had just practically invited him and Jake to move right into Colt's house. Part of him felt that things were moving too fast, but then there was another part that was telling him it felt right. But, all things considered, he still couldn't move into Colt's this early, could he?

"I don't think your dad has thought about that part, but you are both more than welcome to stay here, if you'd like," Colt said, looking at Jake.

"That is what he would like," Charlie said before going back to his cereal. Jake sometimes wished Charlie had a better filter around people, but in this case, Charlie was proving to be quite the effective wingman. Jake nodded while he smiled at Colt. He didn't have to say anything, but his response was enough for Colt to perk up in excitement.

"We can talk about it later, okay? Right now, I need you to put your bowl and spoon into the sink and go upstairs and get ready," Jake said. "I need to stop by the restaurant for a bit before we go to lunch with my mom and dad."

"All right, all right," Charlie said, sliding off the stool. He took the bowl to the sink and then ran upstairs.

"Look, I hope this is not moving too fast," Jake said to Colt.

"Jake, I would tell you if it was. If it were someone I had just met, there is no way we would be moving this fast. But we have a history, and I'm not going to waste another minute without you."

264

CHAPTER 37

"This is...your home?" Charlie asked Jake the moment they pulled into the driveway of his parents' house later that afternoon. There was nothing fancy about the house that Jake grew up in. It was a one-story rancher with stained cedar shakes that wrapped around the house. And just like the restaurant, the house seemed to have also fallen into disrepair over the years. The stained siding had faded, dried out, and splintered since the last time Jake had been there. The yard, which had once been meticulously landscaped by Jake's mom, looked like it had gone the same route as the landscaping in front of the restaurant. Had he known better, Jake would have assumed that both the restaurant and his parents' house had been abandoned.

"It was at one point," Jake said, shocked. "Now it is just a house. Hey, buddy?"

"Yeah?"

"Let's maybe not talk about my relationship with Colt while we are here. Is that okay?"

"You want me to lie?" Charlie asked. Jake felt guilty for asking his son what he thought was a simple favor.

"No. I just..." Jake couldn't think of what to say or why he even felt the need to keep this from his parents.

"Fine. I won't say anything," Charlie said, interrupting Jake to his relief.

Large weeds sprouted out of the multitude of cracks in the sidewalk that led to the front door. Charlie had been hopping over the cracks at first as a game, but had to give up once there were so many that there was no "safe" path to the entrance without needing to step on them. Jake glanced over to the bay window that looked into his parents' living room

265

and saw his mother moving away from it. He wondered how long she had been standing at that window.

"*Hola!*" Consuela said, opening the front door and waving to Jake and Charlie.

"Hi, Mom," Jake said. He wasn't sure what to do, and it was apparent that Consuela had no idea what to do either as the two stood facing each other, bobbing left and right as though they were wondering if they should hug one another. The result was what appeared to be an extremely awkward encounter, which Charlie was fortunately the only witness to.

"Yeesh," Charlie said quietly, unable to hide his response.

"Come on in." In true Consuela fashion, she brushed right past the interaction and ignored Charlie's comment, because not addressing it was more convenient. Nothing had changed in his parents' house. It was the same furniture and in the same exact position. As far as Jake knew, this could have just as easily been 1995, 2005, or 2022 inside his parents' house. The air even smelled old.

"Carlos, Jacob and the little *osito* are here," Consuela said to Jake's dad, who was sitting in the rocking chair.

"*Osito?*" Charlie whispered to Jake.

"It's like saying teddy bear. Hey, Pa! How are you doing?" He had no idea why, but Jake found himself yelling clearly enunciated words, as if his father was hard of hearing.

"*Mijo!* I'm doing good," Carlos said, reaching out and taking Jake's hands in his own. Nearly half of the muscles in his face seemed to be frozen in place as Carlos looked at Jake and Charlie and smiled. "But I'm not deaf. It's good to see you two."

"Your father had his physical therapy this morning, and Dr. Mathison thinks he will make a fast recovery. Can you believe it?" Consuela said.

Jake's father grunted and waved his hands as if he were shooing the voice away from the kitchen. "You were amazing on *Wake Up With Us*, Jacob. I'm so proud of you, my boy!"

"*Ay,* your father must have watched that tiny segment probably a hundred times by now!" Consuela called out from the kitchen.

"How are you, son?" Carlos asked Jake.

"Me? Pa, you were the one that was induced in a coma and went through a stroke. Don't worry about me," Jake replied.

"I do though," Carlos said. This time, his voice was quieter and more hushed. "I worry about you all the time. I'm sure you miss him."

The *him* that Carlos was referring to didn't need to be clarified. Jake knew his dad was referring to Paxton. The two of them had only met on, to Jake's recollection, one occasion and Jake's father was at least courteous to Paxton in a way that Consuela refused to display. He talked to Paxton briefly, smiled, and shook his hand, while Consuela talked to Jake and pretended Paxton was nonexistent. She had refused to say a word, much less look at Paxton, even though he had been standing right next to Jake. Hearing his father speak about the feeling of loss that Jake had felt ever since Paxton's death provided a sense of healing and comfort Jake could have never imagined he'd feel from such a small act of kindness.

"Thanks, Pa," Jake said.

"So, do I call you Mr. Ruiz or Abuelo?" Charlie asked, reminding Jake and Carlos of his presence. Charlie and Carlos looked at Jake as if he were the arbitrator to this question. Jake knew that if he told Charlie to call him "Mr. Ruiz" it may seem cold and cruel. It was the last thing he wanted to inflict on his dad, who was still recovering. But, just like his mother, Jake didn't feel that Carlos had really done anything to deserve being called "Abuelo."

"You can call him whatever you're comfortable with," Jake said diplomatically, which seemed to satisfy Charlie, who shrugged and went to go sit on the couch and watch TV. Jake sensed Charlie was looking for any type of outlet to not be a part of the conversation, considering it was the news that was on TV.

"So, how's the restaurant?" Carlos asked Jake.

"It'll be in a really good spot when I'm done," Jake said confidently. "Pa, how could you guys let it get to that point?"

Carlos sat there silently. For a moment, Jake wondered if it was the stroke that had caused his father to be silent, but something told him it was more than that. "Your mother and I lost our drive. We lost our ambition...when we lost you."

"Pa, you've had a seat at the table at every moment in my life," Jake said. He felt a little angry his father insinuated they had somehow involuntarily "lost" Jake, when they were the ones who so willingly decided to cut off contact and rarely speak to him. "I sent invites and announcements for everything I went through. I made the effort. Can you and Mom say the same?"

Jake knew he had touched a nerve with the silence that followed. He hoped his father truly listened to those words, and by the looks of it, he had. It was his mother who was a fortified wall that he might never be able to get through to.

"Lunch is ready!" Consuela called out. Charlie rushed over to the dining room without needing to be asked a second time. Jake helped his father out of his chair and the two made their way to the dining room.

"Ma, I told you I'd come and help you cook. How'd you get all of this done?"

"Don't worry about it. I rescheduled the physical therapy appointment to an earlier time this morning."

"Smells delicious!" Charlie said, taking a seat at the table.

"I'm glad you like it. I'll give you a little extra," Consuela said. She patted Charlie on the head and scooped the spatula into the enchilada tray, serving a heaping portion to Charlie. To anyone unfamiliar with the dynamics of this family, it may have seemed like a normal gathering. Consuela had a knack for being able to turn on the pleasantries when needed. Unfortunately for everyone in the family, she could just as quickly turn them off.

"*Gracias*, Mrs. Ruiz," Charlie said, taking a spoonful of enchilada to his mouth and causing Consuela to purse her lips.

"*De nada*, Charlie," Consuela said, taking her seat at the table. She unfolded her napkin and remained silent. Jake couldn't believe the expression he could see on her face. He was probably mistaken, but it somehow looked like guilt or remorse. "*Damos gracias al Señor para la comida que estamos a punto de comer.* Amen."

"Amen," the rest of the table said in unison before digging into the food. It was quite unlike the thousands of meals Jake had with his family at this very table when he was growing up. Meals were a time to connect as a family. Often, Carlos or Consuela asked Jake about his day or how school was going. They would talk about the restaurant or what their cousins in California were up to. There was hardly a moment at the table for silence to slip in. However, during this meal, the group ate in mostly silence, lending to the awkwardness that each of them had already been feeling in their own way. Once lunch had wrapped up, Jake and Consuela stood to clear the table in an obvious attempt to escape their current situation.

"I can get this, *mijo*." Consuela sounded incredibly determined to leave the table.

"Sit. The both of you," Carlos said with a quiet fierceness. The tremble and command in his voice caught their attention and caused them both to find their seat once again. "This cannot continue. *Nosotros somos familia*. It's time we start acting like one."

Jake knew the words were intended more for his mother, but his father was speaking to him as well. As much as Jake would have loved for these simple words to repair things, there were years of hurt. Years when Jake felt alone before meeting Paxton. Years where he would see and hear friends talk about their family and all he would feel was jealousy for wanting to have that too with his own. There were those other moments during culinary school when that feeling of loneliness was so consuming that Jake wondered if going on was even worth it, and the only thing that kept him from pursuing those thoughts was wondering if there would be anyone there to grieve for him. He had gone through the emotional trauma of losing his parents and through the stages of grief that followed, as if his parents had died. His heart had gone most of his adulthood with the wounds of the loss of his parents now heavily scarred over. And whenever his parents would reemerge sporadically in his life, like his father had that night at his restaurant, it was sometimes like seeing a ghost. And hearing these words as he sat at his childhood table, now with his own son, was easier said than done.

He sat there quietly, and as much as he wanted to say something, Jake was at a loss for words. He wanted to show his parents the pain they had inflicted on him over the years when they chose to remove themselves from his life, and the only way Jake knew he could do that was through words. Words that he feared would only complicate things and threaten his father's recovery and health.

"It's a nice thought, but I'm not so sure it's that easy, Pa." There was no turning back now, Jake realized. He found himself standing on a thin layer of ice he had to carefully maneuver, if he were to avoid an argument at the table.

"*Mijo*, I'm so sorry we weren't there for you for so many years, but I want to be there for you now." Carlos glanced over at Charlie, who looked like he was watching a car wreck and wished he could be anywhere else besides this table right now.

"Charlie, why don't you take your meal into the other room and go watch TV?" Jake said, noticing the distraught and troubled look on his son's face.

"Ok," he said quietly and quickly grabbed his plate and left the table.

"Jacob, I want to be there for your entire family… And that includes Colt." Carlos said, once Charlie was out of the room.

"*Ay dios mio*," Consuela said, hushed under her breath.

"What?" Jake said, startled. Hearing Colt's name come out of his father's mouth in this conversation made Jake feel as though he had somehow come out of the closet all over again to his parents.

"We know, *mijo*," Carlos said.

"You do?"

"Of course. We've always known," Consuela said, realizing there was no path to reconciliation ahead if she were to keep anything else from Jake. "I knew back when you were in grade school and you two were inseparable. You two were *too* close. I told your father I thought you were gay, and he brushed me off, but I knew. A mother knows…probably before you even knew yourself. It's the reason I told Beth Humphrey that you two couldn't play together anymore. She didn't agree, but respected my request. It's the reason I became friends with Helen Clayton after I saw how you connected with Virginia, and I prayed that maybe she could be the one for you. That was before I realized what a bizarre woman Helen is. If I knew what a bad influence Virginia was going to be on you, I would have never allowed you two to be friends either."

Jake couldn't believe what he heard. His mother had known he was gay nearly his entire life and still thought this was somehow a choice or lifestyle he was choosing to take part in, like some sort of Paleo diet. Jake couldn't believe this information didn't help Consuela realize it wasn't a choice for him. It was biologically programmed, just as the DNA that made his eyes brown. But more importantly was the land mine that Consuela had just triggered. The answers to the questions as to why him and Colt had a falling out were now starting to become clearer. Consuela had deviously been the architect for manufacturing and destroying Jake's friendships when he was a kid.

"And then that Halloween night, I got that voicemail from *him*," Consuela said, stopping herself before realizing it was too late. She had divulged a secret that not even Carlos knew about.

"What are you talking about? You got a voicemail from who?" Jake asked.

"Colton called and basically professed his *gay* love for you," Consuela said. The inflection of disgust was palpable in her voice. "So I..."

"So you texted him, 'Asshole lose this number,'" Jake said, doing everything in his power to control the rage that built inside him as more pieces to the puzzle started to come together. When his parents had finally purchased a cell phone for Jake, it had been on a family plan and all three of their phone numbers were sequential and only off by one digit. Colt must have somehow received Consuela's number by accident when he was trying for Jake, but because the two had practically never spoke after high school until that fateful night, the wrong number was unknown to Colt. It was through her admission that Jake also realized he had inadvertently been outed to his mom by Colt well before he "officially" came out to her. He started to now understand why his mom had grown cold and distant after Halloween night, which Jake just assumed was because he had decided to pursue his love of cooking and go to culinary school back East.

"Oh, Connie, you didn't," Carlos said, shocked.

"I did what I thought would help keep our son on the right track," Consuela said. This time, however, there was no confidence in her reasoning. She had realized there was no "right track" for Jake. There was only "her track," and no matter how hard you pushed against the water, there was no way to change the flow of a stream.

"Mother, no amount of your meddling could have kept me from being my true self," Jake said, his voice quivering. He felt his throat burn and tighten. He knew he was on the verge of tears of anger for everything his mother had done to change the course of his entire life, including removing friends from it. "And in all of that work you did to intervene and force your decisions into my life, what did that result in? Nothing. I'm still gay. I always have been. I always will be. All it did was force a wedge between us so great that it's irreparable."

Tears started welling up in Consuela's eyes and ran down her cheeks. *Crocodile tears*, Jake thought. He knew he was done here and stood up to make his way out of the house.

"You put me in one of the darkest moments of my life, and you did it willingly. Selfishly," Jake said, looking at Consuela, who kept her eyes trained on the table, refusing to make eye contact. "There were moments I thought of taking my own life, and that was because of you. That was 'the path' that your actions put me on. And then, I worked hard. I found a man who believed in me. Who loved me. Who put all of my broken pieces together and made me a better man than I could have ever been through your actions. I worked so hard for everything in my life, whether it was my family or my career. And that was because I knew I didn't have parents I could fall back on if the going got tough or if the floor fell out from underneath me. So, at the very least, I guess I can thank you for giving me the drive and vision to be successful in business and the determination to be the parent to my son that I always wish I had growing up. Charlie, let's go."

Jake headed towards the door and Charlie jumped off the couch without needing to be asked a second time. Jake didn't look back as they left the house and back down the cracked and deteriorating sidewalk. Before they got to the car, they heard the screen door on the porch swing open.

"Jacob!" Jake turned around and saw his father slowly walk down the sidewalk with his cane.

"Dad, what are you doing?" Jake said, running up to his father to help him back to the house.

"I meant what I said. I'm so sorry," Carlos said, tears in his eyes. "Believe me, I had no idea your mother did that to Colton."

"I believe you," Jake said quietly. He could see the words he had directed at Consuela still had a painful effect on Carlos. He wished he could have taken that feeling away from his father, but he wasn't sorry for what he had said to his mother.

"I know it's too late to make amends for the past, but do you think there's a future for you with your dad in it?" Carlos asked.

"Of course, Pa." He stepped forward and Jake wrapped his arms around Carlos and squeezed him tightly.

"If it's okay with you, do you think I could go with you?"

"Sure, come on." Jake helped Carlos into the passenger seat of the car. As they pulled out of the driveway, Jake looked in the rearview mirror and saw the silhouette of Consuela Ruiz standing at the bay window of the living room. He wondered how long she would stand there this time.

CHAPTER 38 – ONE YEAR LATER

Local Celebrity Chef Jake Ruiz Goes Back To Family Roots

By Diana Cosgrove

Chef Jacob Ruiz has always taken bold and ambitious leaps every time he has opened a new restaurant in Seattle. Whether that was with the chipotle-braised short ribs at Beacon Hill Barbeque or the spicy notes that linger on the tongue from the hatch chile margarita at Blue Agave, Ruiz built a portfolio of restaurants that felt authentic to its own cuisine, while staying true to his roots.

It has now been five months since Ridgeline Hotel Collection closed a landmark deal with Chef Ruiz, acquiring the family of restaurants under the Ruiz Kitchens organization. The business acquisition has allowed Chef Ruiz to pursue his latest business venture, bringing him back to where it all started.

This Saturday, July 22nd, the incredible menu of Ruiz y Mijo will once again be available to the public after being closed for the last four months as the restaurant underwent a major renovation and rebranding. However, if you want to experience Chef Ruiz's latest culinary story, it will be about a six-hour drive to the small town of Newport, Washington.

Ruiz y Mijo is the first restaurant that bears the name of the famous chef, as well as his father, Carlos Ruiz. But that isn't the only thing this restaurant has going for it. The restaurant will be Chef Ruiz's mainstay, where he will serve as head chef. Early buzz about this restaurant has tables booked for the next four months.

"It's exciting to see the enthusiasm and support," Chef Ruiz said in response to the reservations. "I am really excited to be cooking beside my father after so many years and share our individual styles with all of our guests."

Earlier this year, Chef Ruiz picked up his belongings and moved back to Eastern Washington to care for his father, who suffered a stroke in June of last year. For now, Ruiz has no plans for opening any new culinary endeavors beyond Ruiz y Mijo, but he hasn't ruled it out.

This isn't all that is new for Chef Ruiz either. After suffering a devastating loss in the death of his business partner and husband, Paxton Cooper, love also seems to be on the menu for Chef Ruiz after reconnecting with his childhood crush, Dr. Colton Humphrey. When asked for a comment about this relationship, Chef Ruiz seemed to glow and simply responded, "Things are going well, both professionally and personally."

Ruiz y Mijo will have a small invitation-only opening on Friday, July 21ˢᵗ before opening to the general public on July 22ⁿᵈ.

CHAPTER 39

"Did you hear about Los Ruiz?" a woman said to her friend in the aisle of the grocery store.

"You mean Ruiz y Mijo? Bob and I are so excited for their grand opening. Their remodel looks beautiful. Really spruces up Newport. We've been trying to get a reservation but they are booked solid," the other woman said. She picked through the produce as though she was some sort of appraiser for Granny Smith apples.

"Are you kidding? You won't catch me there anymore," the woman said, seemingly appalled at the apple woman's enthusiasm for the grand reopening. She was determined to make her opinions known to anyone who could hear as she began to speak even louder.

"Why not? That restaurant's going to put Newport on the map! I'm excited to see how the restaurant helps the rest of the town." The woman tied up her bag of apples and set them in her shopping cart, continuing down the produce section. Unbeknownst to the two women, they had already gained the attention of half the other customers in the produce section.

"Charlotte, you've got to be kidding me. Their son…" the woman said to her friend, as if that would explain everything.

"What about him? He's from here. He grew up here. And I hear he is an amazing chef!"

"Yeah, and a fruity queer at that—OW!" The woman screeched and stopped halfway through her comment. She spun around to find the front of another shopping cart digging into her heels and into the back of her legs. "What's your problem? You clipped my ankle with your shopping cart!"

"I know exactly what I did, *perra*! That chef you are talking about...he is my son," Consuela Ruiz said, pushing the shopping cart a little farther into the woman's ankles as she squealed in pain. "Besides, it looks like your fat ass could stand to skip a few meals, so you won't be missed!"

Consuela walked away, refusing to turn back around to catch a glimpse of the woman's reaction. She knew she had created a problem at the grocery store, but it finally took the hateful words of someone else to realize she had a much larger problem that she had to fix. Carlos had finally caved after several months of staying at Colt's guest house and moved back into the house, but Jake still had not spoken with her. She worried she had lost her son forever now, after the revelations that came out at that lunch a year ago, but she thought she might still get one last chance to make amends for everything she had done. And that chance was tonight.

"Are you guys almost ready?" Jake yelled out from the kitchen at the direction of his bedroom and upstairs.

"Just a second!" Charlie called out from his bedroom.

Jake stood there pacing, realizing he was incredibly nervous for tonight. Sure, he had opened multiple restaurants in the past, but this was different. This was no ordinary restaurant. It had his family name on it. But there was another reason Jake was nervous; he reached into his pocket and turned the small ring box around in his fingers.

"Babe, do you know where my black tie is?" Colt poked his head out from their bedroom. He was shirtless, and normally the sight of a shirtless Colt would excite Jake, but they were already running late and Jake couldn't believe Colt wasn't dressed.

"I set it on the dresser already for you," Jake said, doing his best to mask his frustration.

Colt snapped his fingers and then pointed to Jake. "You are the best!"

"I know. Now go get a shirt on!" Jake said.

"Simply the best!" Colt's voice trailed off into their bedroom.

The sharp clicks of heels made their way down the stairs and Jake turned to see Gigi, who had arrived the night before from Seattle. She was dressed in a black caped blouse with black pants. Her hair was pulled up tight into a bun with a few loose strands falling down around her ears.

"Whoa, whoa, whoa," Jake said. "Don't you look…"

"I believe the word is *stunning*," Gigi interrupted.

"I was going to say like a cross between a businesswoman and a dominatrix," Jake said.

"I'll take that," Gigi said, shrugging.

"Seriously, you look hot! Are you trying to impress someone special tonight?" Jake asked.

"I don't have the faintest clue what you are implying," Gigi said in a tone that meant she was hiding something from Jake and was teasing him to pry it out of her.

"What? Are you serious? Are you dating someone?" Jake asked, his interest piqued, causing him to forget he was still waiting for Charlie and Colt.

"Okay, fine. I've kind of been seeing someone and he's my plus-one tonight," Gigi said.

"Gigi, we don't have plus-ones," Jake said, irritated but wanting to know more.

"Jacob Ruiz, I came here all the way from Seattle. I get a plus-one, okay?"

"All right, fine. But who is this person? Have I met him?"

"Well…"

"Oh my God. Please don't tell me it's someone from Newport," Jake said, racking his brain for any single man in town. "Gigi, is it Jozef?"

"The foreign exchange student? Jeez, Jake, he really made an impression on you while he was here. And no, I'm not in a long-distance relationship with a creepy underwear sniffer from Slovakia." Gigi fiddled with her clutch. "You remember the night we met for drinks and you had to fly out because of your dad?"

"Yeah…" Jake said slowly as he thought about the night.

"Well, you remember that college student in the purple hoodie?"

"The one who thought you were his roommate's grandma?"

"Oh go to hell, Jacob Ruiz," Gigi snapped. "He thought I was Mason's *mother*… I mean his roommate's mother."

"Gigi, you didn't." Jake thought about the guys who had been hanging out around the bar area when he was talking with Gigi. He couldn't even remember what Purple Hoodie looked like, except that the entire group looked like total bros.

"Well, my best friend had to leave for a family emergency, and I had just ordered another margarita," Gigi began. "So, I ended up staying, and Dylan came over and we started talking. And then we started drinking a little more. And then we ended up back at his apartment…for the next three nights. And days."

"GIGI! Why didn't you tell me this?" Jake asked in shock. Gigi was not one to keep a secret, so Jake was floored she had been able to hold on to this one for an entire year.

"I don't know; the timing never seemed right. Plus, you had your own budding romance going on. And then it had been a secret from you for so long, I kind of became superstitious that if I told you, it would jinx it," Gigi said. "Anyway, I thought I'd tell you before you saw him tonight, so we can get past the initial shock here, rather than in front of him."

Jake reached into his pocket and wrapped his hand around the ring box. Gigi had shared something with him, and he felt compelled to return the favor. He was about to tell her of his plans when he heard the familiar thuds of his son making his way down the stairs.

"How do I look?" Charlie asked. He was dressed in a tiny suit with a smaller black tie that was identical to the one Jake wore. He was starting to look like a little man and no longer the tiny boy Jake had raised. It was both an amazing and sad feeling for Jake as he looked at Charlie, who had slicked his hair back with a copious amount of gel.

"You look like a secret agent," Jake said, squeezing his son tightly.

"That's what I was going for," Charlie said.

"Sorry, I'm ready," Colt said, emerging from their bedroom. Jake looked at him, and if he wasn't the most beautiful man in the world, Jake had no idea who was.

"Wow. You look incredible," Jake said.

"Hey, I have to look nice for my boyfriend's big night, right?" Colt said, leaning in to kiss Jake. "We're all ready?"

"Jacob? I forgot to mention I have a gift for you," Gigi said as they got into the car.

"Really?"

"Well, this is your big night and all, so if you and Colt want to have a few drinks to celebrate…"

"Aw, Gigi, you don't have to be our DD!"

"WHAT? Who said anything about that? Oh honey, I'm drinking. Remember, I came here all the way from Seattle. I was going to say that if you want to drink tonight, I will have Dylan drive us back home."

"Who's Dylan?" Colt asked quietly.

"Oh, Gigi's his nanny," Jake said, before feeling the full force of Gigi's clutch collide with the back of his head. He knew he had deserved that, so he couldn't even be angry at her for it.

"So, is Dragon going to be there tonight?" Gigi asked as she put on her lipstick with the visor mirror in the car.

"Her name is Mrs. Ruiz," Charlie said matter-of-factly. "Name-calling is rude."

"You know what? You are so right, little man." Gigi turned around and looked at Charlie and smiled. "Thank you for helping me be a better person."

"You're welcome."

"I just can't believe you invited her tonight, considering everything she did to try and keep you two apart. And look, you two still found your way back to each other. Awwwwwwwww!" Gigi placed her hand on Jake's shoulder as he pulled out onto the highway.

"This isn't just my night. It's my dad's. My mom told me a long time ago he wanted to make his mark on the world, so I pulled out all the stops for this grand opening. And this also means inviting the people most important to him, which includes my mom." Jake said, shrugging as he continued driving down the highway. He was of course terrified Consuela would not be on her best behavior but his dad had assured Jake she would be. His dad told Jake how sorry his mom was and wanted to be back in his life. He reached down to feel the ring box in the pocket of his pants. If his mom was going to be a part of his life, he thought it may be a nice gesture to have her there for when it started again.

When they rounded the corner and saw the spectacle of the restaurant launch party, Jake chuckled. He wondered what his dad thought when he saw it. The restaurant was beautiful and had been almost entirely rebuilt from the foundation, but it was the red carpet, photographers, and a giant spotlight that shot into the sky that helped make this a night unlike any other. This was an event Newport had never seen the likes of, and probably never would again.

"Jake, that spotlight can probably be seen in Canada," Gigi said.

The four exited the car, and they made their way up the red carpet and toward the entrance. Jake and Charlie walked hand in hand, and as they got closer to the restaurant, Jake felt Colt's hand slip into his on his other side.

"You sure about this?" Jake asked Colt. The two hadn't been secretive about their relationship and it was pretty common knowledge, but they didn't advertise it, especially since Colt had already lost some of his patients from the practice.

"Oh, I've never been more certain of anything else in my life," Colt said, and the three made their way to the entrance.

Jake looked back and saw Gigi kissing someone, and Jake recognized him as Purple Hoodie. She took him by the arm and followed Jake. Their age difference was obvious, but so was her happiness, and for that, Jake couldn't have been more thrilled that Gigi had found someone who seemed to make her feel the way Colt made him feel.

"Ah! And here's the 'Mijo' in Ruiz y Mijo." Carlos waved his cane in the air at Jake, nearly taking out a nearby photographer, and yelled, even though Jake was now only a few feet from him. He was talking to a reporter Jake did not recognize. Along with the town's newspaper, reporters from other newspapers had also showed up for the launch. "And this is his beautiful son, Charlie...and his beautiful partner, Colton."

Carlos leaned over to Jake and whispered in his ear, "I can say that, right? Is it weird that I just called Colton beautiful? It's weird. You know, as soon as I said it, I thought to myself, 'Carlos, that's weird.' Never mind."

"Pa, don't worry about it. This is your night," Jake said reassuringly. "Let's enjoy it."

"No, *mijo*, it's our night! I'm so proud of you, my boy," Carlos said, wrapping his arms around Jake and squeezing him tightly. Flashes from cameras went off, and if they were looking for a photo to go along with the opening of a father-and-son restaurant, this was probably that moment. "Come on, let's go inside."

The entire restaurant was unrecognizable from its dingy former self. Jake had a restaurant designer come in and help him re-envision the entire restaurant and also nearly double the size of it. Gone were the faded murals of the walls and the old chairs and booths. In their place, white stucco with arched alcoves and terracotta vases and statues lined the restaurant. Elegant chairs and tables with white linen tablecloths and flowers replaced the cracked vinyl booths. The entire restaurant was enough to trick someone into thinking they had left the small town in Washington and had been transported to somewhere else.

"Oh my God," Gigi said, right after she had gasped when she walked into the restaurant. "Jake, this... Oh my God."

"What do you think?" Jake asked her. She had been the only one who hadn't seen all the changes. The last time she was here, the construction workers had only just finished the framing of the restaurant's addition.

"Honestly, I think this is your most beautiful restaurant," Gigi said.

"Hi. I'm Jake," he said, reaching his hand out to Dylan.

"Jake, it's nice to meet you finally! I'm Dylan!" He said, aggressively shaking Jake's hand. "You're the first person that Gigi's introduced me to. I was beginning to think she was embarrassed of me or something."

Gigi let out a nervous cackle that was neither convincing, nor flattering, and ended up catching the attention of nearly everyone around her. This was followed by a groan by the time she realized what she had done. "Come on, Dylan. If I know Jake, there is an open bar at these launches." She pulled Dylan off toward the bar area of the restaurant.

"Hola, *mijo*," a voice said behind him, and when Jake turned around, his mother stood there. She was dressed in a black sequined gown with white pearls and her hair was curled. He couldn't remember his mother ever being dressed like that in his entire life; she looked beautiful.

"Hi," Jake said quietly. The two looked at each other for a brief moment and Jake leaned forward to give his mother a hug. "Thanks for coming."

"Thank you for inviting me," Consuela said. "Colton, you look very handsome tonight. You both look very handsome."

"Thank you, Mrs. Ruiz," Colt replied. Her mere acknowledgment of Colt was already an exponential improvement, compared to how she had treated Paxton when the two had met.

One by one, guests continued to arrive. Unlike Jake's other restaurant openings, which had become a "who's who" of the Puget Sound, the launch party of Ruiz y Mijo had become more of a "who's who" of Jake's life. Stacy Morrell-Jones-Clovis, soon to be Stacy Morrell-Jones-Clovis-Thompson, had arrived with her new fiancé and immediately picked up a conversation with Helen Clayton. Glen, the restaurant's kitchen cook, who had rented a tuxedo for the evening, even appeared out of the kitchen to mingle with the group. Jake looked around and couldn't be any happier. For the first time in years, he was beginning to feel whole again.

"Can I borrow you for a second?" Gigi walked up to Jake and whispered into his ear. "Is there somewhere private we can talk?"

"Right now? Can it wait?" Jake asked, looking around.

"I'm afraid not. This is URGENT," Gigi said, now in a hoarse whisper, practically spitting in his ear.

"All right, okay," Jake said. "Charlie, can you stay here with Colt?"

"Yep," Charlie said with a devious little smile on his face Jake did not trust.

The two walked into the kitchen area, but Gigi kept pulling him farther back into the restaurant until they were nearly in the linen closet area that was at the farthest corner of the restaurant.

"Are you telling me the nuclear codes or something? What's with all the secrecy?"

"I just want to tell you how proud I am of you," Gigi said. "You were…well, a bit broken a year ago. And I'm not going to lie, I worried every day for you when your dad had his stroke. But now, well, I've never seen you happier. And *that* makes me happy."

Jake's eyes began to well up. He wasn't sure if he had still been riding the endorphin wave he had felt and this just was the catalyst to send him over the edge; he didn't care. "Thanks, Gigi. You have been such a good friend, during my high points and my lows."

The two hugged and when they pulled away, Gigi took her finger to wipe away a tear that was nearly about to fall down Jake's cheek. "And to think," she said, "we have Consuela to thank for really making us become friends."

Enough time had now passed for the two to be able to lightly joke at Consuela's manipulations from their childhood. To be honest, Jake was grateful his mother had at least done that. He would have possibly never had become friends with Gigi otherwise. Unfortunately, that action had come at the cost of his friendship with Colt, but now, thanks to his mother, he had Colt, Gigi, and also Charlie.

Jake's thoughts were interrupted by a flickering of the lights in the kitchen and then everything went dark in the restaurant.

"Oh my God. You have GOT to be kidding me," Jake said in a panic. The entire power had went out in the restaurant and now he and Gigi were standing in pitch black.

"It's okay. I have my phone," Gigi said, reaching into her clutch and turning on the flashlight. "Maybe it was just a breaker fuse or something. Hey, look, we can use this." Gigi held up a battery-operated taper candle that was with the linens. She turned her flashlight off on the phone and switched on the candle.

"Where did that even come from? There was more light on your phone," Jake said. "You want to turn that back on?"

"The candle's more fun," Gigi said. "Let's go figure out what happened."

Jake ran into one of the stainless steel tables and then another cart. He didn't remember that many carts and tables being in their path when he had walked through the restaurant earlier, but his hip and shins now seemed to be finding every single rogue cart in the kitchen. Finally, he stepped out of the kitchen into the dining area and gasped.

As far as his eye could see, every single guest stood there silently. In their hands, they each held the same battery-operated candles Gigi had found in the closet. Jake looked around and saw his father beaming with excitement as he held his candle. Stacy, for some reason, was crying and her mascara had already started running down her cheeks as she held her candle. Jake saw his mother standing next to his dad. She held a candle, but looked nervous, like she was somehow going to get burned by the battery-operated flameless stick. Next to her, Colt's parents, Mark and Beth Humphrey, stood there smiling and holding candles as well. It wasn't until that Jake looked down and saw Charlie holding a candle in one hand and a ring box in the other that Jake realized what was going on. He reached into his pocket to find the box was still there. Charlie held a different one. He turned around to look at Gigi, but instead found Colt there. He was on one knee.

"Oh…my…" Jake whispered.

"Jacob Carlos Ruiz," Colt began. "I have loved you since we were in high school. And then I lost you. I found you again in college on Halloween and you reminded me of how I felt about you. But then I lost you again. You once said in an interview that you want to see potential in something and that it will stand the test of time before you make a commitment."

Charlie walked up next to Colt and handed the box to Colt. Colt opened it, revealing a gold band.

"And before all of our family and friends, I'm asking if you will make that commitment with me and be my husband and partner for the rest of our lives. Will you marry me?"

Jake was no longer holding back the tears that now freely ran down his face. "Yes," he stammered. Colt leaped up and wrapped his arms around Jake, kissing him. The entire restaurant began to hoot and holler. Charlie screamed with excitement. Jake and Colt leaned down and picked him up, embracing each other in a large family hug. Jake wasn't the only one with tears in his eyes, as Charlie wiped away his own.

"I'm going to have two dads again," Charlie said excitedly.

"You always had two daddies, Charlie. Don't ever forget your Daddy Paxton," Colt said sincerely. "But I'd be more than honored to be your dad too."

Charlie squeezed his arms around Jake and Colt's necks, bringing them closer together. "Are you surprised I was able to keep this a secret, Dad?"

"I was," Jake said. He reached into his pocket and pulled out the ring box he was carrying. "I guess you beat me to the punch, Humphrey. But will you marry me too?"

The guests all laughed, along with Colt.

"Absolutely," Colt said. He slipped the ring on his finger and kissed Jake again. He leaned over to Jake's ear and then whispered, "You know, I think there is maybe someone you might want to talk to also."

"Who?"

"Your mom," Colt said. "I actually went and spoke with her before tonight and told her my plans for this evening and she still decided to show up. Jake, she still held a candle."

Jake, Colt, and Charlie made their way back to the rest of the guests and began to receive hugs and congratulatory well wishes from everyone. Jake moved through the crowd until he came to his mother.

"You think we can go sit somewhere quietly?" Jake asked Consuela.

"Okay," Consuela said and followed Jake to a table tucked toward the back of the restaurant.

"*Mijo,* congratulations," Consuela said. There didn't appear to be any insincerity in the comment.

"Thank you," Jake said, unsure of how to respond. Any normal person saying this after a beautiful engagement wouldn't have thought twice about being congratulated, but this was coming from Consuela. "Listen, Mom…"

"Ttt…ttt…ttt," Consuela said, interrupting him. "Let me do the talking first, Jacob. I made an incredible mistake years ago. I'm not talking about the text to Colt, and I'm not talking about speaking with his parents and ruining your friendship with him. Although, I *am* sorry for all of those things, and I hope that one day you will accept my apology.

"I am sorry for not seeing you. I'm sorry for being blind and refusing to acknowledge and support what was in front of my eyes this entire time. You have always been my Jacob, and I have loved every part of you, my son. I'm sorry I pushed you into that dark place in your life. I'm sorry I made you feel you were alone in this world. I will never forgive myself for that and that will be my cross to carry for the rest of my life."

Consuela began to tear up and cry. It was something Jake had only seen perhaps one or two times in his entire life. Seeing his mother begin to cry had a domino effect and Jake felt his eyes begin to well up.

"I see how happy you are with Colton," Consuela continued. "He has always made you happy, and I don't want to be the one to stand in the way. But I do want to be a part of your life. And Charlie's. And Colt's. I want to be a part of your entire family. I guess what I'm trying to ask is… Is there still room in your life for me?"

A Note from Will

Thank you for reading *Is There Still Room In Your Life For Me?* Whether it is a relationship with a child, parent or a love that has been lost over time, I wanted to tell the story of how second chances are never too late. I also wanted to explore the feelings that so many in the LGBTQ+ community experience. The moment someone decides to come out and share their authentic self with their family and friends is deeply personal and a very different experience for everyone. For some, they are greeted with support and for others, they forge a new tribe.

I hope you enjoyed this story as much as I enjoyed telling it. If you have a moment, please leave a review of *Is There Still Room In Your Life For Me?* so that others can hopefully find this book as well. For new authors, this can make a big difference in helping this book be found amongst the millions of incredible stories that have already been told.

If you or someone you know needs help finding crisis resources or is in emotional distress, you are not alone. Call the National Suicide Prevention Lifeline at 1-800-273-8255 to speak with a trained counselor. You can also visit www.thetrevorproject.org to learn more.

ABOUT THE AUTHOR

Will Manwill was born and raised in the northeastern part of Washington state in Newport and now resides in Seattle, Washington with his husband. Will graduated from Gonzaga University in Spokane, Washington with a degree in Criminal Justice but his love of writing never diminished.

In his spare time, Will enjoys exploring the Puget Sound area. When he's not writing, Will is hiking, kayaking, or enjoying that rare sunny day in Seattle.

To stay updated and for more information, please visit www.willmanwill.com.